*Say it Loud: Marxism and the Fight Against Racism*
Edited by Brian Richardson

Dedicated to Julie Waterson

# SAY IT LOUD
## Marxism and the
## Fight Against Racism

**Edited by Brian Richardson**

Bookmarks Publications

*Say it Loud: Marxism and the Fight Against Racism*
Edited by Brian Richardson
Published by Bookmarks Publications July 2013
© Bookmarks Publications
1 Bloomsbury Street, London WC1B 3QE
ISBN 978 1 909026 38 4
Cover design Yuri Prassad
Typeset by Bookmarks Publications
Printed by Halstan Printing Group

# Contents

# Acknowledgements

IN THE true spirit of socialism, this book is the result of many minds and a collective effort. I must begin by thanking Ken, Gary, Hassan, Talat, Weyman, Yuri and Esme for the thought and commitment that they have put into their individual chapters. Meanwhile Sally Campbell our editor at Bookmarks is the unsung hero who spent many months patiently prodding, encouraging and cajoling us and finally pulled everything together. Paul Holborow, Charlie Kimber and Alex Callinicos read various drafts and provided measured and valuable feedback. Thanks also to Claire Dissington and Dave Sellers for their encouragement and support. My ex-flatmate Miriam Ruth is not only an amazing friend; she has also been a great source of strength and someone who has willingly given of her time to read various chapters, accompany me to numerous meetings and seminars and discuss and debate ideas. Particular thanks again to Yuri Prasad for his cover design—and for coming up with the title!

It saddens me to think that many of the people who read this book will never get to meet Julie Waterson, our comrade and friend who died in November 2012 at the age of just 54. For me it was a privilege to work with her for five years during her time as the national organiser of the Anti Nazi League. She was truly inspirational, one of the most principled and dedicated people I have ever met and without doubt the most fearless. On behalf of all of the contributors, this book is dedicated to her. Our modest hope is that it can play some role in enlightening a new generation, reinvigorating others and encouraging the struggle that Julie spent her life building.

# A note on terminology

IN MOST of the chapters in this book we use the term "black" to mean those people of African, Asian, Caribbean, and South East Asian and mixed race descent and other groups who are oppressed and discriminated against on the grounds of their race, culture, colour, nationality or religious practice. A number of points need to be made about this choice of terminology.

The first thing to say is that we recognise that this definition may be problematic for some individuals and groups. It has been suggested for example that the term "black" evokes the specific historic experience of people of African descent and thereby understates that of Asians. Clearly as well, it appears to exclude the experience of Irish people and those from Roma, Gypsy and Traveller communities who, we argue, unquestionably suffer from racism. Indeed, one of the most naked examples of racism in Britain in recent years was witnessed with the eviction of the Traveller community from land they owned at the Dale Farm site in Essex, south east England.

Our aim is not to marginalise and exclude but, rather, to encourage unity. Identity is a very sensitive and, by definition, personal matter. We share our readers' concerns about the use, or misuse of terminology. As Ken Olende's opening chapter makes clear, the idea of "races" is itself scientifically unsound. Yet race clearly exists as a social construct and its impact upon us is deep and profound. We therefore respect the right of every individual to identify themselves as they see fit and according to the terminology with which they feel most comfortable.

One simple reason for the use of the term "black" is for ease of reference. In recent years a myriad of different terms have been used.

As an alternative to "black" there has been a preference for, among others, black and ethnic minority, black and minority ethnic, minority ethnic, BME, black, Asian and minority ethnic and BAME. There have also been fevered debates about whether "black" should have a capital "B" and if so, whether "white" should also be capitalised. And of course, who falls under the rubric of "white"?

Given the frequency with which a book of this nature refers to identity it is, quite simply, easier to read the one-word term "black" than any of the other choices. There are occasions, however, where we cite particular statistics or pieces of research which are broken down into specific ethnic groups.

The final point to be made is a political one. Historically, "blackness" was adopted and recognised as a collective term which encouraged solidarity among different ethnic groups by focusing upon the common experience of racism rather than dwelling upon the areas of difference. Indeed, in the late 1960s and early 1970s, one of the highest periods of struggle, the term "black" was celebrated as the collective term which united people and also drew solidarity from women's rights and gay and lesbian campaigners. As Gary McFarlane demonstrates in these pages, very few people have benefited from the increased obsession with distinct and separate identities which developed in the 1970s and 1980s. Nevertheless, we acknowledge that in recent decades there has been a shift away from the use of the term "black" and that many people who are oppressed by racism would not recognise or define themselves as such. It is for this reason that we use the term "black and Asian" at times in the final chapter.

The aim of this book is to encourage a revival of struggle. We believe that what unites is more important than what divides and therefore we prefer to use a term that reflects the very best history and tradition of solidarity.

# Introduction: Say it loud

**Brian Richardson**

THE WORLD we live in is one of enormous wealth and technological development. Our ability to create, produce, communicate, travel and transport seems limitless and the capacity exists to provide everybody on the planet with food, shelter and a decent standard of living. Yet despite that, it is a world of deep divisions and racism, a belief that some people by their very nature are not simply different but also less deserving of equality, inclusion and a share in society's resources.

Far from eradicating these divisions, the dawning of a new decade has been accompanied by a revival of trends we had not witnessed since the horrors of the 1930s and 1940s when Hitler and Mussolini held power in Germany and Italy respectively. Across Europe far-right and openly fascist groups such as Golden Dawn in Greece and Jobbik in Hungary have risen from nowhere to claim a place at the heart of politics while the Front National in France maintained a position that it had built up steadily over 30 years.

Mainstream politicians and media commentators frequently assert that Britain is different; that "we" are somehow more tolerant, broadminded and committed to a sense of "fair play" which makes these islands immune to such extremism. Such assertions are both dangerous and complacent.

In the spring of 2013 Britain experienced a sharp and significant increase both in racist scapegoating and in fascist activity. The most dangerous and dramatic development was a revival in the fortunes of the seemingly moribund English Defence League (EDL). These racist thugs set out to exploit and avenge the horrific murder of a soldier in Woolwich, south east London, by taking to the streets and fomenting violence against Muslims. Within weeks there was a significant increase in attacks upon individual Muslims and arson attacks upon an Islamic community centre in north London and a school in Chislehurst.

While condemning the activities of the far-right, mainstream politicians took the opportunity to ratchet up the rhetoric, lecturing Muslims about their responsibilities and promising tougher sanctions against "Islamic extremism". An entire community was seemingly being held responsible for the violent adventurist acts of a handful of conspirators.

More broadly, those same politicians were busily outbidding each other with tough talk about the perils of immigration and parading their determination to reduce the numbers of "foreigners" settling in the UK. Prime Minister David Cameron declared his intention to end the "something for nothing society" by "cracking down" on European Union migrants claiming benefits, access to social housing and so-called "health tourism". This was despite the fact that every indicator suggested that foreign migrants are more likely to be in work and therefore paying taxes, less likely to be sick and therefore reliant upon the NHS, and no more likely to be allocated social housing. Far from challenging the lies that lay behind Cameron's pronouncements, Labour leader Ed Miliband meekly apologised for the policies of the government in which he had served and promised that an incoming Labour administration would also be tough on immigration.

The most immediate reason for this game of racist trumps was the dramatic rise to prominence of the UK Independence Party (UKIP), which was threatening to replace the Liberal Democrats as the third force in British politics. Central to its success was a vicious and sustained offensive against Bulgarians and Romanians who, its leader Nigel Farage claimed, were queuing up to flood into Britain as soon as border controls were lifted in 2014. In his desperation to arrest a decline precipitated by his party's participation in the coalition government, Lib Dem leader and Deputy Prime Minister Nick Clegg also entered the fray. He announced that his party would no longer support an amnesty for certain "overstayers". Instead those arriving on permits would be obliged to post financial bonds which would be forfeited if they failed to leave when required.

Such scaremongering exposes the plain, simple and unpleasant truth that racism is alive and kicking in the UK and so are the reasons that lie behind it. At the heart of the analysis in this book is an argument that racism is inextricably linked to capitalism, the social and economic system which predominates today. This is set out in an opening chapter in which Ken Olende explains how racism emerged over time as an ideology that was used to justify the slave trade, the primary source of profits of the fledgling capitalist mode of production. He goes on to analyse how and why racism persists today long after the demise of slavery as a major international phenomenon.

## August 2011: England erupts

The comfortable notion that Britain is a united kingdom largely at ease with itself and with little of the racial tension that afflicts other countries was blown apart by the riots that erupted over four days in August 2011 in a number of English towns and cities. The catalyst for these events was a violent death at the hands of the police. On Thursday 4 August 2011 Mark Duggan, a 29 year old mixed race man, was travelling in a car in north London which was being pursued by officers from Operation Trident, a specialist unit within the Metropolitan Police that investigates so called "black on black violence". The encounter ended with Duggan lying dead on the street from gunshot wounds close to Tottenham Hale underground station.

In the immediate aftermath of the shooting it was alleged that the police had opened fire only after they had come under attack from Duggan, who was characterised as "a well-known gangster".[1] It was widely reported that one of the police officers survived only because the bullet that Duggan had fired had lodged in his radio rather than passing through him.

Whenever a death of this sort occurs, the matter is immediately referred for investigation to a body called the Independent Police Complaints Commission (IPCC). The clue to its statutory function supposedly lies in its title. In keeping with its reputation for bureaucratic toothlessness, however, the initial response of the IPCC was to parrot the police line by declaring, "We understand the officer was shot first before the male was shot".[2]

On the streets of Tottenham a very different account was circulating. Many young people were present as the incident unfolded and insisted that Duggan had been unarmed. They claim that they had been swiftly ushered away from the scene by the police with some having their camera phones confiscated as they were given their marching orders. The inference from these accounts was that the police had something to hide, that Duggan's death had been an act of police brutality.

Within days the Metropolitan Police account of the incident was beginning to unravel. The IPCC was forced to correct its earlier assertion and admit that the police had not come under attack. The fragment of bullet found in the officer's radio had come from his own weapon. Not surprisingly, in the wake of this admission, Duggan's family demanded answers. They waited in vain. By 6 August no explanation or support had been forthcoming from either the police or the IPCC's family liaison officers.

Flanked by a group of around 200 supporters, the family therefore marched from the Broadwater Farm estate where Duggan had grown up and mounted a peaceful but determined demonstration outside Tottenham Police Station. On arrival their demand was a simple one: that a senior police officer should come out and answer their questions. Again they waited patiently, but in vain. The police were too busy stewarding a pre-season Tottenham Hotspur football match. The family felt insulted when a chief inspector, a comparatively junior officer, was finally sent out to speak to them. They demanded to see a superintendent and as they continued to wait the tension grew.

Eventually that anger boiled over allegedly after the police who were protecting their station had roughed up a 16 year old woman who had thrown something at them. By 8.30pm on that Saturday evening the police station had come under attack, and as night fell, hundreds more people took to the streets and a full-scale riot erupted.

In the days that followed, the unrest spread to a number of other London districts including the neighbouring boroughs of Hackney and Enfield, but also Brixton, Peckham, Croydon and Ealing. Beyond the capital, disturbances broke out in Birmingham, Bristol,

Derby, Gillingham, Gloucester, Nottingham, Leicester, Liverpool, Manchester, Rochdale, Salford, Sefton and the Wirral.

Parliament was on its lengthy summer recess and neither the prime minister nor the London mayor Boris Johnson were in the country when the riots broke out. The scale of the uprising demanded a political response, however, so within days Cameron was forced to return from his vacation in Tuscany and convene an emergency debate in the House of Commons.

There was, in fact, very little debate in the Palace of Westminster. Instead politicians from all sides united in a chorus of condemnation of those who had participated in the riots. Little attention was paid to the death of Mark Duggan. Instead the focus was almost exclusively upon the looting that took place in the aftermath of the original explosion.

Cameron led the way by denouncing the events as "criminality pure and simple".[3] He subsequently repeated this claim in a ludicrous "fight back" speech delivered at a youth club in his posh Oxfordshire constituency. Johnson agreed and, indeed, sought to shut down any wider discussion by insisting that there should be "no economic and sociological justifications" for the "violence and looting".[4] Meanwhile, Education Secretary Michael Gove fulminated against the Labour Party's deputy leader Harriet Harman when she tentatively raised a point about the impact of the coalition government's withdrawal of a small weekly grant, the Education Maintenance Allowance, which supported young people who remained in further education.[5]

By the time of the parliamentary gathering, the members of Her Majesty's Most Loyal Opposition, Harman included, had clearly been reminded of their responsibilities by Ed Miliband. Consequently, rather than mounting any sort of meaningful challenge, they simply echoed their government counterparts. Among the most vocal contributors to the "debate" was Hazel Blears. She had been a cabinet minister in the previous New Labour government, responsible for the "community cohesion" that collapsed so spectacularly during the riots. After condemning the "deliberate, organised and violent criminality" she went on to demand that the prime minister give his "full backing to the police".[6]

The hypocrisy of these interventions was quite breath-taking. Cameron and Johnson, former schoolmates at Eton College, had both been members of Bullingdon, a dining club for rich students, during their time at Oxford University. This group was notorious for its drunken and loutish behaviour, its party piece being the trashing of the restaurants in which they had just eaten. When it is displayed by those with power and wealth, such behaviour is, apparently, not "pure criminality", but simply youthful exuberance and jolly japes.

Of greater significance than the idiotic indiscretions of a handful of Tory toffs is a scandal that engulfed parliament two years before the riots. It was revealed in 2009 that many MPs and peers had, in essence, fiddled their expenses and—no other word will suffice— looted millions of pounds from the public purse. Prominent among them was the very same Michael Gove who submitted a claim for around £20,000 including £7,000 to pay for fancy home furnishings. Meanwhile, like Gove, Blears was found to have deployed an accounting scam known as "flipping" to profit from the sale of her second home.

It is a measure of how our society treats the rich and poor that a mere handful of these pampered politicians found themselves hauled before the criminal courts. Blears was able to escape sanction by nonchalantly writing out a cheque and waving it at a TV camera to pay back the £13,000 she had pocketed when her money grabbing manoeuvre was exposed. By contrast, swift and harsh summary justice was meted out to the least fleet-footed of those involved in the 2011 riots.

The police were heavily criticised for their initial leaden response to the disturbances. Prominent among their critics was David Lammy, the parliamentary representative for the constituency in which the uprising had begun. He was praised for his contribution to the House of Commons debate when he demanded to know, "Where were the police?"[7]

The constabulary soon recovered and launched an offensive which in London was codenamed "Operation Withern". By 8 August all leave had been cancelled and 16,000 officers were on the streets, a number apparently unprecedented in the history of the Metropolitan

Police. Many of those deployed came from far beyond the capital with amusing results. Some forces reportedly sent their officers down to London in the most decrepit vehicles, anticipating that the Met would be forced to pick up the tab if they broke down or got trashed in the disturbances.

On a more serious note, within two weeks almost 3,000 people had been rounded up with over 1,000 charged in London alone. In an unprecedented step, magistrates' courts in the capital stayed open through the night to process the first tranche of people arrested and charged with riot related offences.

The criminal justice system operates on the presumption that defence lawyers offer their clients sound and realistic advice about the strength of the prosecution case, the likely outcome and the sentence they can expect to receive if they are convicted. For this to work, it is necessary for the courts to deal with similar cases in a way which is consistent and predictable. When sentencing those who are convicted, courts are expected to follow specific guidelines or previous similar cases unless there is a supposedly "good reason" to do otherwise. Where a sentencing judge does depart from the guidelines or tariffs set in previous cases, he, and it usually is a he, is required to explain his decision in open court.

Many of the people who were caught red handed during the riots pleaded guilty at their first court appearance. They did so in the hope that they would initially be granted bail and that they would receive light sentences and possibly avoid prison altogether. Most were to suffer an immediate double setback. They were routinely remanded in custody and "committed" to the crown court for sentence. The signal from this blanket policy was clear. At that time the maximum sentence that a magistrates' court could impose for a single offence was six months. The powers of crown court judges are considerably greater.

His Honour Judge Gilbart QC, the Recorder of Manchester, was one of the first crown court judges to assert his authority. It is worth noting what he had to say:

> The context in which the offences of the 9th August were committed takes them completely outside the usual context of criminality. For

the purposes of these sentences, I have no doubt at all that the principal purpose is that the courts should show that outbursts of criminal behaviour like this will be and must be met with sentences longer than they would be if the offences were committed in isolation.[8]

This approach was subsequently endorsed by the Court of Appeal. The Lord Chief Justice, the appropriately named Lord Igor Judge, spoke on behalf of them all when he stated that:

There can be very few decent members of our community who are unaware of and were not horrified by the rioting that took place all over the country between 6th August and 11th August 2011. For them, these were deeply disturbing times. The level of lawlessness was utterly shocking and wholly inexcusable.[9]

He proceeded to indicate that:

the imposition of severe sentences, intended to provide both punishment and deterrence, must follow. It is very simple. Those who deliberately participate in disturbances of this magnitude, causing injury and damage and fear to even the most stout-hearted of citizens, and who individually commit further crimes during the course of the riots are committing aggravated crimes. They must be punished accordingly, and the sentences should be designed to deter others from similar criminal activity.[10]

Alongside those participants who had taken on the police or stolen flat screen televisions, trainers and mobile phones therefore, defendants found themselves sentenced to lengthy custodial terms for helping themselves to bags of crisps, bottles of water and scoops of ice cream.

It is important to note that these uprisings were not race riots. They were not a case of blacks versus whites. Racist groups such as the EDL did try to exploit the situation by forming vigilante groups to roam the streets and stir up trouble in one or two areas but their efforts gained little traction. Nor were they simply a "black thing" in the sense that it was only black people that participated. This is, perhaps, best illustrated by the fact that two of the young people convicted, and whose punishment set the tariff for those sentences that were meted out happened to be white.[11]

The multiracial nature of the riots is borne out by the government's own statistics. The first breakdown of those arrested and charged revealed that 42 percent of participants were white, 46 percent black and 7 percent Asian, while 7 percent were categorised as "other".[12] Clearly, however, these statistics do indicate that the uprising involved a disproportionate number of young black males. Race was therefore a key feature of the riots and in their wake the subject was catapulted to the top of the political agenda.

Following the initial foam-flecked denunciations from our political leaders, various commentators and pundits quickly weighed in with their opinions. The most rancid outburst was delivered by the historian David Starkey. His specialist area is the monarchy and British constitutional history, yet somehow he felt qualified to pronounce upon black youth culture. In a notorious appearance on the BBC's flagship current affairs programme *Newsnight*, he began by arguing that Tory politician Enoch Powell's infamous "Rivers of Blood" prophecy about the dangers of immigration had been proved right. He then proceeded to mimic Jamaican patois and claimed that those white people who had participated in the riots, the "chavs" according to him, had "become black".[13]

Starkey was swiftly and widely condemned, but many of the underlying points that he sought to make have been articulated elsewhere in less extreme form. In particular, politicians, the police and press have become increasingly obsessed with the supposedly malign influence of gangs. We were repeatedly told that gangs had been at the heart of the disturbances, temporarily laying aside local rivalries and coordinating their plans via text messages and other social networks and media.

Arguments about gangs and black youth culture are not new. It has long been suggested that too many black youth are simply uninterested in getting their heads down, working hard at school, gaining qualifications, holding down a proper job and raising a family. Instead of this they supposedly buy into a "ghetto fabulous" and nihilistic "get rich quick or die trying" lifestyle, promoted by "urban" music and MTV. The consequences of this are, apparently, a lack of respect for anyone but themselves, lack of discipline in school or at home and the establishment of the aforementioned gang culture.

A particular bone of contention for many commentators is the apparent absence of strong black male role models. Again this is, supposedly, because too many young black men are not interested in assuming their parental responsibilities. It is argued that they are more than happy to impregnate their sexual partners and readily boast about their numerous "babymothers". This is of course the ultimate assertion of their manhood. They are unwilling, however, to play any meaningful role in the upbringing of their offspring. Others are simply unavailable to raise their children as their criminality has caught up with them and they are detained in one of Her Majesty's prisons. This, in turn, places an often intolerable burden upon mothers who are left literally holding the baby.

There is a further question which arises from these assertions, namely whether the problems we need to address are confined to men. It is often argued that whatever institutional problems they face, black women are forging ahead, gaining good results at school, moving on to further and higher education and making progress in the labour market.

The initial consensus that the riots were just pure criminality could not last indefinitely. Within weeks of the uprising the *Guardian* newspaper and the London School of Economics had published an outstanding piece of research entitled *Reading the Riots* which exposed the inadequacy of those original political assertions.[14] Citing the Ministry of Justice's own statistics, the research showed that the vast majority of people involved were not associated with gangs. The participants were multiracial and a disproportionate number had been excluded from school, had few, if any, qualifications and had previous criminal convictions. Most significantly, the rioters came from, and the uprisings occurred in, some of the most deprived parts of the country. Geographically, however, these areas are cheek by jowl with some of the most prosperous. In short, *Reading the Riots* told a tale of deep and widespread alienation, social exclusion and inequality.

After the original fires had burned out and the rhetorical temperature had cooled down, parliament eventually convened a "Riots Communities and Victims Panel"[15] to look at the causes of the uprisings and to make recommendations to the prime minister. That in itself exposes the fact that, far from being a proportionate and measured response, the original debate had simply been a hysterical play for the cameras.

Meanwhile David Lammy responded rapidly with a book entitled *Out of the Ashes* which sought to "offer a way forward for Britain that is both practical and inspirational".[16] The significance of his intervention cannot be underestimated. Tottenham is one of the major centres of black Britain. Indeed, Lammy argues that it is now the most ethnically diverse constituency in the country. It is no coincidence therefore that Tottenham was one of the first constituencies to elect a black MP, back in 1987. The Labour Party's defeat at that general election was catastrophic, but a beacon of hope was supposedly lit by the election of Bernie Grant alongside Diane Abbott, Keith Vaz and Paul Boateng. In chapter 2 Gary McFarlane examines the history and legacy of the struggles that led to that breakthrough.

Grant's reputation had been cemented two years previously when the very same estate where Mark Duggan was to grow up exploded with rage. Grant was the leader of Haringey Council, which includes Tottenham, at the time. Instead of calling for crackdowns and curfews, or criticising the alleged shortcomings of black communities, he declared that the police had "got a bloody good hiding" during the Broadwater Farm riots. He was widely condemned by politicians and pundits, but local voters repaid him for defending and supporting them by choosing to send him to represent them at Westminster. When he died prematurely in April 2000, many Labour supporters wanted his wife and political soul mate Sharon, a white English woman, to succeed him. One of the main arguments used to defeat her and propel Lammy into the candidacy was that the seat should remain occupied by a black representative.

The perspective presented in this book is unashamedly closer to that of Bernie Grant than his successor. We argue that at the heart of the uprisings both in the 1980s and again in the new millennium was a rage against the racism that blights the lives of black people in Britain. In the first instance these young people were striking back against their most immediate and visible oppressors in the form of the police force.

In the immediate aftermath of the riots these arguments gained little purchase. Cameron was the first to claim that "these riots were not about race", by which he meant that racism had not been a causal factor. Racist policing was, we were told, a thing of the past. Within eight months of that assertion, however, a series of shocking revelations exposed the endemic racism that continues to infect the Metropolitan Police. It began when the *Guardian* ran a story about a young black man who had the good sense to record the racist abuse he received from a police constable on his mobile phone. Following his own arrest, the same youth then witnessed another black male being assaulted in the custody suite at Forest Gate police station in east London. The initial response of the Crown Prosecution Service (CPS) to these allegations of harassment and bullying was that these officers had no case to answer.

The CPS was soon forced into a hasty reassessment and the newly-appointed Metropolitan Police Commissioner Bernard Hogan-Howe issued a video statement to his staff insisting that he was shocked and that he would not "stand for any racism or racists" in his ranks.[17] Many of us listened to these words with a sense of weary recognition. Precisely the same promise had been made by Hogan-Howe's predecessors in the 1980s and 1990s. The reality is that actions speak far louder than rhetoric. In the decade after the publication of the Stephen Lawrence Inquiry Report, following the bungled investigation into the black teenager's murder, just one police officer was dismissed for racist conduct. Twenty others received some sort of sanction, usually a fine.[18]

## Institutional racism

If our assertion about the persistence of racism is true, it throws up a number of questions about why and what, if anything, can be done to eradicate it. A central argument that runs through this book and flows from a Marxist analysis of racism's origins is that it is not simply about individual attitudes and behaviour. Of far greater significance the prejudice and discrimination that emanate from the institutions that control and dominate society. It is this institutional racism that lies behind and explains the behaviour of the police. As Hassan Mahamdallie observes in his chapter examining the extraordinary and groundbreaking Stephen Lawrence Family Campaign the British political establishment was reluctantly forced to acknowledge this reality as a result of the public inquiry into the death of the black teenager. Mahamdallie demonstrates that Sir William Macpherson's recognition of institutional racism in the police and wider society was hard won.

Macpherson characterised it as:

> the collective failure of an organisation to provide an appropriate and professional service to people because of their colour, culture or ethnic origin. It can be seen or detected in processes, attitudes and behaviour which amount to discrimination through unwitting prejudice, ignorance, thoughtlessness and racist stereotyping which disadvantage minority ethnic people.[19]

There are significant weaknesses in this formulation. Nevertheless, it was a major concession and a tribute to the courage and determination of Stephen's parents Doreen and Neville, their family and supporters.

Recognising racism and eradicating it are two quite different things, however. This book will demonstrate that the commitment of politicians and state institutions to tackling racism was inadequate, short-lived and swiftly sidelined.

### Islamophobia
Far from being eradicated, an especially virulent form of anti-Muslim racism came to dominate the political landscape in the aftermath of 11 September 2001 (9/11). The pivotal event of the 21st century has undoubtedly been the suicide attacks which claimed the lives of almost 3,000 people in the US on that day. The fact that the perpetrators carried out this mission in the name of Islam unleashed

an unprecedented wave of Islamophobia which has become a defining feature of the new millennium.

In Britain many of us who live in London and who love the city will never forget the 7 July 2005 (7/7). That was the day on which suicide bombing arrived on these shores when a series of explosions rocked the Underground network and mangled a double decker bus in the city centre.

As was the case with 9/11, the 52 people killed and 790 maimed by the four bombers on 7/7 were innocent victims who did not deserve such a horrific fate. They were not the warmongers and profiteers responsible for the oppression of Muslim people and the occupation of their homelands. Indeed, it is almost certain that many of those people will have been anti-war and opposed to the invasions of Afghanistan and Iraq.

I was one of the people who made it into work on that fateful morning. Minutes after my arrival I heard with horror the news about the suicide attacks. That evening there was a mood of defiance among the hundreds of thousands of Londoners who were forced to walk for miles in order to get home. One of the emotions that I felt on that long march was a sense of revulsion that the perpetrators will have looked at the faces of ordinary commuters from all backgrounds on those packed trains before detonating their deadly devices.

Anger at such actions, though understandable, is nevertheless an inadequate response. Moreover, it is potentially dangerous and reactionary as it can all too easily lead to the total demonisation of Islam and hostility to all Muslims. As Talat Ahmed argues in her chapter on the rise of Islamophobia, this is precisely what has occurred in the wake of 9/11. She also demonstrates, however, that anti-Muslim racism is not a completely new phenomenon. Instead what we have witnessed is the sharp intensification of a process that had begun decades before.

The recognition of this is what enables us to make sense of events such as 9/11 and 7/7. Suicide bombers and jihadists are not simply hapless fools brainwashed into sacrificing themselves by the promise of virgins in the afterlife. They are young men and, less frequently, women embittered by the misery meted out to their brethren in

*Say it Loud*

places like Palestine. In short, 9/11 and 7/7 were blowbacks. On those mornings a small quantity of the violence inflicted on largely Muslim populations over decades was hurled back at the imperialist West.

Suicide bombing has proved to be quite literally a dead end, not simply for those immediately involved but for the millions who have been obliterated in revenge attacks upon Muslim countries. Dissuading potential "jihadists" will not be achieved by retaliatory violence, threats or pious lectures about civic responsibility. Nor is it enough to issue patronising appeals to the "law abiding majority". Instead, we argue, the starting point must be principled opposition to imperialist wars and religious persecution.

The then Prime Minister Tony Blair's chilling response to 7/7 was an announcement that "the rules of the game have now changed".[20] He was, for once, true to his word, introducing a raft of reactionary measures which encouraged the police to go on the offensive and which stoked up hostility towards Britain's Muslim population. This rewriting of the rules put paid to any prospect of far-reaching change in the aftermath of the Stephen Lawrence Inquiry. The impetus for change that was initiated by the inquiry report was quickly and emphatically sidelined as new priorities took over.

Even if that had not been the case we do not believe that Macpherson's proposals for reform would have met with lasting success. This is not because we agree with the pessimistic argument that all white people are irretrievably racist and that the interests of black and white people cannot be reconciled. On the contrary, if as we argue, racism has not been an ever existing feature of human history, then by definition, it is not something that is built into the DNA of all white people. If that is the case, it raises at least the possibility that white people can be active participants alongside blacks in the struggle to eradicate it. The questions that then arise are whether that can be achieved and, if so, how that can be brought about.

## Obama and the dream that died
The primary historical focus of this book is upon Britain, but it is impossible to ignore developments elsewhere, particularly in the United States. The early prosperity of that country was founded on

slavery, and yet in 2012 Barack Hussein Obama was voted in as president of the world's superpower for a second term of office. Having been born in Hawaii and spent much of his life in Indonesia, Obama, the son of a white American mother and black Kenyan father, is very much a man of mixed heritage.

Sadly the record of Obama's presidency is not so much mixed as overwhelmingly negative. The simple fact of his election victories gives the lie to notion that black people can never—and as far as racists are concerned should never—prosper and be voted into the White House. It is therefore a sign of the progress that has been made since that very building was built by slaves. His election victories have proved to be the highlights rather than the catalyst for far-reaching change. The fatal shooting of a black youth, Trayvon Martin, by a Hispanic neighbourhood patrolman in 2012 once again exposed the racial fault lines that continue to blight a country that is far from united. Internationally Obama's language is more eloquent and temperate than his predecessor but his actions have included an acceleration of drone strikes which have killed innocent men, women and children. So what does that tell us about racism in the 21st century and what does the record of a man swept into office on the strength of the inspirational collective slogan "Yes we can!" tell us about the strategy of "getting black faces in high places"?

### 21st century Britain—a mixed story

These words are being written in the spring of 2013 within weeks of the death of Margaret Thatcher, the prime minister who dominated much of the period under discussion in these pages. She was a hugely controversial and divisive character who pioneered many of the attacks upon multiculturalism that have been resurrected three decades later. Within two years of her first election victory the riots that Gary McFarlane discusses had rocked the establishment and given a glimpse of the bitter struggles that were to be typical of the 1980s.

The pomp and pageantry of Thatcher's funeral were illustrative of the imperial past that the British ruling class pines for. It was very white, very male and typified by a display of military power out of all proportion with Britain's role in the modern world.

Commentators were quick to claim that the funeral had been a marvellous event, something that Britain does better than any other country and one which had brought the nation together. The real truth is that Britain remains deeply divided, not least on the subject of race. One week after conducting Thatcher's funeral, the Bishop of London, Richard Chatres, presided over a memorial service to mark the twentieth anniversary of the murder of Stephen Lawrence. Again therefore it was an occasion for reflection which revealed that the Lawrence family are right to argue that they have been denied justice and that a legacy worthy of Stephen's name has not been built.

In many respects both domestically and abroad the balance sheet for black people is grim. It would be wrong to conclude that the picture is unremittingly gloomy, however. As the *Guardian* journalist Gary Younge among others has noted, one of the most important developments in Britain is a significant rise in the number of children born to parents from different ethnic backgrounds, so called "mixed race" children.[21] In less than a decade, from 2001 to 2009, there was a 50 percent increase from 672,000 to 989,600. This intermingling of ethnic groups and cultures is indicative of the fact that in most towns and cities black and white people live, work, study and socialise together with ease.

But there can be no room for complacency. Racism will not simply fade away as different ethnic groups become more familiar with each other. The frequency with which mainstream politicians turn to scapegoating immigrants and asylum seekers and the periodic resurgence of the far-right are indicative of the fact that race remains a touchstone social and political issue.

There is a fine tradition of black and white working class unity against both the violence of organised fascists and the institutional racism of our rulers. For those of us who were born in Britain, it has been those struggles that have made this country a better place in which to live than the one our ancestors arrived in and it is that which gives us hope that lasting change is possible. Yet many of the gains we have made have been reversed while others such as a broader and more inclusive school curriculum are under attack.

"Say it Loud", accompanied by the refrain "I'm Black and I'm Proud!" is, of course, the title of one of the most famous songs by the great soul singer James Brown. The fact that the song was released in 1969 is indicative of the influence of the burgeoning Black Power movement that Yuri Prasad discusses in his chapter on the lessons from America, which concludes with a brief assessment of the presidency of Obama. Brown's message was contradictory, promoting self-advancement and "black capitalism" as much as collective action. Many of the episodes we consider here are ones in which the participants have spoken loud and shaken the system, but the message and demands have not necessarily been clear, coherent and consistent.

### What is to be done?
The final section of this book is therefore dedicated to addressing the vexed question of what is to be done. Weyman Bennett discusses the vital task of building a united front to marginalise the fascists both in Britain and abroad and ensuring that they are not able to grow and present a barbaric solution to the social economic crisis. Following Yuri Prasad's assessment of the American experience, Esme Choonara then picks up the baton, critically analyses a number of alternative approaches and considers what positive strategies and proposals we should be prioritising. Can we renew the fight for reforms or do we need to campaign for separate black spaces and centres of power? Where are the black leaders of today and what role, if any, can white workers play in the struggle for race equality?

We are not alone in our assertion that, more than anything else, the 2011 riots revealed something about the class divisions that persist in the 21st century. The Runnymede Trust, a leading and highly respected race equality think-tank, produced an excellent report which explodes the myths that abound about gangs and urban disorder. Its authors argue that:

> What is telling about the...Home Office figures released on the disorder is that it is not participation in criminal associations that unify the population involved. What unifies them is that they derive predominantly from the poorest sections of our society... The conclusion we must derive from this is thus clear. The riots are essentially issues of class not criminal association. The issue at hand is how we understand this class".[22]

The challenge is not simply to understand, but to integrate those who supported or participated in the riots into a wider movement that can struggle against oppression, inequality and exploitation. Our focus is on how our class in itself can become a class for itself. We end with an unequivocal call for unity in the firm belief that together black and white workers can consign racism, and all forms of oppression and exploitation, to the dustbin of history. In so doing they can transform the history of this millennium and make a better world for all of humanity.

## CHAPTER I

# The roots of racism

Ken Olende

BRITAIN IS a racist society. Black and Asian people face discrimination in education, jobs, housing, and at the hands of the police and the criminal justice system. Many people believe this is because racism is part of human nature and will always be with us. Others think racism is just an irrational hangover from the past that has been in retreat in the 250 years since the Enlightenment and can be put behind us as we arrive in a post-racist society. Some, mostly in the media and among the rich, try and blame the victims—saying that people suffer from racism because they segregate themselves from the rest of society.

Marxism offers another explanation and a practical solution. The development of racism is intimately entwined with that of capitalism. Racism is in the material interest of the people who run our society and to get rid of it we have to challenge that system.

### What is racism?

Scientifically, race is a meaningless concept. Thankfully, serious attempts to classify people by race stopped being acceptable after the Nazi horrors of the Second World War. Before then it was common for people to be defined by racial types and specific traits that supposedly went along with their types. For example, it seems bizarre now that Raymond Arthur Dart, an important scientist who discovered the human ancestor Australopithecus, believed races could be clearly and precisely divided into types, and that it was possible to tell how much of which type made up the bloodline of a population. He calculated the racial type of South Africa's black population to be "51.2 percent Negroid, 25 percent Bush, 22.3 percent Caucasoid and 1.5

percent Mongoloid" in 1937.[1] These races were assigned moral values. Some were apparently "industrious"; others, like the African Bush, "merry, dancing, carefree".[2]

Even at their peak of popularity, some could see that such classifications were racist nonsense. The great black US anti-racist W E B Du Bois was able to point out as early as 1915:

> In fact it is generally recognised today that no scientific definition of race is possible. Differences, and striking differences there are between men and groups of men, but they fade into each other...[3]

Regrettably, such ideas of innate difference still occasionally resurface, as when Richard Herrnstein and Charles Murray attempted to rehabilitate ideas of scientific racism in their 1994 book *The Bell Curve*. So to this day mainstream organisations such as the American Anthropological Association have to state that there is no scientific substance to such beliefs. In 1998 it issued a statement saying:

> Evidence from the analysis of genetics (eg, DNA) indicates that most physical variation, about 94%, lies within so-called racial groups. Conventional geographic "racial" groupings differ from one another only in about 6% of their genes.
>
> Racial myths bear no relationship to the reality of human capabilities or behaviour. Scientists today find that reliance on such folk beliefs about human differences in research has led to countless errors.[4]

This is true, but the argument needs to be taken further. In fact racism, along with the concept of "race", is a relatively new development that came with capitalism. Its emergence goes along with the rise of a new class and a new way of ordering the world.

The great black Marxist C L R James argued that racism came out of the Atlantic slave trade, which was:

> so shocking, so opposed to all the conceptions of society which religion and philosophers and others had (despite St Paul and his "Slaves, obey your masters"), that the only justification by which humanity could face it was to divide people into races and decide that Africans were an inferior race.[5]

Only a Marxist argument can explain how racism emerged when it did and how it can be challenged. In order to show this however we have to define certain things. First, what exactly do we mean by "racism"? Second, if it emerged with capitalism what do we say about previous prejudices? And why does racism remain influential long after the demise of the Atlantic slave trade?

In his book *Racism, Resistance and Revolution* Peter Alexander defined racism as "discrimination against a group on the grounds of some imputed inherited characteristic, such as colour".[6] As a core position that still stands, though we need to consider prejudices that are supposedly cultural, such as modern Islamophobia or the Turkish government's objection to Kurds, both of which are supposed to disappear if the oppressed change their cultural identity. We will return to this issue later.

Racism links to other forms of prejudice. In itself it is neither logical nor consistent. Again and again, however, the idea that a certain group of people are inherently different lessens and then returns. It has appeared in the past with the Irish, Jewish people and most recently with Muslims in Britain. But centrally, racial discrimination emerged alongside the Atlantic slave trade, which accompanied the rise of Britain as a capitalist state and a world power. As it has developed it has become a powerful way to divide people who might threaten capitalist rule.

The development of racism as it exists today can be roughly divided into three phases. First there was the horror of the Atlantic slave trade. Second was the period when the globalising of capitalist empires made racism a worldwide phenomenon. Finally we have the development of racism related to immigration.

## 1    Slavery, capitalism and the birth of racism

Slavery was central to early capitalism and racism became its justification. Racism evolved entwined with capitalism over three centuries. Both have changed, but they are still intimately connected and we will not see the back of racism while capitalism survives. Capitalism emerged in northern Europe—particularly in Britain and Holland—as a new economic system based around sale for the market. For it to replace the previous feudal system a wholesale shift in ideas and social organisation was required.

One of the key developments was the triangular slave trade, where manufactured goods from Britain were taken to the west coast of Africa and traded for slaves. The slaves were transported to the Americas on the second side of the triangle, where they were sold to work on plantations. Finally the products of those plantations—sugar, cotton and tobacco—were brought back to Britain on the third leg. These were sold and the process began again. The profits were astronomical.

Capitalists pushed the idea of universal trade and the "free market". As Chris Harman put it, "Market relations rest on the assumption that, however unequal people's social standing, they have an equal right to accept or reject a particular transaction".[7] Such ideas were expressed in the slogans of the bourgeois revolutions: "All men are created equal" in the US, and "Liberté, égalité, fraternité" (Liberty, equality, brotherhood) in France.

Earlier societies had certainly not considered these to be self-evident truths, and therefore their rulers had felt no need to justify straying from them. But the massively profitable Atlantic slave trade—based on brutally forcing some people into inequality of the most extreme kind—dominated the capitalist's income. How could the capitalist resolve this contradiction? In 1911 the black US Marxist Hubert Harrison argued that:

> to the credit of our common human nature, it was found neces-
> sary to reconcile the public mind to the system of slavery. This was
> effected by building up the belief that the slaves were not really
> human: that they belonged to a different order of beings... One
> broad, general implication of this belief seems to be the denial of
> social, political and economic justice to all people not white.[8]

The ideas of racism developed first among the planters in the West Indies and the Americas and it was here that they took their most extreme form.

When Europeans had first arrived in the Americas they had forced

Native Americans to work for them, but a combination of overwork and European diseases led to a catastrophic population decline. The British then imported indentured labour from England and Ireland. Indentured labourers were bound to work for an employer for a fixed period of time, to pay off a debt—sometimes a conviction or just the cost of travelling to the Americas. They were not paid wages and could be bought and sold by employers. For much of the 17th century there were more indentured labourers than slaves on the plantations. Though there was a time limit on indentured work, the labourers often died before their working life ended. The planters found that imported African slaves could do the work, and if they died there was a plentiful further supply available. Historian Eric Williams observed:

> Here then is the origin of Negro slavery. The reason was economic, not racial; it had to do not with the colour of the labourer, but the cheapness of the labour. As compared with Indian and white labour, Negro slavery was eminently superior... This was not a theory, it was a practical conclusion deduced from the personal experience of the planter. He would have gone to the moon, if necessary, for labour. Africa was nearer than the moon.[9]

The slavers tried a series of justifications, including Noah's curse on Ham from the Bible. They argued that black people were descended from Ham and as such were born to serve. In the end they preferred a more forward-looking myth, one that fitted with the developing new scientific taxonomies. Black people were a different, and inferior, species.

An early opponent of these developments spotted the class relations that caused the bigotry in a book called *The Negro's and Indian's Advocate* published in 1680. As a Christian the author, Morgan Godwyn, was outraged that planters told him that to convert black people to Christianity would lead to "the overthrow of their estates, and the ruin of their lives, threatening even the utter subversion of the island".[10] Godwyn reports that the slave owners were not confident in their ideas of black inferiority and spread them in whispers. He decided that the planters believed what they did out of "avarice".

Nevertheless, the ideas took root. A century later the same slave owners' descendants proudly displayed their prejudice in books such as Edward Long's *History of Jamaica*, published in 1774, which aimed to show that black people can be observed to be subhuman. While his book claimed to be a scientific treatise it contains passages like the following about black people:

> When we reflect on the nature of these men and their dissimilarity to the rest of mankind, must we not conclude that they are a different species of the same genus?... That the oran-outang and some races of black men are very nearly allied, is, I think, more than probable...nor, for what hitherto appears, do they seem at all inferior in the intellectual faculties to many of the Negro race... The amorous intercourse between them may be frequent... An oran-outang... has in form a much nearer resemblance to the Negro race, than the latter bear to white men.[11]

Though most people in Britain had never seen a black person the ideas of the slavers gained currency, particularly at the top of society. So the Enlightenment philosopher David Hume wrote in 1753 that he was:

> apt to suspect that negroes, and in general all the other species of men (for there are four or five different kinds) to be naturally inferior to the whites. There never was a civilised nation of any complexion other than white, nor even any individual eminent either in action or speculation. No ingenious manufacture among them, no arts, no sciences.[12]

But even as these ideas caught on, examples emerged to directly contradict them. So former slave Ignatius Sancho, who wrote poetry, plays and music, began to publish in London in 1782. Sancho mixed with other Londoners, including the artist Thomas Gainsborough—who painted his portrait—the writer Samuel Johnson and the actor David Garrick.[13]

This vast change in ideas had an immediate effect on people's lives in Britain's new colonies in the Americas. Historian Brian Kelly has looked at social relations in Chesapeake Bay, Virginia, then under British control. He explains that it is:

likely that during the first few decades of the 17th century, the line between servitude and slavery had not yet been sharply fixed. Both servants and planters used the terms interchangeably.[14]

This wasn't considered strange at the time, as vast numbers of people suffered various forms of unfree labour. Around 20 black people were imported into Chesapeake in 1619. They fitted into a general pattern of forced labour. At the time it was considered cheaper to use indentured workers from England and Ireland than to buy slaves. The rulers' view of indentured servants was not high. One said Virginia could serve as "a sink to drain England of her filth and scum".[15]

Kelly argues that it was:

not uncommon during the first half of the 17th century for Africans, Europeans, and Indians to work alongside one another and even to share the same living quarters. No sharp racial division of labour had yet emerged to prescribe which work would "belong" to a particular group. From the fragmentary historical record that does survive we know that at least some white workers were conscious of the common lot they shared with blacks. One servant-poet wrote that "We and the Negroes both alike did fare/Of work and food we had an equal share".

He quotes from a 1647 investigation into the death of a Dutch servant at the hands of his master. An overseer testified about a visit he made to the servants' quarters, where he found the servants' co-workers distraught, and asked them why. He reported:

The Spanyard made answer and said Lord have mercy upon this boye hath been killed by b(l)owes, his conscience told him. Tom Clarke said Lord have mercy upon us that ever it was my hard fortune to come to this countrye for, if this bee suffered, it maye bee my turne to morrowe or next daye. The Negro said Jesus Christ my mayster is not good. And they all wept bitterlye.[16]

Furthermore, though planters were concerned about "mixed" marriages what they meant by this was unions between servants and free persons of any race. Their main worry was not about "racial mixing" but about property rights.[17]

Until 1670, though most black people in Chesapeake were slaves, there were still black freemen who owned property and controlled their own unfree labourers. That year, however, a law was passed to outlaw what had by then become an aberration.

## Resistance

One reason for these attacks was a determination by the rich to break up the solidarity that the poor of whatever race showed in resisting planters. Servants had led a series of uprisings in Virginia from 1663. Planters' fears of solidarity among the lower classes were a key factor that encouraged them to aggressively push a racist agenda. They were obsessed with effective exploitation. Race only became an issue where it complemented their needs.

The most serious of these uprisings was Bacon's Rebellion in 1676. In that year Nathaniel Bacon, a member of the Virginia colony's landed elite, confronted the governor over a number of grievances including attacks by Native Americans. He gained support by appealing to the poor, both black and white. His rhetoric tapped into widespread class resentment. He told his followers, "The poverty of the Country is such that all power and sway is got into the hands of the rich, who by extorious advantages, having the common people in their debt, have always curbed and oppressed them in all manner of ways".[18] The rebellion was suppressed and Virginia's rulers saw to it that the situation would not be repeated.

Kelly calls the experience of Chesapeake in the 17th century a process of "inventing race".[19] He concludes that:

> the turn toward slavery—arrived at piece by piece, as a response to specific material constraints and demands—was simultaneously a turn toward a racially stratified society, and the changes introduced in the basic structure of the economy were accompanied by a funda-mental transformation of social relations. By the middle of the next century, the Chesapeake had been transformed into a rigidly seg-regated society based on the exploitation of black slave labour and propped up by an elaborate system of racial ideology.[20]

## Global development and the primitive accumulation of capital

The ideas of racism fitted with the masters of the new global markets. As capitalist economies developed they drew in capital from around the world to build them. Initially Britain was far behind Spain and Portugal in extracting wealth from Africa and the newly discovered Americas, but its system of investment eventually enabled it to match and overtake its rivals, who stagnated despite the gold they had looted from the Americas.

In *The Wealth of Nations* economist Adam Smith praised the discovery of the Americas as it raised "the mercantile system to a degree of splendour and glory which it could never otherwise have attained to".[21]

Slavery was key to capitalists building up the money that would fund industrialisation—the process Karl Marx called "the primitive accumulation of capital".[22] In his monumental history of the Atlantic slave trade, *The Making of New World Slavery*, Robin Blackburn concludes, "Industrialisation in Britain was decisively advanced by its success in creating a regime of extended primitive accumulation and battening upon the super-exploitation of slaves in the Americas".[23]

The slave plantations were crucial sources of cheap raw materials for emerging industries, as markets for British goods and as a source of considerable profit. A large portion of the money made from slaves was invested in industrial production—in canals, railways, ships and new productive techniques. As Marx put it, "The veiled slavery of the wage-earners in Europe needed, for its pedestal, slavery pure and simple in the New World".[24] The slave trade built English cities like Liverpool, which grew from a modest population of 5,000 to 78,000 during the 18th century, and Bristol, which expanded from 20,000 to 64,000.[25]

Marx suggested that:

Direct slavery is just as much the pivot of bourgeois industry as machinery, credits, etc. Without slavery you have no cotton; without cotton you have no modern industry. It is slavery that has given the colonies their value; it is the colonies that have created world trade, and it is world trade that is the precondition of large-scale industry. Thus slavery is an economic category of the greatest importance.[26]

## Prejudice before capitalism

The argument that racism emerged alongside capitalism does not mean that there were no prejudices in earlier societies. In many ancient societies there was prejudice against foreigners, and rules limiting the role of immigrants. For instance in classical Athens, only the children of citizens could become citizens.[27] Pre-capitalist class societies were riddled with prejudices of various sorts but racism was not one of them. Even societies built on slavery such as ancient Greece and Rome did not categorise people on the basis of "race".

Skin colour, the most common definer of "race" in the modern world, would have seemed a particularly poor marker to the Mediterranean civilisations of the ancient world. To them people with darker skins were as likely to be "civilised" as those who were lighter. The earliest of these civilisations, Egypt and Babylon, came from the south of the Mediterranean, where people's skins tended to be darker. Greek historians such as Herodotus accepted their debt to the civilisations of North Africa. Though Greece and Rome were both based in what is now Europe, they did not see themselves as European civilisations. Their civilisation was based around the Mediterranean Sea. People from North Africa were part of such a civilisation. Barbarians from the north of Europe were not.

The Roman Empire dominated the whole Mediterranean region. The Roman Emperor Septimius Severus was of North African descent, as were the playwright Terence and three early popes.[28] Some modern historians have carped that these figures may have been of mixed descent or that sections of the ruling class had come from other parts of the empire so they might have been "white", but that is to miss the point. The kind of "racial" division that seems logical today was meaningless in these societies.

It is also true that skin colour could be an issue. In England black was associated with death, mourning and evil. Devils were often depicted as black. This is not the same, however, as dismissing entire continents as subhuman, but that dismissal is made easier by comments such as those of the English traveller and writer Thomas Herbert who reported in 1629 that Africans were "fearful black", "devilish savages" and "devils incarnate".[29]

Most people didn't travel and were deeply suspicious of strangers. Knowledge of the wider world was very limited.

Civilisations as far apart as Medieval Europe, China and South America often looked down on people who were outlanders or looked different and had different customs. For instance in China, "in 760 several thousand Arab and Persian merchants were massacred at Yangchow by insurgent bands led by T'ien Shen-kung, and a century later, in 879, it was also the foreign merchants who were attacked at Canton by the troops of Huang Ch'ao".[30]

In Medieval Europe the main division was religion. Rulers defined themselves as part of Christendom rather than Europe. But there was no room for smug superiority as neighbouring Islamic states were more advanced technologically and beyond them lay India and China, legendary for unimaginable wealth revealed through spices and manufactured goods.

Within Christendom the church put down heresy with all the enthusiasm it used against other religions. And descendants of heretics could be persecuted for generations. Medieval Europe was not unchanging. By the time Europeans sailed to the Americas, they could revel in how much more advanced their technology was than that of the people they met.

None of this is to suggest that there were no ethnic divisions or awareness in the pre-capitalist period. The complex hierarchies of modern racism developed by building on and expanding existing prejudices.

### Anti-Semitism

The situation of Jewish people is central to understanding the history of racism. Jewish people have undergone a series of different oppressions.

As Abram Leon argued in *The Jewish Question*, Jewish people spread through the Mediterranean region of the ancient world as traders. In so doing, they became what he calls a "people class". People who were not part of this class converted over time to the dominant religion in the region, first Christianity and then Islam.

Jews were not always in a disadvantaged position, even in Medieval

Christendom. Leon notes that in the 9th century under the Holy Roman Emperor Charles the Bald, the sale of impure precious metals was punished by a whipping for serfs, but a fine for free men and Jews.[31]

This class became marginalised in the late medieval period as other groups wanted to become merchants and traders. Many Jewish traders were pushed into money lending. Jews became associated with money lending and hated for that. Other traders moved down the social scale becoming tinkers and were pushed to the margins.

The persecution of Jews in the late Middle Ages was regarded as religious and could be ended by conversion and the abandoning of "alien" cultural practices. This differed from the later anti-Semitism, which saw the Jews as a race rather than a religious group.

The relation between local lords and religious authority changed over time, partly as Catholic authority established itself across Western Europe. The crusades were part of this process. One historian writes, "For the pope this was an opportunity to reassert the supremacy of the Roman Church both in Europe as well as in the countries of the eastern Mediterranean".[32]

And reasserting this authority meant that "many on the crusades cooperated in massacring not only vast numbers of Muslims but so too Jews and those Christians that the Vatican deemed heretical".[33]

### Slavery before the Atlantic trade

The massive scale of the Atlantic slave trade marked it out as thoroughly different from anything that had existed before, in Africa or anywhere else in the world. This scale is missed by people who claim that, while the Atlantic slave trade was barbaric, it was just one of many brutal societies. It is true that forms of slavery were normal in much of Africa at this time, and forms of unfree labour were common around the world. The first European slave traders in Africa joined in with an existing trade.

The slave trade most often compared to Atlantic slavery was that from across the Sahara to the Arab world. Apologists for imperialism often point out that the Saharan trade went on for longer than the Atlantic trade. But around 3,000 slaves a year were taken to the Middle East at the peak of the trans-Saharan trade. The comparable figure for the Atlantic trade was 80,000—and those slaves heading for the Caribbean who survived the "middle passage" could expect to be worked to death.

Africa's various forms of indigenous slavery also differed in character from the Atlantic system. A typical example is Sudan, where slaves were not transferable from one master to another. They had traditional rights and could own property. Slaves of the ruling class could themselves own slaves.

Slavery had been key to the economy of large sections of the ancient world, particularly Greece and Rome—though in a non-racialised society the question of who was enslaved depended far more on who was defeated in battle or owed tribute. Until the growth of the Atlantic trade most slaves in Western Europe came from Eastern Europe, indeed the English word "slave" comes from "Slav". Slavery generally declined in importance as the Roman Empire gave way to feudalism.

The Catholic church had no particular qualms about enslaving fellow Christians, a view it changed once Christendom came into conflict with expanding Islamic powers, which held that believers should not be enslaved.[34] In early Islam Jews and Christians were also not to be enslaved, though this changed over time.

When the first Portuguese traders arrived on the African coast in the late 1400s they may have tapped into existing trade routes but they justified their actions as a means of conversion—and in this guise they gained the pope's support for their enterprise.[35]

The Muslim prohibition of enslaving co-religionists partly explains the trans-Saharan trade, which in principle if not always in practice avoided the capture of those who shared the faith. When they could be captured prisoners from Europe were also enslaved. Slaves in the Islamic lands filled a number of roles, including military and administrative, that would have seemed absurd to those who would claim that black people were subhuman.

As the slave population of the Americas increased, the European rulers came up against a problem. If it was not permissible to enslave fellow Christians how could they justify their brutal system? The growth of the belief that the slaves were in their natural role helped salve their consciences and the church shifted its position.

*Say it Loud*

### The horrors of middle passage

Between the early 16th century and 1870 up to 13 million slaves were transported to the Americas. It is likely that as many as 21 million people were captured in order to get that many live slaves across. This is in a period when the total population of Africa was in the region of 50 million. The trade devastated economies. It removed much of Africa's most productive labour and it created skewed, militarised societies.

When discussing the slave trade the sheer horror of what took place should never be forgotten. The slave traders were well aware of how unacceptable their actions appeared to most people in Britain and went to great lengths to disguise the reality from the public. Relatively few slaves actually arrived in Britain because of the triangular nature of the trade and it was therefore possible for slave traders to peddle all sorts of fanciful stories.

The former slave Olaudah Equiano famously wrote an autobiography, in which he recalled his experience on the middle passage:

> The closeness of the place, and the heat of the climate, added to the number in the ship, which was so crowded that each had scarcely room to turn himself, almost suffocated us. This produced copious perspirations, so that the air soon became unfit for respiration, from a variety of loathsome smells, and brought on a sickness among the slaves, of which many died, thus falling victims to the improvident avarice, as I may call it, of their purchasers. This wretched situation was again aggravated by the galling of the chains, now become insupportable; and the filth of the necessary tubs, into which the children often fell, and were almost suffocated. The shrieks of the women, and the groans of the dying, rendered the whole a scene of horror almost inconceivable.[36]

Once they arrived in the Caribbean slaves could expect to be worked to death on plantations. Yet a manual for planters could recall, "How pleasing, how gratifying...it is to see a swarm of healthy, active, cheerful, pliant...Negro boys and girls going to and returning from the puerile work field".[37]

The brutality is epitomised by the notorious story of the *Zong*, which set sail from West Africa with a crew of 17 and 470 slaves. In a difficult passage seven of the crew and 60 slaves died, and more fell ill. The captain calculated that if the slaves died a natural death the ship owners would have to bear the cost. If he could claim they had died in an attempt to save the ship he could claim them on insurance. Thus he threw his "cargo" overboard. In an insurance claim he said that the ship had run out of water and he had no choice. The truth came out, but in an ensuing court case the solicitor general defended the ship owners, stating that prosecution for murder "would be madness; the blacks were property". And thus the case was tried simply as an issue over a lost cargo between owners and insurers.[18]

In many ways the 19th century slave owners of the American South treated their slaves better, because they had to get them to reproduce, once there were no more coming from Africa to replace them. But this was a relative shift. Former slave Moses Grandy recalled how heavily pregnant women were still forced to do their shift in the field and that "a woman who gives offence in the field and is large in a family way, is compelled to lie down over a hole made to receive her corpulency, and is flogged with the whip".[39]

### Resistance and revolt against slavery

The same capitalists who worked black slaves to death had shown no greater mercy to the white indentured labourers who preceded them. These were also the people investing in early factories which were death traps. The difference between the experience of factory workers and slaves was one of degree rather than kind. Both systems faced concerted resistance from the outset.

The great black Marxist C L R James was outraged at the way the unending resistance to slavery by the slaves themselves has been written out of history. He writes:

> In America the Negroes made nearly 150 distinct revolts against slavery. The only place where Negroes did not revolt is in the pages of capitalist historians.[40]

News of the French Revolution affected all classes in St Domingue, then the richest colonial property in the world. Adam Hochschild writes:

*Say it Loud*

News from Europe spread with lightning speed because at white dinner tables, as one resident put it "every person has his own waiting man behind him". "To discuss *The Rights of Man* before such people... What is it but to teach them that power dwells with strength and strength with numbers".[41]

Slaves rose up and showed that they understood and fought for the values of the French Revolution far more closely than their masters. Toussaint L'Ouverture, who came to lead the rebellion, swore allegiance to the values of the revolution and swore by them until he died, betrayed by French generals. In a letter from the leaders of the slave revolt to the colonial assembly in St Dominique, in 1792, Toussaint declared:

> Yes, gentlemen, we are free like you, and it is only by your avarice and our ignorance that anyone is still held in slavery up to this day, and we can neither see nor find the right that you pretend to have over us... We are your equals then, by natural right, and if nature pleases itself to diversify colours within the human race, it is not a crime to be born black or an advantage to be white.[42]

He proceeded to demand liberty under the auspices of the French Revolution.

But the biggest lesson for the slavers was the efficiency of the risen slaves. They first beat one French army, then the cream of Britain's forces who thought they could easily walk in while France was otherwise occupied and finally an army of Napoleon Bonaparte's. Britain sent more men to fight in this campaign than it had to defend the rebellious American colonies. It is difficult to think of an equivalent today—beyond fighting off invasions by both Russia and the US.

Many historians have made much of the slaves' violence, but as James points out in his masterful book on the revolt, *The Black Jacobins*, the slaves were:

> surprisingly moderate, then and afterwards, far more humane than their masters had been or would ever be to them. They did not maintain this vengeful spirit for long. The cruelties of property and privilege are always more ferocious than the revenges of poverty and

oppression. For the one aims at perpetuating resented injustice, the other is merely a momentary passion soon appeased... Compared with what their masters had done to them in cold blood, what they did was negligible.[43]

But after three brutal assaults by European armies the restraint shown by the ex-slaves to the whites was long forgotten. The newly independent state of Haiti, freed by former slaves, represented a powerful beacon of liberation and a threat to authority of the Western regimes. The imperialist powers began their long revenge—first by crippling Haiti with foreign debt after France outrageously demanded "reparations" for property damaged by the slave revolts, then by military threats, invasions and occupations, most notably by US troops.[44]

### Britain's black population

As a direct result of the slave trade a significant black population built up in Britain. Two black men imprisoned for begging in London during 1773 received upwards of 300 black visitors.[45] Not all black residents were slaves or ex-slaves though. By the 1780s at least 50 school children sent by wealthy West African parents were getting their education in the Liverpool area.[46]

What really concerned the authorities was the fact that slaves were often regarded as fellows by ordinary people. Magistrate Sir John Fielding warned slave owners in 1768 that it was highly risky to try and recapture runaway slaves as they have "the mob on their side".[47]

And it wasn't just those who had met black people who adopted this attitude. At a mass meeting organised by radicals in Sheffield in 1794 thousands of artisans unanimously passed a resolution calling for the emancipation of black slaves:

"Wishing to be rid of the weight of oppression under which we groan, we are induced to compassionate those who groan also", declared the Yorkshiremen, before pledging to "avenge peacefully ages of wrongs done to our Negro Bretheren."

Adam Hochschild described how Thomas Clarkson's campaign against the slave trade started with a meeting of just 12 people. They formed themselves into a committee with what must have seemed to their fellow Londoners a hopelessly idealistic and impractical aim—ending the British slave trade.

This business was dominated by British ships, which at that point carried about half the slaves taken to the New World. Starting a movement in Britain to outlaw this trade in 1787 was as utopian a task as starting a renewable energy movement in Saudi Arabia today.[48] But the movement took off immediately, particularly among the new urban masses who were inspired by the radical libertarian language of the French and American revolutions.

Slavers used all the best public relations of their day in an attempt to undermine the campaign. In a particularly modern touch a letter to *The Gentleman's Magazine* suggested in 1789, "Instead of slaves, let the negroes be called assistant-planters; and we shall not then hear such violent outcries against the slave trade".[49]

People petitioned parliament, though few had the right to vote. Every literate inhabitant of a small town or village signed some of the petitions. The campaign gathered factual information to undermine the slave owners' false claim that Africans were happier as slaves. Equiano toured the land, speaking and selling his book.

Hochschild concludes:

> The British slave trade was abolished in 1807. When it became evident that British slavery itself was not going to wither away and die as a result, the movement revived in the 1820s, pushing for the emancipation of the slaves.[50]

Working class organisations—that were now starting to agitate over issues such as child labour and factory conditions—saw the connections between the slaves and their own lives. They paraded during the election campaign with signs that read "End slavery at home and abroad". The campaign was partly successful as arguably the first mass campaign, but the slave owners and Britain's rulers were also heavily influenced by the increased danger of holding slaves—as the slaves kept revolting. For example, some 20,000 Jamaican slaves led by Samuel Sharpe staged a huge uprising in 1831, the largest ever seen in British territory. It was suppressed but only after fierce fighting.

Slavery was abolished in the British Empire in 1833. It was no longer as important economically, but there is no reason to believe it would not have dragged on for a great deal longer if it was not for constant rebellions by the slaves and hostility in Britain. Britain's rulers certainly didn't abolish slavery out of sympathy with its victims. The 1833 abolition act set aside £20 million in compensation, but all for the slave owners, not the former slaves, who now found themselves paying rent to their former owners.[51]

Impoverished former slaves were left with few choices as to where to work. In the Caribbean many made the only choice available to them, working as smallholders or share croppers rather than agreeing to continue labouring on plantations.

## 2   Racism and empire

Black nationalists, who argue that black people require some form of autonomous organisation, and liberal anti-racists both say that Marxists downplay race and other forms of oppression in favour of class. For Marxists class division is not only the root of oppression, but also opens up the possibility of ending oppression. Whether in Chesapeake or in modern times, our rulers push racism because they know that it divides the forces that could challenge their power. This explains why racism remains now, long after the slave trade that it developed out of has passed into history.

Marx argued that the existence of racism offers real benefits for capitalists. He developed his understanding by watching divisions between Irish immigrants to England and "native" workers. His arguments show that there is nothing specific to any particular characteristic such as skin colour. Racism is about division and exclusion, not a real difference of interests.

He explained:

Every industrial and commercial centre in England now possesses a working class divided into two hostile camps, English proletarians and Irish proletarians. The ordinary English worker hates the Irish worker as a competitor who lowers his standard of life. In relation to

*Say it Loud*

the Irish worker he regards himself as a member of the ruling nation and consequently he becomes a tool of the English aristocrats and capitalists against Ireland, thus strengthening their domination over himself. He cherishes religious, social, and national prejudices against the Irish worker. His attitude towards him is much the same as that of the "poor whites" to the Negroes in the former slave states of the USA. The Irishman pays him back with interest in his own money. He sees in the English worker both the accomplice and the stupid tool of the English rulers in Ireland.

This antagonism is artificially kept alive and intensified by the press, the pulpit, the comic papers, in short, by all the means at the disposal of the ruling classes. This antagonism is the secret of the impotence of the English working class, despite its organisation.[52]

In his book *Race and Class* Alex Callinicos has shown how this passage outlines the materialist explanation of racism in modern capitalism. He points to three conditions Marx identifies for the existence of racism. First, there is economic competition between workers. This is reflected in the labour market under capitalism in the form of different wage rates. Callinicos writes:

Particularly in periods of capital restructuring when labour is deskilled, capitalists (being what they are) are tempted to replace established skilled workers with cheaper and less skilled workers. If the two groups of workers have different national origins, and probably therefore also different languages and traditions, the potential exists for the development of racial antagonisms among the two groups of workers.[53]

Racism can be used both to exclude new workers and to drive workers from positions they have already attained. For instance in the northern cities of the United States black workers were pushed out of skilled jobs—as dockers, construction workers, coachmen, stablemen and barbers, for example—by unskilled Irish immigrants in the 1840s and 1850s.[54]

Second, the ruling class keeps renewing racism. This is not simply a capitalist conspiracy, however. The kind of labour the bosses require shifts over time as old industries decline and new ones emerge. In such circumstances immigrant workers may provide the best source to meet those needs.

Third is the fact that racist ideas can appeal to workers. The result in mid-19th century Britain was, according to Marx, a situation where the English worker "regards himself as a member of the ruling nation". Such workers believe that they have something to gain from identifying with the bosses rather than the immigrant labourers they work alongside. But, as Marx argues, this merely strengthens the ability of capitalists to exploit all workers.

Racism grew up with the slave trade, but it was consolidated and entrenched through empire. With the building of empire we see the extension of racism to create a great web of different kinds of races. Bigotry was expanded and kept modern by linking it with scientific developments in taxonomy and evolution. Charles Darwin's theory of natural selection is not in itself racist, but it was quickly taken up as part of the justification for inequality among people and peoples. Darwin himself accepted some of this false logic, commenting, "The civilised races of man will almost certainly exterminate, and replace, the savage races throughout the world".[55] Racists crowed about how much further white people had evolved. And during high imperialism all kinds of distinctions between various supposed European races were discovered.

It became a common sense that has never really disappeared that European or "white" civilisation had always been more advanced than those of other societies. The flowering of earlier non-European civilisations including those in Egypt, India and China was always difficult to explain and reconcile with this.

It has only been since the growth of capitalism that a continent such as Africa has been seen as universally backward and lacking in history. Previously travellers were ready to acknowledge its development and achievements. The Moroccan explorer Ibn Batuta—who had travelled across China, India and the Middle East—said of Kilwa, in modern Tanzania, east Africa, which he visited in 1331, that it was "among the most beautiful of cities and elegantly built".[56] Similarly in about 1602 a Dutch trader reported of Benin in West Africa:

> The Towne seemeth to be very great, when you enter it. You go into a great broad street, not paved, which seemeth to be seven or eight times broader than the Warmoes Street in Amsterdam... The Houses in this Towne stand in good order, one close and even with the other, as the Houses in Holland stand.[57]

It was the Atlantic slave trade that really damaged the continent. By the time of the Berlin conference in 1884 and 1885 it seemed ripe for division between the European powers. This period is the peak of paternalist racism, exemplified by Rudyard Kipling's poem, "The White Man's Burden":

> Take up the White Man's burden—
> The savage wars of peace—
> Fill full the mouth of famine
> And bid the sickness cease;
> And when your goal is nearest
> The end for others sought,
> Watch Sloth and heathen Folly
> Bring all your hopes to nought.[58]

The subjects of empire are no longer described as animals or sub-human. They are now ungrateful children who have to be brought up with tough love.

As with the planters who told tall tales about how well the slaves were treated, the reality of life for subjects of the British Empire was rather different from the propaganda. In 1897 Sir Arthur Hardinge, the first British governor for what would become Kenya, said, "These people must learn submission by bullets—it's the only school; after that you may begin more modern and humane methods of education".[59] Historians like Niall Ferguson romanticise the colonial period, saying that while it may have been exploitative it brought the benefits of Western education, medicine, infrastructure and science.[60] The truth is that where these benefits occurred they were a by-product of extracting materials and creating markets for the colonial powers. Moreover, colonial subjects were continually held back. For example, Africans in Kenya were banned from growing the most profitable crops, such as coffee. The fact of the ban is evidence that the settlers' farming methods were not inherently superior. It was required because African farmers represented serious competition.

As the imperial reach of the capitalist powers spread around the world the ideas of race spread with them. The non-scientific concept could be shaped to include a few races—perhaps just white, black, brown, yellow—or many. Britain's rulers in particular became experts at creating and exploiting ethnic divisions. Attitudes to India changed as the empire developed. Traders and soldiers in the 18th century often chose to live like the established rulers, in what they saw as a civilisation that they could both learn from and exploit. Marriage to local women was not unusual. But as the racial politics of empire spread, the small minority of British rulers came to see themselves as a superior and separate group. Such attitudes were made fully concrete after the Indian rebellion of 1857. The subcontinent was brought under direct rule from Britain, where before it had, at least in theory, been run by the East India Company. One justification for this change was the barbarism of the Indian rebels, who had demanded an end to British exploitation. Marx pointed out the hypocrisy of this position:

> To find parallels with the Sepoy atrocities, we need not, as some London papers pretend, fall back on the Middle Ages, nor even wander beyond the history of contemporary England. All we want is to study the first Chinese war... The English soldiery then committed abominations for the mere fun of it; their passions being neither sanctified by religious fanaticism nor exacerbated by hatred against an overbearing and conquering race.[61]

He is referring to Britain's brutal military humiliation of China, known as the First Opium War (1839-1842), because its cause was Britain insisting on having free trade rights to export opium from India to China. After China's defeat European powers and Japan took control of huge parts of China. They built "concessions" in every major city—zones where foreign law, not Chinese, ruled.

## Other unfree labour

Slavery was not the first form of unfree labour to be used by capitalists. We have already discussed the role of indentured labour, in which people were forced to work for a fixed period of time. After the end of the slave trade a version of indentured labour returned to provide labour around colonial empires—sometimes called "coolie" labour. Colonialists had no compunction about simply ordering forced labour as well. Particularly significant are the use of Indian and Chinese labourers both inside India and in other parts of the British Empire, and across the Pacific Rim and in the US. This little-remembered traffic formed another part of capitalism's great migration of peoples.

The island of Mauritius in the Indian Ocean provides a useful example. Here as many as one in seven slaves had come from south India and after slavery was abolished through the British Empire in 1838 India remained a primary source of labour. In 1840 the territory received 18,000 labourers from India.[62] One plantation owner noted the benefit of the coolie system in 1835: "The cost is not half that of a slave".[63] Mauritius had a complex history as most slaves were African, but some were Indian or even Chinese. Once slavery was abolished the majority of coolies were Indian, but some were African—mostly from Madagascar. However, some Africans were people who had been captured as slaves then rescued by the British navy and sent to perform unfree labour in Mauritius.[64]

A century later coolies were defined as:

> Indian, Malaysian, Chinese, Polynesian and Japanese coolies, most of whom work in countries situated in the tropics, but governed by Europeans. For the most part they are employed on the plantations, but also work in the mines and as navvies on various kinds of projects, such as railway or canal construction.[65]

Often coolie labour could be moved around colonial empires to undercut local workers. In the late 19th century western states of the US such as California were encouraging the arrival of Chinese and Japanese workers. After 1924, when legislation blocked this, workers from the Philippines were used. By the start of the Second World

War there were 78,000 Chinese-Americans and 127,000 Japanese Americans on the west coast.[66]

## Nationalism

No study of racism can ignore the growth of nationalism, another product of the development of capitalism. Like racism the idea of the nation is now so universal that many people assume it has always existed.

The success of mercantile trade from Britain and Holland based on centralised states led other powers to follow. More competition between powers led to more centralisation. Each developed their own nationalism—and these were progressive in as much as they advanced society socially, away from the mystic ideas of feudalism. The ideas of nationalism should not be romanticised as they went along with the development of empire and new forms of brutal repression. For a time, however, they tended to increase human unity and rationalism. At their peak with the French and American revolutions they liberalised religious tolerance and opposed regional oppression. Chris Harman suggests that:

> Nationalism grew up as part of the ideology of capitalist development. The idea of the nation is inseparable from a range of other ideas associated with the bourgeois revolution. If nationalism has conquered the globe, with every individual anywhere in the world today slotted into one national identity or another, it is because capitalism has conquered the globe.[67]

In its link with capitalism nationalism bears some similarities to division into races. Marxists do not say race is irrelevant because we believe that class is the dominant division in society, and the same is true of nationalism. Socialists who want to end oppression must take the side of the more oppressed nationalities in the same way that they must identify with those who suffer from racism.

As Harman put it, people's identification with a subsidiary nationalism depends on:

> the extent to which the old state carries through policies that can be seen as involving oppression along national lines. The classic

*Say it Loud*

form this takes is discrimination against those who speak a certain language—as with the Turkish government's attempts in the 1980s to ban Kurdish or the Sri Lankan government's insistence that Sinhalese, not Tamil, is the official language. Although the middle classes suffer most, workers too face problems every time they come in contact with the state—with its police, its courts, or even its post offices.[68]

And national differences can shade into racism. So some groups that are culturally oppressed can find that minor or transient cultural differences are exaggerated to become treated like inherited characteristics. Perhaps the most obvious case in Britain is the repeated attempt by cartoonists and commentators to suggest that Irish people are somehow inherently different and inferior.

Sometimes individuals can seem to escape prejudices based on culture or religion. So some Kurds have taken leading roles in Turkey having abandoned their culture, as Marx and Disraeli abandoned the traditions of Judaism. However, a cultural difference can become a racial one, as the attack on Jews in Europe in the first half of the 20th century shows. While there is no such thing as race, racism has an objective reason to exist and persist.

The most extreme form of reactionary nationalism, fascism, first developed in Italy after the First World War. It emerged from the fear of sections of society like the petty bourgeoisie—small business owners and shopkeepers—that they would be marginalised in the great class struggles that exploded after the First World War. The core aim of fascism was to counter the strength of the working class. While racism is often a key way to do this, Mussolini's movement did not use anti-Semitism until it became linked to Hitler's Nazis in Germany. European fascism is, however, forever linked to the terrible racist crime of the Holocaust. Since then it has been harder for fascists to win mass support if they show their true colours. It also destroyed the intellectual respectability of scientific racism, forcing racists to shift the terrain on which they present their ideas of division to that of culture.

In Germany, where the working class movement was both

stronger and better organised than in Italy, the call to blame the Jews made more sense. Jews could be characterised as poor immigrants undercutting the income of native workers, as communists destroying the fabric of society and as finance capitalists squeezing small shopkeepers. Meanwhile the Nazis presented themselves as the defenders of national productive capital against Jewish parasitic capital.[69] Ultimately, the piling of outright lies on top of distorted half truths does not make for a logical or coherent explanation of the world, but as with other racist stories the Nazi myths were largely there to cover up truths that rulers did not want seen. This is not to say that the Nazis did not believe their own racist filth. Towards the end of the war when the country was hamstrung by labour shortages, it made no sense to exterminate a slave labour force. But the fanatics running the war believed that this was part of a final solution to a "Jewish problem" that was otherwise insoluble.

## The United States: The sharpest arguments

Though this book focuses primarily upon Britain and its role in the development of racism, we cannot ignore developments in the United States, which have impacted on the spread of both racism and anti-racism for more than a century.

The United States has been unusual among capitalist states in the degree to which its development has been overtly connected to racism. The existence of plantation slavery in around half of its states clustered in the South skewed its development. By the middle of the 19th century the existence of the slave states had become the central issue in US politics. As the country grew by creating new states on land seized from Native Americans to the west an economic and moral row developed about how such states should be constituted— with slave or free labour.

Contrary to the popular view that the US has moved steadily away from a racist past, in several periods it has made progress and then regressed. The vote had been removed from all free blacks in the South by the early 18th century. In the first half of the 19th century Northern states passed similar anti-black voting measures.[70] In the new territories to the west black people had by and large had the vote, but as they became states this right was removed: in Ohio in 1803, Indiana in 1816, Illinois 1818, Michigan 1837, Iowa 1846, Wisconsin 1848, Minnesota in 1858 and Kansas in 1861.[71]

By the 1860s the newly formed Republican Party, led by Abraham Lincoln, wanted new states being established in the west to use wage labour rather than slave labour. It saw the Southern plantation economy, which was dominated by the Democratic Party and run on slave labour, as a block on further economic development. Initially the Northern leadership were happy for slavery to continue in the Southern states as long as it did not expand westward. Their hope was that this would enable them to avoid a full blown military confrontation. These hopes were dashed and civil war broke out in 1861.

At its heart, this was a struggle over the most efficient ways to make profit. As the confrontation progressed, however, the Northern leaders were forced to adapt. Once the Southern states had broken away and war commenced, they realised that they could only win by promising freedom to the slaves and recruiting black soldiers in order to disrupt the Southern economy. It was practical necessity therefore that drove the radicalisation of the North—not any pre thought out ideological plan. The North's eventual victory in 1865 was in no small measure due to the active support of slaves and former slaves.

President Abraham Lincoln is widely praised as the "Great Emancipator" who issued the 1863 Emancipation Proclamation which freed all slaves living in rebel territory not yet controlled by Lincoln's army. Two years later he forced through the 13th Amendment to the Constitution which enshrined the abolition of slavery throughout the country. Far from simply being the grateful recipients of Lincoln's benevolence, it was the activity of the slaves that had been central in making him come to this position.

## Douglass and Delany
Frederick Douglass was a former slave who became a key anti-slavery campaigner, as well as an advocate for the rights of women, Native Americans and recent immigrants. In his early campaigns he worked alongside Martin Delany with whom he established the anti-slavery paper *North Star*. Delany, who is sometimes called the "father

of black nationalism", was far less convinced than Douglass that racism could be overcome. In the 1850s he argued that black people would have to leave and set up their own state. In 1854 Delany led the National Emigration Convention in Cleveland, Ohio. He put forward the argument for black emigration in "Political Destiny of the Colored Race on the American Continent". The convention approved a resolution stating, "As men and equals, we demand every political right, privilege and position to which the whites are eligible in the United States, and we will either attain to these, or accept nothing." However, when the civil war broke out Delany saw the potential to change the US itself and not only encouraged black men to join the northern army, but signed up himself.[72]

After the war he worked for the Freedmen's Bureau, the government organisation that was set up to help former slaves, and then became a politician in the Republican Party—then still the most radical mainstream organisation. His experience disillusioned him, however, and made him think that change was not possible inside the US.[73] He returned to talk of black separatism but was surprised at how unpopular his ideas were with black people in the South. He "found it dangerous to go into the country and speak of colour in any manner whatever, without the angry rejoinder, 'We don't want to hear that; we are all one colour now'."[74]

In contrast, Frederick Douglass held a class analysis of racism, not dissimilar to the one put forward in this book. He argued that:

> The hostility between the whites and blacks of the South is easily explained. It has its roots and sap in the relation of slavery, and was incited on both sides by the cunning of the slave-masters... They divided both to conquer each.[75]

And that hostility was actively built and maintained through the development of segregationist movements like the Ku Klux Klan and later the racist "Jim Crow" laws.[76]

Delany denied that this was relevant, saying that the fight for black freedom was not "a question of rich against poor or the common people against the higher classes, but a question of white against black—every white person by legal right being held superior

*Say it Loud*

to a black or coloured person".[77] These two different analyses of racism and how to fight it have recurred throughout the 150 years since Delany and Douglass's time.

## Reconstruction

There was a social crisis across the devastated Southern states in the aftermath of the war. Its whole social system had collapsed and there was no clear plan for what would replace it. This opened a space for radical change. In the years of Radical Reconstruction from about 1868 to 76 the vote was extended to black people and the Republican Party extended its support from blacks to poor whites by appealing to them on a class basis. One statement declared:

> Let the slave holding aristocracy no longer rule you. Vote for a con-
> stitution which educates your children free of charge, relieves the
> poor debtor from his rich creditor...and more than all places you on
> a level with those who used to boast that for every slave they were
> entitled to three fifths of a vote in congressional representation.[78]

Social change spread across the South. For instance, Mississippi's 1868 constitution created a racially mixed public school system, and hundreds of schools were built. Fourteen black congressmen and two black senators were elected. Over 800 public legislators were black. All were from the South.

However, in what was still a rural economy, most of the land remained in the hands of the former slave owners. Northern capital-ists had no taste for the confiscation of property to give the former slaves or the poor whites somewhere to farm. Most of the Northern rich felt more comfortable dealing with the former slave owners than the radicals in their own party. Consequently, by the end of the 1870s the old Southern elite had been allowed to re-establish its rule through a campaign of electoral fraud and savage Ku Klux Klan violence. This was a catastrophe for the ex-slaves but also a his-toric defeat for poor whites. A Mississippi poll tax aimed at excluding blacks from the vote also reduced the white electorate from 130,000 to 68,000.

The mass Populist movement established in the 1890s fought

valiantly to take the South in a different direction. Populist leader Tom Watson said of the typical Southern white and black man:

> You are kept apart that you may be separately fleeced of your earnings. You are made to hate each other because upon that hatred is rested the keystone of the arch of financial despotism that enslaves you both.

When black Populist Reverend R S Doyle was threatened with lynching, 2,000 whites came to defend him. Black people also held positions in the leadership of the movement. The South's rulers saw this as a return to Reconstruction and dealt with it in the same way. A combination of repression and an ill-advised deal with the Democrats—who had adopted some of the movement's rhetoric—finished the Populists. Their vote reached 1.5 million in 1894, but totally collapsed in 1896. This disintegration brought despair. Tragically, the Populists' own leader Watson would re-emerge as a vicious racist. It was in this period that the Jim Crow laws were established. And between 1882 and 1903, 2,060 black people were lynched.

Once again the misery was not restricted to black people. In Louisiana the black electorate fell by 90 percent and the white by 60 percent. Continuing segregation held back white workers' ability to resist. Those demanding wage increases or better working conditions could be threatened with replacement by cheaper black labour.

In the early 20th century the competing strategies of Booker T Washington and W E B Du Bois led the struggle against racism. Washington believed discrimination would end once black people had shown through education and hard work that they were worthy of equality. He set up the Tuskegee Institute as a centre for such education. By 1915, however, Du Bois's more radical ideas were dominant. He demanded equality and was a leader of the new multiracial National Association for the Advancement of Colored People (NAACP). Rather than focusing on the masses, however, he still looked to organising a minority of black people, what he called the "talented tenth".

The development of a layer of black political leaders raised the question of unity with white workers' organisations. Experience throughout the last century shows that where white socialists have made their black comrades welcome and have shown they are serious about tackling racism, black people have been happy to work with them. Both groups have benefitted. Unfortunately, all too often black radicals have been pushed aside by white activists and then blamed for separating. The example of Hubert Harrison,[79] an important and innovative Marxist in the early years of the 20th century, shows this.

Harrison had arrived in New York in 1900 from the West Indies.[80] He worked as a full-time organiser for the Socialist Party in New York and argued for an organised strategy to recruit black workers. He also demanded that the party stopped allowing racism within its ranks and posed the question:

> Southernism or socialism—which? Is it to be the white half of the working class against the black half, or all of the working class? Can we hope to triumph over capitalism with one half of the working class against us?[81]

Unfortunately, the party's response was to continue welcoming racists and Harrison left. Though he worked with the International Workers of the World (IWW) for a time, by 1915 he was coming to "race first" politics. Harrison's shift was a tragic response to the behaviour of the left in this period. Take, for instance, William Z Foster, a former member of both the Socialist Party and the IWW, who would become a leading Communist and who wrote a history of the great steel strike of 1919. A section of this attacks black workers for their "open hostility" to organised labour, complaining that they were prepared to be used as strikebreakers and took a "keen delight in stealing the white men's jobs". Harrison responded by asking why "any self-respecting Negro leaders" would encourage black workers to "join forces with the stupid and short-sighted labour oligarchy which refuses to join forces with them".[82] This question has been repeated in various forms through anti-racist struggles from that point on. It has only been when white workers have seen their joint interests, as they would in the 1930s, that progress for both has been made.

With the intensification of Jim Crow and the backlash against black people at the end of the First World War a new movement emerged, a mass movement based on the slogan "Stand up you mighty race". It was an exclusively black movement very firmly led by the Jamaican Marcus Garvey.[83] By the early 1920s his Universal Negro Improvement Association (UNIA), based in Harlem, New York, claimed 2 million members.

Garvey preached race pride and argued that since black and white could not live together they should separate, with black people returning to Africa. He was a contradictory figure. Sometimes he railed at the "inferiority" or "laziness" of black people and demanded that the better elements pull themselves up to a level where they could fit in with the world of great empires. Sometimes he raged at the systematic racist oppression of Africa and black people in general.

Garvey's most famous project was the Black Star shipping line. This was initially intended to promote black-owned trade around the Caribbean and make travel cheaper. When Garvey managed to get one battered old liner running it seemed to prove the power of black self-help against the weight of white US society. The shipping line went bankrupt, but Garvey said, "We succeeded in the sense of our desire for success." He meant that he had proved that black people could organise themselves and thus prepared them for future successes.

But the UNIA was not central to the huge struggles in the US in the 1930s, when it refused to work with Communists around the vital Scottsboro Boys case—in which nine black men were convicted in Alabama of a rape that had never happened. Garvey was eclipsed partly because of endless attacks from the US state, but largely because the tactics the Communists put forward bringing black and white workers together proved more effective. The story of this united resistance is taken up in chapter 7 on the struggles in the US.

## 3  Britain and immigration

Just as racism developed alongside capitalism so resistance to racism and capitalism have often worked in tandem. In Britain, where both have existed for hundreds of years, that tradition is oldest. Immigrants and white workers have joined together at the high points of the movement for workers' rights right through the 19th and 20th centuries.

In 1819, the same year that the British state showed its contempt for demands for reform by killing 15 people and injuring hundreds more in the Peterloo Massacre, a debate was held in London with the contentious title, "Has a slave an inherent right to slay his master who refuses him liberty?" The argument that slaves had exactly this right was put by Robert Wedderburn, himself the son of a slave. An audience of artisans and labourers enthusiastically accepted the proposition. After the vote Wedderburn commented, "Well, gentlemen, I can now write home and tell the slaves to murder their masters as soon as they please".[84]

And though Wedderburn only mentions men, women were also active. For instance Mary Prince published an autobiography in 1828. Her story is a reminder that slavery continued even in Britain itself after the abolition of the trade.[85] The book went through three printings in its first year, helping to galvanise the anti-slavery movement.

In the years following the end of the slave trade the number of non-white people in Britain appeared to decline. In fact there was no mass exodus. Instead intermarriage with the local population simply meant that black people became less visible. Racism did not disappear, however. The majority of immigrants to Britain in the 19th century came from Ireland, and, as we have previously indicated, they faced terrible oppression. Large-scale permanent migration from Ireland started after the actions of British rulers caused the famine of the mid-1840s. Those who could afford it fled to the US but others were forced to travel to Britain. By the 1880s some 1.5 million people of Irish origin lived in Britain—about 3 percent of the population. Bigots portrayed the Irish as a separate race, reduced in caricature to apes, and encouraged English workers to blame them for their own poverty. Irish workers lived in the worst housing and bosses attempted to use them to undercut other workers' wages.

## Chartism
It is no coincidence that two of the leaders of the world's first radical democratic workers' movement, the Chartists, were immigrants.

Its national organiser Fergus O'Connor was originally from Ireland; William Cuffay, the elected leader of the Chartists in London, was both an immigrant and black.

The movement sought to organise across the national and colour divide, boldly declaring, "Irishmen resident in London, on the part of the democrats in England we extend to you the warm hand of fraternization; your principles are ours, and our principles shall be yours".[86] The establishment *Times* newspaper knew its enemy, reporting with disdain that "Cuffay is half a nigger. Some of the others are Irishmen. We doubt there are half a dozen Englishmen in the whole lot".[87]

Despite heroic struggles and mass appeal, the Chartist movement was eventually defeated. Cuffay was transported to Tasmania despite running his own powerful defence in court. His indomitable spirit meant that he was unbowed and carried on organising in Tasmania.

Racist ideas that were swept away during periods of solidarity and struggle became entrenched in the decades of defeat that followed. The majority of people in Britain came to identify with the empire, despite the fact that it left them living in poverty.

The situation was to change with the emergence of the New Unionism in the 1880s, which brought a new wave of Irish activists into politics. Again many of the leaders of the new movement were of Irish descent, including Will Thorne of the gas workers and Ben Tillett, one of the leaders of the great 1889 London docks strike.

### End of Empire

In the West the Second World War was sold at the time and is remembered as a war to defend democracy. In his provocative essay, written just before war broke out, socialist writer George Orwell pointed out the hypocrisy of this position when he wrote that in any discussion about defending the democracies against totalitarianism, "The unspoken clause is always 'Not counting niggers'."[88] There was no democracy on offer for the subjects of empire, vastly more numerous than the people living in the countries that ruled them.

In the years after the war colonial powers like Britain and France aimed to go back to business as usual. This was not quite so simple and they found it now necessary to talk about independence at some undefined time in the future. In reality the colonisers only left when they were forced out.

Much current ethnic tension in the Global South can be traced back to the racist policies of the colonial empires. Perhaps the clearest example is the partition of India to create Pakistan. Chris Harman argues that, in an attempt to limit the influence of the Gandhi's Congress independence movement, the British imperial authorities:

> turned to the Muslim League as a counterweight to Congress. They claimed it represented all Muslims and gave it control of several provinces despite its poor performance in the 1937 elections. Its best known leader, Mohammed Ali Jinnah, now embraced the demand for a separate Muslim state—one he had previously opposed— even though it was impossible to draw the boundaries of such a state without including within it very large numbers of Hindus and Sikhs and excluding the very large numbers of Muslims who lived in Hindu majority areas.[89]

As India gained independence Britain aimed to consolidate in other parts of its empire. After Indian independence the colonial office stated bluntly, "Africa is now the core of our colonial position; the only continental space from which we can draw reserves of economic and military strength." But this scheme unravelled in a decade. C L R James commented, "Nothing in modern history was more startling than the rapidity with which...African states achieved political independence".[90] During 1960 a total of 17 African countries gained independence from their colonial masters. This was the highest in any single year and, as British prime minister Harold Macmillan said, it signalled that "the winds of change" were blowing across the continent.

Most of the new African leaders talked about socialism and in the immediate aftermath of independence came real improvements in education, healthcare and industrial production. The demise of this progress and the breathtaking corruption of many leaders have been used to resurrect racist claims about the nature of non-white people. The real truth is that it was pressure from Cold War politics and the world economic crisis of the 1970s that threw these plans off kilter, not any genetic disability of Africans to run a state or Arabs and South Americans to maintain democracy.

For all that the colonial period may have finished, recent wars in Iraq and Afghanistan and the renewed scramble for Africa with the millions of related deaths are reminders that imperialism still straddles the world.

## Immigration controls

There is a long history of the ruling class attempting to scapegoat immigrants—often created by their imperialist policies—by blaming them for poverty and poor housing. Speaking in parliament in 1902, for example, Tory MP William Evans Gordon suggested that:

> Not a day passes but English families are ruthlessly turned out to make room for foreign invaders...Romanians, Russians and Poles. Rents are raised 50 or 100 percent... It is only a matter of time before the population becomes entirely foreign...The working classes know that the new buildings are erected not for them but for strangers from abroad; they see schools crowded with foreign children, and the very posters and advertisements on the wall in a foreign tongue.[91]

This racist diatribe is remarkably similar to current statements on the dangers of immigration and equally inaccurate.

Such racism paved the way for the first immigration controls in Britain: the Aliens Act of 1905, which defined some groups of migrants as "undesirable" and was the first to limit immigration. The eastern European immigrants who were the target of such outrage in this period were Jews fleeing pogroms. They joined the Irish in facing the bulk of racist oppression in Britain.

The ruling class as a whole has a contradictory attitude to immigrants. It needs extra workers to expand the economy. At the same time, migrants provide a useful focus to divert anger over poverty, job losses or lack of services. This means that even at times when the ruling class has encouraged immigration to boost profits, it has also whipped up racism.

At the end of the Second World War there were less than 25,000 black people in Britain, yet racism and bigotry were rife. The view of

*Say it Loud*

British superiority was pushed by our rulers through events such as Empire Day, but accepted by the majority of workers.

Coming out of the war Britain was desperately short of labour and actively encouraged immigration from its empire. Many subjects came to "the mother country" with high hopes, having been taught in colonial schools about Britain's tolerant values and democracy. Campaigning journalist Paul Foot wrote of the period after the 1950 election:

> For the new Tory government and the labour hungry employers, this must have seemed a heaven sent gift. The Commonwealth citizens came in freely... They cost the government nothing [and it could not be] held responsible for the accommodation and integration of the new workers.[92]

In general trade unions reacted better to immigrants than other parts of society, and where there was struggle workers were more likely to come together. However, there were also examples of unions taking an overtly racist stance. For example in 1948 the National Union of Seamen tried to stop black workers getting jobs. At that year's union conference the assistant general secretary told the delegates, "In quite a few instances we have been successful in changing ships from coloured to white".[93] In 1955 Wolverhampton bus drivers staged an overtime ban against the employment of immigrant staff. The Transport and General Workers Union (TGWU) insisted on a quota of how many black workers could be employed.[94]

The largely working class immigrants organised themselves to defend their conditions where trade union support was tardy or hostile. In Bristol black workers were refused jobs as bus crew on the publicly owned transport service—despite a staff shortage. The colour bar was operated with the support of trade unionists in the TGWU at the relevant bus stations. One shop steward suggested, "People were fearful of an influx of people from elsewhere [on the grounds it] would be reducing their earnings potential".[95] Local West Indian immigrants, inspired by the US civil rights movement, set up a boycott. After several months of a growing campaign workers on the service voted to end the bar. In September 1963 the company employed its first five non-white crew members.

The battles of black and Asian workers to establish themselves in the workforce and the union movement continued through the 1960s and into the 1970s, and these struggles will be taken up in the next chapter.

The dominant form of modern racism emphasises distinctive cultures. People of "different cultures" are no longer dismissed as inferior, as long as they stay where they came from and don't migrate to the West. The truth is that there is nothing peculiarly "British" about the nature, attitudes or behaviour of people from these islands. The British Isles, like any other part of the planet, have been settled by waves of migration. For example it was the Romans who founded London.

But it has been capitalism that has resulted in the greatest movements of people in history. First were slaves and indentured labourers—Native American and then English and Irish and millions of Africans on the middle passage. Then came the great migrations to find work in the 19th century from Europe to the US, China and India around South East Asia. This continues to the present day.

People moved because they were pushed off their land, in many cases persecuted and forced to flee, or were simply looking for work and a better life. The scale of movement was made possible by developments in transport, particularly the railway and the steamer. This is not incidental to capitalism's development—the system could not work without it.

The establishment had never been keen on permanent settlement by non-whites. But its attitude was pragmatic. Just weeks after the *Empire Windrush* brought the first post-war immigrants from the Caribbean in 1948 Labour prime minister Clement Attlee replied to a group of Labour MPs who opposed non-white immigration, saying:

> It is traditional that British subjects...of whatever race or colour... should be freely admissible to the United Kingdom. That tradition is not...to be lightly discarded, particularly at a time when we are importing foreign labour in large numbers. It would be fiercely resented in the colonies themselves.[96]

*Say it Loud*

But he qualified this by adding, "If our policy were to result in a great influx of undesirables, we might...consider modifying it".[97] Such an attitude leaves a lot of space to decide who might be undesirable and to whom.

Labour's position has always been highly contradictory. In opposition in 1958 front bench spokesperson A G Bottomley made a principled stand in the House of Commons: "We on this side are clear in our attitude towards restricted immigration...we are categorically against it".[98] Paul Foot studied the reaction when Labour took this pro-immigration stance. In the same year that Bottomley made his bold declaration Labour actively opposed a Tory act to restrict commonwealth immigration. Foot observed that "opposition brought the Labour Party rewards both in votes and spirit... A Gallup Poll...showed a sharp slide from 76 to 62 percent in the number of people who favoured the act".[99] By taking a lead, Labour helped to shift public opinion against the Tories' racist immigration controls.

However, in 1962 the Tory government imposed the Commonwealth Immigration Act. This was the first legislation that restricted entry by British citizens from the Commonwealth—in practice it applied only to non-whites.

Labour dramatically revised its position on immigration controls after the 1964 election campaign in Smethwick in the West Midlands. Here the Tory candidate, Peter Griffiths, ran an overtly racist campaign. Gangs of children were organised to chant, "If you want a nigger neighbour, vote Labour".[100] Importantly for the Labour machine, Griffiths won with a 7.2 percent swing in a general election that Labour won overall. Rather than holding firm against Tory bigotry, Labour accepted that racism won votes and from that point onwards a cynical and opportunist game of racist trumps became a feature of the election trail.

By 1968 the Labour government was imposing its own more draconian laws. In March of that year the right wing press and the Tories whipped up a scare that Asians in Kenya who held British passports might "flood" into Britain. In response, the Labour government rushed an immigration bill through parliament in a day and a night.

It was a blatantly racist law that restricted the right of Kenyan Asians to enter into Britain.

This was when Enoch Powell marked another watershed in racism, when he made his notorious "Rivers of Blood" speech in Birmingham that April. What made this nasty piece of racism so damaging was that he was a front bench Tory MP at the time. Powell himself had worked without complaint in the Tory governments of the 1960s that oversaw Commonwealth immigration. His speech pretended to deal with reality while trading only in racist myths and lies. He claimed that an unnamed constituent had complained that "in this country in 15 or 20 years time the black man will have the whip hand over the white man". Powell appeared to agree, painting an apocalyptic picture of a country torn apart by race riots.[101]

Racists gained confidence and there was an immediate increase in attacks on black and Asian people. Some groups of workers even rallied to Powell—dockers in the East End of London and porters in the Smithfield meat market took strike action in support of him. On the day of the strike Terry Barrett, the only docker who was a member of the International Socialists (the forerunners of the SWP), made a lone protest against racism. At the time he was isolated, but the situation changed over the following years as the dockers became more militant and came to understand the need for unity.[102]

Powell was taking a gamble that he could swing the mood to the right and eventually position himself to become leader of the Tory party. He lost. He was sacked from the shadow cabinet. The real beneficiaries were the Nazi National Front, whose vote began to creep upwards in the early 1970s.

### Labour's failure

Since its foundation in 1900 the Labour Party has always taken a contradictory position on fighting racism. Tony Cliff suggests, "In a way the Labour Party is a replica of British capitalist society. Its oligarchy is centralised and its masses, while alienated and rebelling against the system, nevertheless still accept its main values".[103] From the beginning the Labour leadership had been in favour of reforming British capitalism so that its wealth could be re-divided more equitably. Initially therefore this meant holding onto the wealth of empire. In government it adopted the divide and rule policies of the establishment, including immigration controls.

The Labour Party is different from the Tories in that it is not an openly ruling class party. It includes many members who are committed anti-racists and who are part of broader struggles for change. However, Labour is dedicated to change without challenging capitalism and its party machinery is committed above all to winning elections. In office and in its ideology, it is committed to running a capitalist state with all that entails—competing with other capitalist countries and defending "British interests" on a world stage.

This commitment to the nation state and to reformism is why Labour has such a rotten history of scapegoating and imperialist war, despite the good intentions of many of its members. Its strategy of changing things through parliament and "from above" also means a reluctance to encourage the sorts of militant class struggles that would lay the basis for black and white unity. Its politics are often permeated by a pessimism about white working class people—hence pandering to right wing ideas over immigration and multiculturalism, instead of challenging them.

## The socialist tradition

But the British left has another tradition that reaches back to Wedderburn and Cuffay and the Chartists, through the Socialist League to which William Morris and Eleanor Marx belonged. It is a tradition of unity from below but, far from being automatic, it is one that had to be fought for and renewed.

The Communist Party (CP) was founded in 1920, taking up the radical tradition and generalising the experience of the Bolshevik Revolution that had just occurred in Russia. The CP combined a focus on workers' day to day struggles with a strong commitment to anti-racism and anti-imperialism. It immediately took up international issues including opposition to the Amritsar Massacre in India and support for Egyptian national liberation.[104] In addition it stood Shapurji Saklatvala, a candidate of Indian descent, in the working class constituency of Battersea North in South London during the

1922 general election. Saklatvala won, beating his nearest rival by more than 2,000 votes.

This tradition of socialism related directly to people who were fighting colonialism. One of the most important black figures in the movement was George Padmore. Born in Trinidad he moved to the US in the 1920s and became a communist. By 1929 he was in Moscow where he was appointed head of the Negro Bureau of the Red International of Trade Unions.[105] From 1931 Padmore was editor of the international communist paper *Negro Worker*. He eventually broke from the Comintern because of Stalin's Popular Front strategy, which attempted reconciliation with the Western powers partly through toning down criticism of Britain and France's colonial empires. Padmore settled in London, where he founded the International African Service Bureau to continue his work to liberate Africa from colonialism.

In 1945 Padmore organised the Pan African Congress in Manchester attended by Kwame Nkrumah and Jomo Kenyatta, who would go on to become the first presidents of Ghana and Kenya, and a new generation of black leaders.

### Conclusion

The high levels of racism faced by new immigrants to Britain in the 1950s and 1960s were challenged on three fronts, by familiarity, class struggle and anti-racist action. The crudest racial stereotypes are hard to maintain when black and white people live in close proximity to each other. More importantly, as we shall see, when workers moved into struggle and began to win their demands, they were less likely to accept the scapegoats they were offered by the establishment and the press. In the process of striking attitudes change as workers discover who their real allies are. Finally, as we shall see in the next chapter, as the 1970s progressed, active anti-racism played an important role, as oppressed people demanded respect and equality and white socialists and trade unionists acted to challenge the racism that makes us weaker.

Experiences in Britain and the US were radically different in the post-war years but both show that the best way to fight for the rights of people suffering from racism and of immigrants is to combine the struggle with that for wider working class rights. Where white socialists have taken this issue seriously, as with the Communist Party in Harlem and Alabama, the battle of Cable Street in east London or the Anti Nazi League across Britain, unity has been powerful.

The Communist Party exposed a weakness in American radicalism in the first part of the 20th century in that it marginalised race as a central issue, seeing it as negated by class. As James P Cannon put it, "The old theory of American radicalism turned out in practice to be a formula for inaction on the negro front—and—incidentally, a convenient shield for the dormant prejudices of the white radicals themselves".[106]

Racism is not simply an outdated set of ideas, however. It survived slavery precisely because it is of so much value to the capitalist class. The capitalist system constantly renews and reinvents racism, so all anti-capitalists and anti-racists must be constantly vigilant and prove in practice that our methods are the most effective ways of challenging racism.

Because racism is integral to capitalism there can be no victorious class struggle against capital that downgrades or ignores it on the basis of class unity. Race is socially constructed, but now that it has been established, it is also a social fact—one that cannot be ignored or marginalised by anyone hoping to change our society. The following chapters will look at how racism has changed in recent decades and the specifics of how to fight it today.

# From confrontation to compromise: Black British politics in the 1970s and 1980s

**Gary McFarlane**

As we have established, the position of black people in Britain has been shaped and determined both by the needs of capitalism and by the continuing struggle against racism. Immigrant labour had been a convenient necessity in an economy desperate to recover from the ravages of the Second World War. By the late 1960s, however, these workers had increasingly come to be seen as a burden. Anti-immigration politics provided the main organising focus for racists and fascists in post-war Britain and this became more evident as the pace of Britain's imperial and economic decline quickened. The concerns of the state changed accordingly. Initially the authorities maintained a perspective of temporary domicile for the new arrivals. Over time the priorities changed, from control at the borders to control within as well.

Most African-Caribbean, Indian and Pakistani migrants arrived with a similar view. Their hope was that residence in Britain would be a passing phase and that they would be able to save enough money to return home in style. That aim was to remain unrealised: by the 1970s two fifths of the "immigrants" were now born in the country.

There was in turn a change in attitude towards dealing with racism from those who were the subjects of state policy. Not surprisingly, the first generations of black and Asian migrants had, at times, been reluctant to challenge racism in all its guises. This could be accounted for by worries about the precariousness of their new position and the expectation that their stay in the "mother country" would be only temporary. The British born black population were to prove far less reticent. Faced with racism both from the state and from fascist thugs on the streets, they increasingly asserted that they were "Here to stay, here to fight!"[1]

The struggles that began to emerge in Britain were partly inspired by the United States where a growing militancy had seen the civil rights movement grow over into the Black Power movement of Malcolm X, and later the Black Panthers. This was reflected in Britain, albeit with important differences. The struggle in the US was characterised by a class-divided but otherwise largely homogenous community with a shared experience rooted in the enslavement of African descendants. In the UK it was not only the descendants of African slaves who faced racism, but also those from rural roots in the Indian subcontinent and indeed from middle class ones in colonial East Africa.

The lived experience of racism for Britain's black communities also differed markedly in terms of residential segregation from that of their American counterparts. In the United States residential districts with 100 percent black populations were commonplace; in the UK there are still no parliamentary constituencies in which a single ethnic minority makes up a majority of the population.

There were also important differences in the experiences of Britain's black communities. Although anti-immigrant sentiment was the key driver of racism, the impact of immigration legislation varied between African-Caribbeans and their Asian counterparts. As we shall see, in the struggles of the 1970s African-Caribbeans were primarily concerned about police racism and racism in the education system. Meanwhile those from India, Pakistan or Bengal were focused on immigration controls, both the rules to keep black and Asian people out of the country and the constant raids and threats of raids to round up "illegal immigrants" that the state directed at those communities. Nevertheless, there were struggles that found Asians and African-Caribbeans fighting side by side, chief among those being the fight against fascism and specifically the National Front.

Each community was subject to the casual racial prejudice of the majority of the population. In addition they faced institutional racism maintained and promoted by state policy.

Britain's rulers did little to hide their belief that immigration was a necessary evil. As such it was always seen from the perspective of something that held inherent dangers for the "host community" and therefore had to be controlled. When the labour shortages of the 1950s and early 1960s began to wane these questions assumed greater importance for the state and the racists who wanted to turn back "the tide" of "coloured" immigration. The Tory Enoch Powell was the arch rabble-rouser of racist hate, claiming the nation was digging its own grave by letting black people in. Powell and growing sections of the press demanded that immigration be stopped and even reversed.

### Immigration controls

The effect of Powell's racism on mainstream politics quickly translated into ever more draconian immigration controls, firstly from the 1964-70 Labour it, and then from the Tory administration that succeeded them in 1970. The Immigration Act of 1971 brought an end to all primary immigration from the "New Commonwealth"—namely the black countries. In the future only "patrials"—those from the white Commonwealth—would have the right to reside in the UK.

The Tories were only following in Labour's shameful footsteps. After all, it was the previous Labour government that had rushed the Kenyan Asian Act through parliament in March 1968 to prevent non-white British citizens in Kenya from entering the country. Prime Minster Harold Wilson claimed, unconvincingly, that the reasons behind the new legislation were "geographical", not "racial". The 1971 act, which came into effect two years later but operated retrospectively, gave carte blanche—otherwise described as "reasonable suspicion"—for immigration officers and police to hunt down "illegal immigrants". The entry of dependants of those already in the country would be strictly regulated at the discretion of British consulates in the country of emigration.

The 1824 Vagrancy Act allowed the authorities to arrest a person on suspicion of being about to commit an offence. This law, which was routinely used to target African-Caribbean youth, would also

*Say it Loud*

now be used against "over-stayers" and other "illegals". A special unit of the police known as the Illegal Immigration Intelligence Unit, employing informers, was created to harass and spy on communities. Much of the focus of the Asian community fell on battling to get family members and relatives into the country and, once in, to avoid being arrested in "fishing raids" and deported.

The plight of Asian people from East Africa was a growing concern, dramatically increased by Idi Amin's expulsion of Asians from Uganda in 1972. The Joint Council for the Welfare of Immigrants became the major organisation providing legal and campaigning aid around these issues.

Perhaps the most shameful and notorious practice invented by the authorities to police the communities and deter people from seeking entry in the first place was virginity tests. This deliberate degradation of women by subjecting them to vaginal examinations was supposedly required to determine "marital status". The practice was not banned until 1979 after the case of a 35 year old Indian teacher forced to undergo "a gynaecological examination" at the hands of a male doctor was brought to light by the *Guardian* and after the Indian government had condemned the "humiliating and obscene" practice.[2]

In the same year the Campaign Against Racist Laws organised a march that attracted around 20,000 people, making it probably the largest mobilisation on the streets against the racism of immigration controls. The march was predominantly Asian in composition. The largest previous march took place in 1969 and was led by the Black People's Alliance, counting both African-Caribbeans and Asians among its participants.

### Police racism

Black people had to contend with racism throughout society to varying degrees, from blatantly racist TV programmes that purported to make fun of the racists, such as the thoroughly misguided *'Til Death Us Do Part* and *Love Thy Neighbour*, to the virulent racist chanting that would greet black footballers, often from their own supporters. Nowhere was the racism worse, though, than among the ranks of the police, and they made this clear to the black people they came across.

Black people were routinely harassed, arrested and beaten by police making ready use of the notorious "sus" laws that allowed police to stop and search at will. Meanwhile a campaign to highlight street robbery as a supposedly new crime of "mugging" that was the province mainly of black youth took off in the early 1970s. This provided the police with further excuses for their racist violence.

In 1973 the government published a White Paper on Police-Immigrant Relations, not to draw attention to racist policing but to warn of "a small minority of young coloured people...anxious to imitate behaviour among the black community in the United States".¹ The scene was set for blanket oppressive policing of African-Caribbean youth in the inner cities. The police in London formed the Special Patrol Group (SPG) to carry out this task, which they set about with relish. In Lewisham, south east London, for example, they stopped 14,000 people in 1977 and arrested 400 in an operation codenamed Police Nigger Hunt.

The police aggression brought a fitting response. Battles broke out with the police at the Brockwell Park fair in Brixton, south London, in 1973, in Chapeltown, Leeds, in November 1975 and at the Notting Hill Carnival, west London, the following year.

The Notting Hill Carnival had grown in size every year since its inception in 1965. By the 1970s it had become the largest street festival in Europe, a site of music and revelry. For the police it was an opportunity for the mass harassment of black youth. They intended to do this in style in 1976 when 1,600 officers were mobilised for the clampdown. By the third day of the carnival at around 5pm the police made one arbitrary arrest too many. The youth turned on them and fought back in what turned out to be the biggest explosion of civil unrest seen in mainland Britain since the Battle of Cable Street drove Mosley's Blackshirts off the streets of east London in 1936. The zone of insurrection spread to encompass the area round Ladbroke Grove and fighting with the police went on into the night. Over 300 police officers were injured and 35 police vehicles damaged or destroyed.

The police managed to arrest 60 people but the ferocity of the fightback limited their ability to detain more. They had no riot equipment and were unable to reply effectively to the constant fusillade of rubble raining down on their heads and vehicles. Contrary to how some in the media tried to portray it, this was not a race riot but an uprising against the police. Years of pent up rage against racist police had exploded in the face of the authorities.

The government didn't respond by addressing the concerns of the rioters. There was no disbanding of the SPG, for instance. Instead they tooled up the police to be ready for the next fire. Anyone who had witnessed the routine harassment and violence that the black residents of Notting Hill had to put up with would have known that it would only be a matter of time before the powder keg was reignited. The case of the Mangrove Nine should long since have dispelled any myths about the universal benevolence of the police.

## Mangrove

The Mangrove restaurant in Notting Hill, owned by Frank Critchlow, was the subject of numerous raids by the police because it was a place where black people gathered. It was in essence a community centre where you could eat, meet and organise. That was crime enough for the police who succeeded in getting an order to shut it down in 1970.

A demonstration held in its defence was brutally attacked by police. People fought back and, of the many arrested, nine were charged and brought before the courts. By the conclusion of a 55-day trial, towards the end of 1971, the corruption and racism of the police and the courts had been exposed to all, and the defendants, who included Critchlow and political activist Darcus Howe, were acquitted.

Critchlow would continue to be hounded by the police right through to the end of the 1980s. In 1989 he was tried once more, this time for allegedly dealing heroin. Again he was acquitted and subsequently won an action against the Home Office for false imprisonment, battery and malicious prosecution. The police commander responsible for the Notting Hill area by this time was Paul Condon who, as we will discover, went on to become a highly controversial Metropolitan Police Commissioner.

The state's attempts to nip the bud of black resistance through judicial means arose again in the charging of the editor of a radical magazine called *Grassroots* with "encouraging the murder of persons unknown". This occurred after an article from the US Black Panthers' newspaper describing how to make a petrol bomb was reproduced.

## Cricket lovely cricket

New black identities were forged through the experience of racism and resistance in the 1960s and 1970s. This can be clearly illustrated through a slightly unlikely medium—cricket, a sport exported by British colonialism alongside racism and empire.

In the colonies the game was yet one more way in which the colonial masters asserted their superiority over "the natives". Eventually they allowed those they ruled to take part. They even allowed the colonial subjects to be represented in the national team.

But cricket to the colonial populations wasn't just a game. It came to be seen as a zone of struggle in which the battles for independence and dignity—the overthrow of colonialism and racism—could be played out. Every match the West Indies played was followed intently by the folks back home. C L R James, the great Trinidadian Marxist and cricket lover, explains:

> I haven't the slightest doubt that the clash of race, caste and class did not retard but stimulated West Indian cricket. I am equally certain that in those years social and political passions, denied normal outlets, expressed themselves so fiercely in cricket (and other games) precisely because they were games... They could be fought out without violence or much lost except pride and honour. Thus the cricket field was a stage on which selected individuals played representative roles which were charged with social significance.[4]

The West Indies team, drawn from all the islands of the English-speaking Caribbean, played its first internationals—or test matches—in the 1930s and included black players, most notably Learie Constantine, who was a close friend of C L R James, and George Headley. Later the team included "the three Ws", Everton Weekes, Frank Worrell and Clyde Walcott at the batting crease and the bowling spinners Sonny Ramadhin and Alf Valentine. These players brought pride to the West Indian people when they beat England in a series of matches in England for the first time in 1950.

It was not until 1960 though that the team had its first black captain in Frank Worrell, and it had required an orchestrated campaign led by C L R James to achieve this.

Despite occasional victories over England and Australia, the "Windies" were still seen as somewhat lightweight—good for a bit of entertainment but lacking in stamina, backbone and tactical nous. This perspective was, of course, infused with racism. All of that changed in the mid-1970s and it was no accident. Trinidad and Jamaica had gained independence in 1962 and it was the independence generation who spearheaded the rise to dominance of West Indian cricket.

The West Indies cricket team embodied a unity that could not be achieved in the political and economic sphere. The idea of a post-independence West Indies federation never became a reality as the islands (and Guyana, which is part of the South American mainland) failed to overcome their differences. By contrast, the cricket team was able to bring together West Indians of Asian and African descent. It wasn't just people in the islands that supported the Windies. The hundreds of thousands of people from the Caribbean living, and struggling, in Britain were also inspired by their endeavours, and support for the team helped to foster a sense of collective identity among the diaspora.

If anyone was in any doubt that politics was an integral part of cricket, Tony Greig, the England captain during the West Indies tour in 1976, made it abundantly clear. The six foot plus, white blond Greig, originally from apartheid South Africa, proclaimed his intention to beat the West Indians by declaring, "If they're down they grovel. I intend to make them grovel."

This was interpreted as nothing less than a declaration of war and the West Indians were up for the fight. The West Indies' fast bowlers, Andy Roberts and Michael Holding, were going to make Greig and his team mates pay.

Alongside his battery of brilliant fast bowlers, Windies captain Clive Lloyd could also call upon the majestic batting of Gordon

Greenidge and Viv Richards and he built an indomitable team spirit. The West Indies crushed England, winning three of the five matches and drawing the other two.

That triumph was to establish a pattern of success that would last for 20 years. Black Britons packed the venues whenever the Windies were in town, and created a carnival atmosphere as their heroes steamrollered England.

The hostile bowling tactics adopted by the West Indies in the 1976 series were no different to those of the English team in the famous "bodyline" tour of Australia in 1932-33 or those of the Australians against the West Indies that we highlighted earlier. Nevertheless Lloyd's team was condemned for supposedly "unsporting behaviour". It was argued that the deployment of such belligerent tactics was "just not cricket". The Windies were accused of cricket "terrorism" and "savagery" in the none too subtle racially tinged howls of the mainstream press.

The success of the West Indies cricket team played a remarkable role in bolstering the confidence of their compatriots living and struggling in Britain. Throughout this period test matches were screened live on the BBC. For a full six hours a day those unable to attend in person could nevertheless revel at the sight of Holding running in to bowl or Richards blasting the ball to the boundary. Those without access to a television could tune in to *Test Match Special* on the radio.

This was a time when very few black people appeared on screen at all and those who did were invariably portrayed negatively or in subservient roles. The Windies demonstrated in glorious technicolor that black people could fight and win.

The other great sporting hero whose exploits boosted the African diaspora in the 1960s and 1970s was Muhammad Ali. Born and raised as Cassius Clay in Louisville Kentucky, the fleet-footed and fast talking boxer changed his name and joined the Nation of Islam after returning with a gold medal from the Rome Olympics in 1960. As a professional he famously took on and beat several British boxers including the much loved Henry Cooper. All of the bouts were watched by African-Caribbeans with excited expectation of victory over those brought up to consider themselves superior to black people. He never let them down.

Ali's proud membership of the Nation of Islam marked him out as a fighter for black liberation more obviously than the West Indian cricketers. Nevertheless, the politics of struggle against racism were still there, perhaps displayed most explicitly by the team's outstanding performer the Antiguan Viv Richards. He wore his politics on his wrist—a sweatband emblazoned in Rastafarian colours. In Stevan Riley's brilliant 2010 film *Fire in Babylon* Richards describes the feelings of the players after Greig's comments in 1976, making it crystal clear that cricket, as played by the West Indies against England, was part and parcel of the struggle against racism: "We stepped beyond the sport to where there was a whole load of other things that needed defending rather than the cricket ball itself."

Cricket against England for the Caribbean countries was therefore more than just a sport, and so it was too for the Indians and Pakistanis, and for the migrant communities residing in the "mother country". Matches represented a battle for victory over old colonial masters. All were happy to fail what would come to be Tory politician Norman Tebbit's "cricket test" that demanded of migrants their support for England in sporting matters to prove themselves worthy of the privilege of living in the country. Tebbit of course never expected Britons abroad to do the same in relation to their host countries.

### Employment patterns and workplace struggle

The colonial prejudices that informed the establishment and employers' view of the different ethnic groups helped to determine patterns of employment. Many African-Caribbeans were directed to the service industries such as transport and health. Meanwhile Asians were widely employed in the mills, textile factories and associated trades and in the most menial and dangerous industrials jobs elsewhere, such as paper mills, plastics factories and foundries. African-Caribbeans were also present in many of these places but in smaller numbers.

Employers were only too happy to foster divisions in the workplace but it is worth noting that there were surprisingly few racist strikes in which white workers walked off the job in protest at having to work with black workers. At the same time however, unions colluded with employers in channelling black workers into the worst jobs at lower wages.

The opportunism of trade union leaders was quite disgraceful. To maintain trade union effectiveness at the workplace black workers had to be unionised, but all too often when these workers looked for support it was absent or offered only grudgingly. This was not always the case, however. The better organised a workplace and the more political its leadership, the more likely black workers were to be unionised and treated on an equal basis. For example the Communist Party was strongly represented in the car plants and engineering, less so in textiles where many Asian workers were employed.

In 1972 a number of strikes broke out in the textile industry over pay and conditions. At Crepe Sizes in Nottingham two thirds of the workforce were black, mostly from Pakistan and occupying the most poorly paid positions. Many worked 84 hours a week for a meagre £40.08 and were fed up of racist bullying by management and discriminatory practices that denied them proper canteen and toilet facilities. Workers began to join the TGWU union, resulting in five being sacked. Enough was enough and the workers struck unofficially. After a solidarity campaign had developed union officials came under pressure to make the strike official. The management eventually capitulated, reinstated the victimised workers and agreed to recognise the union.

Later that same year, at Mansfield Hosiery in Loughborough, another strike by largely Asian workers erupted. This time the demand was for higher wages and an end to discriminatory practices that reserved certain jobs for white workers, denying promotion to Asians. Again the union, this time the National Union of Hosiery and Knitwear Workers, was slow to make the strike official. This was consistent with its previous approach of refusing to back Asian workers' demands on promotion. In this case the workers occupied the union offices to demand official support and got it, but it was not wholehearted. The strike would be supported over wages, but, outrageously, the white workers would not be called out with their Asian brothers and the specific grievance on promotions was not addressed.

*Say it Loud*

After 12 weeks on strike and with the backing of community and black political groups and the left the strike won. Out of it the strike committee called a conference against racism in the unions and was supported by many trade union branches from, for example, the Amalgamated Union of Engineering Workers (AUEW), the National Union of Public Employees (NUPE) and the National Union of Mineworkers (NUM). Left wing trade union leaders such as Ernie Roberts from the AUEW were among the speakers.[5]

There were also strikes involving predominantly African-Caribbean workers in engineering plants. Two important strikes took place in London, one in Stanmore in 1972 and one in Southgate. At Stanmore Engineering the AUEW supported the strikers' wage demand and awarded strike pay. The workers escalated the action by staging a sit-in. Crucially however, it failed to call on workers in other firms to refuse to handle products from Stanmore and the strike lost after the employers won an injunction to remove the occupiers who were then sacked. The other strike, at US multinational ITT, saw black workers striking to break into the more skilled areas of the plant. The strikers were not only opposed by the employer but also by the craft unions, which organised the most highly skilled workers. Hence the Electrical Trades Union opposed the strike. There was support from the local branch of the AUEW but not the national union. This strike also ended in defeat.

Perhaps the most famous of the strikes over racism took place in 1974 at Imperial Typewriters in Leicester where two thirds of the workforce were Asian, this time mostly women and mostly refugees from Uganda. The strike won but with no thanks to the TGWU which, in failing to challenge the racism of the white workers at the factory, refused to back the strike, claiming that procedures had not been followed correctly. Support from the community and left-led union branches and organisations proved crucial to keeping the strikers out. Money rolled in from, among others, the Southall Indian Workers Association (IWA), the Birmingham Sikh Temple and the Birmingham Anti-Racist Committee. On the minus side, the fascist National Front agitated around the dispute, as they had at the Mansfield Hosiery strike, even attempting to intimidate workers at the factory gates.

The Imperial strike was eventually successful, but the factory was closed shortly afterwards by US parent company Litton Industries. Instructively therefore, the racism of white workers at Imperial ultimately only succeeded in making it easier for the bosses to shut their factory:

> When Littons decided to close its two UK factories in 1974, the Leicester plant put up no resistance, while the Hull workers occupied their factory in an attempt to save their jobs. The Leicester workforce, weakened and demoralised by racist divisions, was in no position to fight back over the closure, and black and white workers alike lost their jobs.[6]

The dispute at Grunwick, a film processing factory in west London, became a cause celebre of the British trade union movement when half of the workforce of mostly Asian women, predominantly from East Africa, went on strike to demand union recognition in 1976. One worker in particular, Jayaben Desai, became an inspiring leader in the struggle. As fate would have it, the owner of the factory was an Anglo Indian called George Ward who had no qualms about exploiting Asian women. Despite the stalling and foot-dragging at the top of the labour movement by the Trades Union Congress and the Labour government, the women were able to attract the support of thousands of Britain's most militant trade unionists, not just in words but in action:

> It was the mass picket that transformed the strike... It was the arrival in Willesden of thousands of trade unionists from all over Britain which was to reassure the strikers that they were not, after all, alone and that besides the right wing section of the labour movement there was also a left wing, a radical and a militant section which responded with class feeling to the call of all workers in struggle, whether male or female, manual or clerical, black or white.[7]

The strike went on for two years and its height saw 20,000 trade unionists converge on the plant for a mass picket in July 1977, led by Arthur Scargill and the Yorkshire miners. This was a proud day for British trade unionism, which showed that solidarity could trump racism.

Again it was the trade union bureaucracy, rather than racism, that held the struggle back. Postal workers sought to show concrete support by refusing to move Ward's products. The courts ruled such action, known as "blacking", was illegal. Instead of backing their members, the union bureaucrats prevented them from defying the courts. Ultimately the Grunwick strike went down to defeat but it had set an important benchmark for the British trade union movement. It demonstrated that class unity could be forged in action and racism challenged head on. Black workers had forced the issue and the best traditions of class solidarity came to the fore.

## Racist violence

The rising level of racism orchestrated by the Powellites and the Nazi National Front backed up by the media came to a head in 1976 over the prospect of more East African Asians coming to Britain, this time from Malawi. A climate of hatred permeated the air and, as is so often the case, it led to racist murders on the streets. In particular the death of Gurdip Singh Chaggar in the centre of Southall, west London in 1976 unleashed a ferocious response from black people who were further enraged by a police force that decided that the murder was not necessarily racial. In 1968 when Powell made his "Rivers of Blood" speech and dock workers had marched in support of him the reaction from black people and the left was timid. This time there was a militant response.

The Asian Youth Movements were key components of that militancy. They gave direct political and organisational expression to the generational difference the 1970s heralded. The movements in Southall, Bradford, Birmingham, Sheffield, Leicester, Manchester and elsewhere came together to defend their communities and combat violence from the fascists. They also took up campaigns over racist immigration laws. They were open to working with the radical left and indeed many of their members had come from those ranks:

> The Southall Youth Movement considered itself more radical than the "old guard" who were connected with the IWAs and the Communist Party. Many members of the youth movements had moved in and out of Trotskyist organisations, and although some

later ended up hostile to the far-left, there is no doubt that they were influenced by its politics and methods.[8]

In east London a Bangladeshi Youth Movement was formed, again in response to a racist murder, that of Altab Ali, a 25 year old clothing worker in Tower Hamlets, east London, in May 1978. In Newham it was the murder of Akhtar Ali Baig in 1980. Asian youth made it clear that racist violence would be answered. They also recognised that the widest possible unity in action against the racists and fascists was necessary and to that end they were happy to work with the left, notably the International Socialists (IS), forerunners of the SWP. It was members of IS who removed the sign put up by Robert Relf, an NF member, outside one of his properties in 1976 which declared, "For sale to an English Family", in blatant violation of the Race Relations Act 1976 which outlawed such discrimination. The sign was ceremoniously burned at one of the demonstrations organised by the Southall Youth Movement.

The NF was gaining in strength by the mid-1970s, terrorising black communities, openly assaulting black people and "Reds" and breaking up meetings not just of socialists, but of liberals. The NF's national organiser, Martin Webster, won a frightening 16.2 percent of the vote in the 1976 West Bromwich by-election.[9]

The heightened fascist violence saw the NF march through predominantly black areas under police protection with the aim of intimidating the local population. But the Nazis' strategy came to a shuddering halt in Lewisham in August 1977. Here an alliance of forces comprising the IS and local youth numbering around 5,000 was able to break through police lines and smash the NF march. Victory at the battle of Lewisham led to the formation of the Anti Nazi League (ANL).

The ANL succeeded in building a mass organisation of black and white people to confront the fascists and prevent them from organising unopposed. At the same time, and just as importantly, it challenged their lies head on with mass leafleting drives and the distribution of thousands of stickers with the help of School Kids Against the Nazis (SKAN) and similar groups for trade unionists, gay people, musicians and so on. Instead of allowing the NF to pose as a legitimate political party that was merely concerned about race, the ANL exposed its fascist agenda. The NF's members weren't just racist—they also wanted to destroy trade unions, democracy and all opposing political parties.

The ANL aimed to split the NF's soft racist supporters from its Nazi core, and it succeeded. The SWP initiated the formation of this mass movement by bringing with it the lessons of the 1930s in Germany where sizeable left forces had failed to unite in opposition to the rise of Hitler. Britain in the 1970s was going to be different.

A parallel and complementary development was the establishment of a cultural movement, Rock Against Racism (RAR). The origin of RAR reads like the stuff of legend. Two young music lovers, Roger Huddle and Red Saunders, both members of the International Socialists, wrote a letter to the *New Musical Express* magazine protesting at the drunken declaration of support for Enoch Powell by rock guitarist Eric Clapton at a Birmingham concert in 1976. What particularly horrified Huddle and Saunders was the fact that Clapton had made his name in the 1960s playing rhythm and blues, the classic black American music genre. Moreover, he had revived a flagging career in the mid-1970s with a cover of Bob Marley's "I Shot the Sheriff". Huddle and Saunders wrote:

> Come on Eric...you've been taking too much of that *Daily Express* stuff and you know you can't handle it. Own up. Half your music is black. You're rock music's biggest colonist. You're a good musician but where would you be without the blues and R&B? You've got to fight the racist poison otherwise you degenerate into the sewer with the rats and all the money men who ripped off rock culture with their cheque books and plastic crap. We want to organise a rank and file movement against the racist poison in music. We urge support for Rock Against Racism. PS: Who shot the Sheriff, Eric? It sure as hell wasn't you![10]

A series of carnivals against the Nazis sealed the deal, so to speak. A generation of young black and white people was won to the cause. Most notable was the march of 100,000 from Trafalgar Square through the East End to Hackney's Victoria Park in 1978 for a concert celebrating multiculturalism and defiant resistance against the NF.

Punk rock and reggae provided the soundtrack of the anti-fascist movement. Indeed reggae, which originated in Jamaica, now saw the flowering of its first British-based acts. Up until this time it had been artists such as Jimmy Cliff and later the cross-over success of Bob Marley who were most representative of the genre. Both were influenced in their different ways by socialism and the struggle against oppression. Their radicalism, whether "hidden" in the case of Jimmy Cliff or open in Marley's case, was firmly anchored in the Jamaican experience. Although the experiences that Cliff and Marley articulated were relevant to British youth, it was not quite the same "Babylon".

From the 1970s on, a new breed of reggae musicians emerged who spoke to the experience of black youth who were told they were British but found themselves treated as second class citizens and subjected to oppressive racist policing. In the vanguard of this new British roots reggae were the likes of Birmingham's Steel Pulse, Misty in Roots in Southall and Aswad from London's Ladbroke Grove. Steel Pulse, formed in 1975, had initially been turned away from Birmingham's reggae venues because of their Rastafarianism. They soon became stalwarts of Rock Against Racism, the band members' black nationalism presenting no barrier to them throwing in their lot with white punk bands such as The Clash. The album *Handsworth Revolution* railed against police racism and the fascists. Alongside The Clash's cover of reggae classic "Police and Thieves" and that band's overt appeal to white youth to take a leaf out of the book of their black compatriots in "White Riot", *Handsworth Revolution* was the cultural expression of what black and white unity in struggle could and had achieved. RAR gigs nearly always featured both punk and reggae bands, and it is no exaggeration to say that this conscious insertion of anti-racist political energy into the music scene was incredibly influential.

The NF hadn't given up on its provocations, however, and announced that it was holding an election meeting in Southall as part of its 1979 general election campaign. The authorities allowed the gathering to go ahead and the police mobilised in massive numbers to protect it. Again there was an alliance of the IS and other anti-fascists and the local black community, this time mostly Asian, to build a counter-demonstration aimed at stopping the march, which was scheduled for 23 April. The Nazis were smashed and humiliated but the police, in the form of the SPG, took their revenge on the anti-fascists by bludgeoning Blair Peach, a teacher and member of the SWP, to death. Over 30 years would pass before the truth, that the police had told "easily recognisable lies", was finally admitted. The report which drew this conclusion was written at the time of Peach's death, but no action was taken against any of the officers involved.

There were those who criticised the ANL for waging a targeted war against fascism, accusing it of ignoring wider racism and not opposing immigration controls. In fact a motion was passed at the ANL conference in 1978 against all immigration controls but supporting it was not made a condition of membership. Instead the ANL's strategy was one of seeking the widest possible unity in action against the fascist threat with the aim of bringing mass mobilisations to bear against their organisation and ideas. It was a strategy that worked. And it helped to create a wider culture of opposition to racism.

Some on the left tried to argue that it was Margaret Thatcher's election victory in 1979 that led to the decline of the NF, after she effectively co-opted the fascists' anti-immigrant racism. However, the movement against the NF had already broken the backbone of the fascists' organisation by the time of Thatcher's election. So by the general election in 1979 the Nazis' vote had fallen to just 1.3 percent. And in the 1981 Greater London Council elections the Nazis got just 2.1 percent of the vote compared to 5.7 percent in 1977. The NF's national organiser, Martin Webster, admitted in 1981 that it was the impact of the ANL that had driven them back: "The sheer presence of the ANL had made it impossible to get NF members on the streets, had dashed recruitment and cut away at their vote."

The NF had been destroyed both as a fighting force and as an electoral vehicle. Exposure of the NF as being a fascist organisation undermined their support. Also anyone considering joining the party would have to steel themselves to be physically confronted at every turn.

Despite the success of the ANL and other forces in driving the fascists back, a much wider and deeper racism remained that was crystallised in the enduring popularity, at one level or another, of anti-immigrant racism. For that battle to be won there needed to be a war not just against the fascists that bred out of the racist scapegoating and economic decline, but against the capitalist system that gave rise to racism. That required a socialist struggle against the cause—capitalism—to uproot the symptom: racism.

Yet it would be wrong to underestimate the wide and lasting impact of the ANL's success for black people in Britain. It was captured by Darcus Howe in his speech at a memorial meeting for SWP member David Widgery, whose book *Beating Time* is still the best cultural history of the resistance and celebration of those times. The pioneering socialist journalist Paul Foot recorded that:

> Howe said that he had fathered five children in Britain. The first four had grown up angry, fighting forever against the racism all around them. The fifth child, he said, had grown up "black and at ease". Darcus attributed her "space" to the Anti Nazi League.[11]

The dregs of the NF continued to organise into the early 1980s. The Asian youth movements had largely gone into decline by this time but in 1981 it was members of a split from the Bradford Youth Movement that organised resistance to a planned fascist invasion of the area. Petrol bombs were stockpiled for the defence. The police found some of the petrol bombs and arrested and charged 12 people. A huge defence campaign was launched with the defendants' lawyers arguing that they were engaged in legitimate preparations to protect their community. The jury at their trial agreed, acquitting all 12 and making legal history.

The anti-fascist struggles of the 1970s saw Asians and African-Caribbeans fighting a common enemy alongside other activists and in that sense there was a unity of purpose in those struggles, even if they took place in different localities with the mobilisations tending to reflect those demographics.

Many of these advances took place at a time of rising class struggle. This background created a context for unity in which black and white people could fight back together for the common advance of all. But as that working class struggle went into decline in the second half of the 1970s it became harder to make the case for united action. The fag end of the Labour government at the end of the 1970s did much to disorientate and weaken the working class and embolden the bosses. The result was the election of Margaret Thatcher which ushered in a period of defeat for workers.

### Riots: The fire last time

In a series of planned assaults on the unions the Tories were able to weaken resistance and drive up unemployment. Those at the bottom of the pile would suffer the most and it wasn't long before the ruling class heard from them, when the unemployed, black and white, rose up in April 1981 in Brixton and in July across the country against hopelessness and racism.

The Scarman Report published in response to the Brixton uprising and the Macpherson inquiry into the murder of Stephen Lawrence capture the meaning of two decades in the history and struggle of black people against racism in Britain. Two decades, each of which was transitional: the 1980s, from united combat to something less so; the 1990s, from a trumpeting of battles thought won to a realisation of a war far from finished.

The Brixton riot unleashed a shockwave of black-led working class anger in a similar vein across the country. It threw the state onto the defensive. The uprising shattered the comfortable notion that Britain was immune to the problems of urban decay and racial oppression and to the angry uprisings that had shaken the US.

The urban rebellions in fact began the year before Brixton in Bristol on 2 April 1980, when the police raided the Black and White Café in the St Paul's district, the inner-city home to the African-Caribbean population of the city. The police were in the habit of raiding the cafe, on this occasion using the pretext of selling alcohol without a licence. Two hundred or so black and white youths attacked the police as they removed alcohol from the premises. Running battles with the police ensued for several hours and by the time the dust settled 25 people had been injured, mostly police officers. Indeed such was the ferocity of the fightback that the police were forced to retreat time and again, leading the local chief constable to lament, "Surely we should be advancing, not retreating?" The headline in the *Daily Telegraph* the following morning screamed, inaccurately given the level of involvement by white youths, "19 Police Hurt in Black Riot",[12] wrongly blaming the disturbances on poor parenting in the black community—a false narrative that has continued to the present day.

When all hell broke loose in Brixton a year later, on 10-12 April 1981, the scale of the disturbances was even greater. Petrol bombs were used on a wide scale, a bus was hijacked and driven at the police, dozens of cars were burnt out and a number of pubs burnt down, and scores of shops were looted. It required thousands of police to "restore order".[13]

Although the exact triggers of the Bristol and Brixton riots differed, as did the causes of the riots that followed elsewhere, a combination of police racism, racist attacks and unemployment laid the basis for the rebellions. Also it wasn't just African-Caribbean and working class white kids doing the rioting. In July rioting broke out in Southall when police provided protection for fascist skinheads going to a gig in a local pub, beating up an Asian woman on their way. Asian youth were enraged and launched an attack on the pub. The police were eventually forced to evacuate the fascists and were unable to prevent the pub from being burnt to the ground by the youths who broke through their lines.

On the same day as the Southall riot, Toxteth in Liverpool exploded. It took the police two days to take back control. This was followed by Moss Side in Manchester, Handsworth in Birmingham and countless others. These were now referred to by the media and authorities as "copycat" riots in an effort to infer that they were lesser affairs. In many cases this was not the case at all. Though disturbances in places such as Gloucester and Bedford were undoubtedly smaller-scale affairs, in other areas including Hounslow and Woolwich in London, Leicester and Leeds Chapeltown militant pitched battles were fought with police.

Anger at racist harassment at the hands of the police was clearly one of the sparks that ignited the riots. But these were multiracial riots, reflecting the widespread disaffection and anger felt by young working class people in general. In many of the confrontations it was Asian youth that were to the fore and in all the riots white youths played their part to some extent.

The Tories had brought mass unemployment to Britain and black people were disproportionately affected. However, black people were a minority of the overall population and therefore a minority of the unemployed. This can be seen in Handsworth, for example, where 31 percent of the population were black in 1977 but 60 percent of the unemployed were white.[14] So when black and Asian youth took to the streets against police harassment and/or racist attacks they found many white youths, alienated for other reasons, more than willing to join them.

What did the rebellion mean from the perspective of revolutionaries, black and white, who wanted to see an end to racism? Had the struggle been advanced? Could the energy of the rebellion be harnessed and channelled into lasting militant organisation against a racist society?

These questions had been raised before by a plethora of both black nationalist and revolutionary left organisations. The US was often looked to as a template but there was a big difference. The urban insurrections of the 1960s and early 1970s in the US were predominantly all-black affairs because black people lived in ghettoes, unlike in inner city Britain. Imaginative and heroic though many of those struggles in the US were, as we shall see in chapter 7, those black organisations that did grow roots such as the Black Panthers, could not find a way to successfully sustain a challenge to capitalism.

Perhaps the most influential of black separatist groups in Britain were those aligned with the Race Today Collective, which produced a monthly magazine of the same name edited by Darcus Howe. The biggest success of Race Today was the protest march it organised in response to the fire at a house party in New Cross, initially thought to be the work of racists, in January 1981. Thirteen black teenagers were killed but the police made no serious attempt to investigate the cause of the fire, blaming it on the partygoers themselves. Around 20,000 marched in protest, with slogans such as "Blood Ah Go Run If Justice No Come". This was a real achievement, but *Race Today* wasn't able to build on the anger by creating a larger and more effective organisation in its wake.

*Race Today*'s ultimate failure flowed from its political outlook:

> There is one distinctive position we had to maintain...that we had to come through on our own as blacks, independently... The main vehicle of that must be our willingness...to develop independent movement... The black working class will be in charge... The black struggle has an independent validity and vitality of its own.[15]

When the riots broke later in the year, the response from *Race Today* and other black nationalist groups was to try to create black defence campaigns, despite the fact that many of those arrested were white. This approach in effect hampered the creation of any campaigns, black-led or otherwise. Chris Harman lays bare the limitations of the rhetoric and strategy of the black nationalists:

> The demand for physical forms of black self-defence is certainly quite correct if a black locality is under attack from the Nazis or the police. But to be effective, black self-defence has rapidly to pass over into defence involving anti-racist white workers and youth as well, to encompass industrial action from the mixed workforces of the large factories as well as just fighting on the streets. To refuse to encourage this because of a commitment to "black autonomy" is to endanger black lives.[16]

Socialists defend the rights of oppressed people to resist— including where they organise separately. However, there is still an argument to be had about what strategy can actually take the struggle forward. Without linking the fight for black liberation with that of the working class as a whole it is impossible to win. Black workers are part of the working class and as such work and strike with their white brothers and sisters. It is that experience of being exploited collectively by the employer that has eroded the prevalence of racism inside the workplace, combined with the overt challenge to racism by black workers and white anti-racists.

The orientation on unemployed youth and the act of rioting as agency and method was also mistaken. By definition the unemployed stand outside the collective struggle at the point of production and as such are notoriously difficult to organise. Combine that with an emphasis on insurrectionary methods deployed in large-scale rioting and the error of a "street" focus is magnified. Riots are an expression of anger at injustice and oppression, but they are by nature short-lived—they go up like a rocket and come down like a stick. They rarely last more than a few days. In the case of the 1981 riots two days was the maximum time a "liberated zone" was held before the state reasserted its control by re-establishing its monopoly of violence. As it turned out, in the absence of a wider challenge to its power, the state was able to regain its balance fairly quickly and for sure used the riots to expand its armoury of repressive weaponry and laws.

## Rastafarianism

Black nationalism, or separatism, does not just take the shape of formal organisation—it also exists as a common sense in the struggles against racism. During the riots of the early 1980s it was clear that a layer of young black men in particular identified with the symbols of Rastafarianism. As Britain's African-Caribbean youth became more conscious of the racism they faced, the Jamaican-developed religion of Rastafari had grown in popularity. The roots of the religion and its appeal are best understood as an Afro-centric response to the legacy of racism in Jamaica.

Despite gaining independence from Britain in 1965 ideas of black racial inferiority still lived on in the former colony, so that the lighter your skin the higher up the social order you could rise. It was no accident therefore that the country's first leaders were very light skinned. Rastafarians consciously turned their back on this neo-colonial mind-set. They argued that it was by freeing the mind "from mental slavery" as Bob Marley suggested that liberation would follow.[17]

This was an approach firmly embedded in the mould of the black consciousness movement. There was also something of the counter-culture about Rastafarianism, certainly helped by the movement's insistence on the spiritual centrality of smoking marijuana. The notion that the leader of black liberation could be an Ethiopian King called Haile Selassie, a ruler who was happy to exploit and oppress his own people, was more difficult to reconcile. But this didn't matter. What did matter was the historical fact of Ethiopia having an older Christian tradition than Europe and being an African kingdom that was the last to fall to the imperialists. This is what made it stand out as a zone of biblical and historical significance from a black perspective.

However, the possibility of achieving liberation simply by freeing the mind from backward ideas was even less realistic in the UK than in Kingston, Jamaica. To change social conditions would require a struggle involving not just black people but the working class of the white majority. An Afrocentric black nationalist response that sought to break away from the world as it existed would always find it difficult not just to achieve liberation but to engage and recruit beyond a narrow stratum of African-Caribbean youth. Nevertheless, "in their locks and dress and music the Rastafarians signified their deadly opposition. They were to some extent the 'burning spear' of the new resistance".[18] The assertion of black pride in the face of racism can be an important component of a wider struggle. However, the lack of organisation as an avowedly political force beyond the "personal is political" cultural nationalist response meant that their impact was limited.

## The Scarman Report
The scale of the uprisings in Brixton and elsewhere shook the state and forced a response in the form of the Scarman Report written by law lord Leslie Scarman. He was forced to acknowledge that social deprivation was a root cause of the Brixton riot and how that deprivation was worsened by "racial disadvantage". However, in the summary of his report he did not use the word racism once in respect to the police or any other institutions. He began his summary by suggesting:

The police do not create social deprivation, though unimaginative, inflexible policing can make tensions which deprivation engenders greatly worse. Conversely, while good policing can help diminish tension and disorder, it cannot remove the causes of social stress where they are to be found...[19]

Throughout his report Scarman denied the existence of institutional racism to focus instead on individuals, with proposals for how "racially discriminatory behaviour by police officers can be avoided". At the same time he set his face against any changes in legislation on the police.

In time-honoured tradition, Scarman also suggested that black people themselves were to blame for the problems they faced. He homed in on supposed deficiencies in black culture and black families, bemoaning the incidence of single parent families, and claiming that the impact of "British social conditions on the matriarchal extended family structure of the West Indian immigrant" had created a destabilising environment. He suggested that young African-Caribbean people are "a people of the street...they make their protest there...and some of them live off street crime", and their hostility towards the police "whom they see as pursuing and harassing them" has "infected older members of the community".[20]

Scarman's other main conclusion in terms of policy was the advancement of "positive action" to promote equal opportunities. His positive action is not to be confused with the positive discrimination of targets and quotas. Scarman's solution was far less radical and, because it didn't countenance the possibility of institutional racism existing, the ability to make good on the objectives came down to education—challenging attitudes and prejudices, not the structures of inequality.

In Scarman's world black people "perceived" institutional racism to exist. This is not the same as admitting that it actually does exist. He conceded that there was some racial prejudice in the police force "which does manifest itself occasionally in the behaviour of a few officers on the street". This could be corrected through better police training aimed at "an understanding of the cultural backgrounds and attitudes of ethnic minorities". None of this was any different to the commonly held view of racism as something that can be educated away. Crucially, the focus of change was being moved from structures and institutions to individuals and attitudes.

Despite Scarman's inability to address the real causes of the riots, the state was forced to make a shift in how it dealt with discontent. The Tory government set about a twin track approach of coercion and co-option to attempt to create a buffer between itself and the most discontented sections of society. Kalbir Shukra summarises it this way:

> Scarman accepted that "hard" policing (such as stop and search operations) would still be necessary in the future in areas characterised by severe social problems. The question for Scarman was how policing could be enforced without provoking further outbreaks of disorder... Some of the report's recommendations were implemented through a new dual state strategy of repression and containment. This meant that running concurrently with increasing repression in the form of hard policing measures were new state interventions which were designed to create greater public trust and confidence in official institutions.[21]

This meant an acceleration of attempts to channel off some "community leaders" into state-sponsored schemes and "ethnic projects". The Tories approved over 200 new "ethnic projects" in the year after the riots, while traditional spending on similar "ethnic schemes" more than tripled. The aim of such funding was to create a range of self-help organisations and businesses in which black entrepreneurs would play a key role. This new black middle class would have a stake in the system and could be encouraged to neutralise threats to its stability.[22]

The 1980s therefore represented a bridge for activists to go from challenging power from below to a conscious effort to challenge from within. It was a process that found its natural outlet through the vehicle of the country's primary organisation committed to progressive reform—the Labour Party.

At the heart of our analysis is the argument that racism cannot be reformed away. This does not mean that reforms in themselves are not worth fighting for and cannot make a difference. Unfortunately, however, the barriers to equality are so deeply entrenched that they lead us to the conclusion that they are an integral part of the current economic and social set-up.

The "reforms" offered by Scarman and others in the 1980s failed as a solution to racism but, for the state, they succeeded at the level of incorporating a section of the oppressed population into overseeing their own oppression. Some of the radicals who came out of the confrontations with the state in the 1970s made their peace with old enemies in the 1980s and 1990s, even as they claimed to be continuing the fight. That this sleight of hand could be achieved so deftly is more to do with the bankruptcy of reformist and black nationalist ideas than it is with the authors of the betrayal as such.

### The undermining of the anti-racist struggle

Even before Scarman the establishment had accepted multiculturalism but it sought to do so on its own terms. A legal framework of racial equality had been partially established in the 1970s, notably as a result of the Race Relations Act 1976. This was not simply bequeathed from on high but was the product of the struggles for recognition that we have highlighted. In this sense this shift was a gain for the anti-racist movement.

The multiculturalism of the establishment had two guiding principles. Firstly, the over-riding objective of the policy was to assimilate a problematic "alien" culture into the "host" community. Secondly, different cultures were recognised but only in the context of a dominant British—and "white"—culture.

The clearest expression of this approach was probably to be found in the words of the then leader of the opposition, Margaret Thatcher, on 27 January 1978 in a television interview, when she declared, "People are really rather afraid that this country might be rather swamped by people of a different culture." Thatcher continued making explicit her belief in the manifest superiority of British culture: "And, you know, the British character has done so much for democracy, for law and done so much throughout the world that if there is any fear that it might be swamped people are going to react and be rather hostile to those coming in".[23]

Multiculturalism, against this background, was shorn of any radicalism and hitched to the needs of the state. From this new framework flowed the need for a professional class of administrators to refashion British life and bring equal opportunities to all.

This development coincided with the growth of a black middle class. In the case of the African-Caribbean middle class many of the employment opportunities were in the public sector, precisely the place where the new legislation could be most successfully policed because political will could be brought to bear more effectively, if not at a local level, certainly at a national one.

The new social movements against the oppression of black people, women, and lesbians and gays that had come to the fore in the 1960s and 1970s had found allies in the workers' movement and the left. There was at that time a sense of a bigger prize of social revolution in which different oppressed groups could make common cause. Nevertheless, alongside this there was also a strand of "common sense" in the movements that held to the idea that only those who experienced oppression could successfully fight it.

As those collective struggles for change waned and the workers' movement in particular seemed to go on to the defensive in the late 1970s, the ideas that only those who experienced oppression could understand or fight it became more prevalent and influential. Taken to their logical conclusion, these ideas came together under the umbrella label of "identity politics". The failures of the movements to follow through on the overthrow of "white society", or of "patriarchy" or "straight" society, led activists to begin viewing the differences between oppressed groups as more important than what had previously been seen as points of unity. Each oppressed group had to assert its own distinct identity. The logic of these politics was fragmentation of the struggles, competition between oppressed groups, and a turn away from campaigning for wider change in society.

The state intervened to promote this fragmentation by fostering fierce competition for state funds. As A Sivanandan observed of the aftermath of the 1981 riots:

The ensuing scramble for government favours and government grants (channelled through local authorities) on the basis of specific needs and problems served, on the one hand, to deepen ethnic differences and foster ethnic rivalry and, on the other, to widen the definition of ethnicity to include a variety of national and religious groups—Chinese, Cypriots, Greeks, Turks, Irish, Italians, Jews, Moslems, Sikhs—till the term itself became meaningless (except as a means of getting funding).[24]

Capitalism as such was no longer the enemy, but instead whites, men or straight people. Each oppressed group could then be internally divided in a hierarchy of oppression in which, for example, black lesbian women would be at the top.

These developments were reflected in wider society by a shift of those associated with the New Left of the 1960s and 1970s into the Labour Party. The Labour Party therefore became the new home for most of these one-time revolutionaries. In the case of black radicals, it wasn't so much their organisations that moved over, for there weren't any of substance, but rather the leading individuals.

Those who didn't join Labour found other, equally tempting, methods of promoting change from inside the system. For example Farrukh Dhondy became editor for multicultural programmes at the newly established Channel 4 Television. In this role he commissioned the excellent *Bandung Files*, an "Afro-Asian current affairs magazine programme" that ran from 1985 to 1991. Tariq Ali and Darcus Howe were brought in as the programme's joint editors. Howe was also the moderator for a debating programme with a remit to discuss issues of concern to the black community called *The Devil's Advocate*. Elsewhere an organisation was created aimed at getting black people into the media and multicultural programming into the mainstream. This organisation, the Black Media Workers Association, didn't outlive the opening up of Channel 4 to some black perspectives and subsequent "ethnic slots" on other stations.

For many black people there was already an orientation towards the Labour Party. African-Caribbean voters in particular continued to show great loyalty towards Labour, despite that party's consistent habit of bending with the wind of anti-immigrant racism, whenever a gust was blown up.

Although the Tories were in power nationally the Labour Party ran many of the town halls in Britain's urban centres. Also on the ground it still had a large and active membership that was further invigorated by the left's attempt to capture the leadership of the party that came to a head in left wing MP Tony Benn's campaign for the deputy leadership in 1981.

## Labour Party Black Sections

The context of the turn to the Labour Party was the pessimism about the possibilities of wider change created by Thatcher's victory and the declining level of open class struggle. In this context, winning reforms seemed more realistic than attempting to challenge the whole system, and this was combined with a genuine hope that Labour could be shifted to the left. The Labour Party Black Sections were one manifestation of this leftward lurch in the party. They succeeded in drawing into their orbit hundreds of activists up and down the country who thought carving out a space in the Labour Party, a party that would one day win an election and form a government, seemed a much surer way to achieve change than rioting in the streets or confronting the state. There may have been much talk of extra-parliamentary action, and indeed there were plenty of marches and demonstrations in the early Thatcher years, as well as strikes, but at no time were they seen as central by the Labour lefts or the Black Section leaders. It was electoral politics that filled that role.

A clutch of black MPs were elected to parliament in the 1980s: Diane Abbott in Hackney, Bernie Grant in Tottenham, Paul Boateng in Brent and Keith Vaz in Leicester. The mood of unstoppable change among black reformists was captured, with brazen hyperbole, by Boateng in his 1987 general election victory speech: "We can never be free in Brent until South Africa is free too. Today Brent South, tomorrow Soweto!"

It seemed as if the Black Sections movement was onto something. If it could achieve its stated aim of constituting a black section in the party, with a similar constitutional standing to the women's section, a permanent power base could be established from which to launch an assault on the "white-dominated leadership".

But it wasn't the whiteness of the Labour leadership that meant they always equivocated when it came to being consistent fighters against racism; it was their reformist political outlook, an outlook that would have its effect on the small number of black MPs as well. The Labour leadership is the political expression of the trade union bureaucracy, a social layer that plays a very specific role in society—standing between capital and labour in their attempt to negotiate the rate of exploitation. The strategy of reformism—winning elections and using the state to make changes—subsumes everyone in the Labour Party, both right and left. In fact a generation of Labour activists would find that, rather than changing the Labour Party, it was the Labour Party that changed them.

Writing in the *Guardian* in 2008 Marc Wadsworth, one of the leaders of the Black Sections, argued that the "movement" had been a success:

> Despite [internal opposition to its establishment], Black Sections won. We achieved a 500-fold increase in African-Caribbean and Asian representation in town halls around the country, four black council leaders, four black MPs, and Bill Morris as the first black trade union general secretary. On top of that, black self-organised groups were formed in trade unions and even by police officers. And the TUC created places on its general council and executive for black representatives.
>
> Urged by our communities to state our policies, we published the influential Black Agenda document in 1988.
>
> By 1990, the Labour Party finally changed its constitution to embrace the Black Socialist Society that we brought into being.[25]

Black Sections leaders quite rightly waged a battle against a Labour Party that had always been slow to deal with racism both internally and externally, especially when in office. This was reflected in the lack of black candidates at both national and local level. Many respected activists met resistance from the Labour establishment.

Martha Osamor, former deputy leader of Haringey Council,

was the frontrunner for the Vauxhall parliamentary seat of Stuart Holland who resigned in 1989. In his crusade to drive the socialist grouping Militant from the party, however, Labour leader Neil Kinnock had changed the constitution so that all candidate shortlists for parliamentary seats had to go before the national executive committee. Osamor was barred from the shortlist on the spurious grounds that she had been accused, falsely, of misusing the funds of charities connected to the council. All the other black candidates were also rejected with the exception of TV journalist Wesley Kerr, but he withdrew in protest. The seat that Osamor sought to contest, and which includes Brixton, one of the capitals of black Britain, was eventually won and held for decades by Kate Hoey.[26]

Despite the persistence of its fight for positions there was an abject failure to carry this tenacity through to the streets and the workplaces. The Labour Party Black Sections did not call a single demonstration and at no time attempted to build a mass movement outside parliament. Black Sections were a success for those who won the positions Wadsworth holds up as trophies. As Wadsworth made clear, its focus, ultimately, was on the selection committees for parliamentary seats—a fight for positions inside the Labour machinery with the aim of winning elections.

It was in local government that the agenda of identity politics and piecemeal incremental reforms came into its own. Although not in power nationally Labour trumpeted its relevance in local government through the "dented shield" policy. This held that if cuts were forced upon local authorities by the Tory government, it was better that they were implemented by Labour councillors who would do their best to protect frontline services. More than that, Labour councils would introduce reforms to advance the interests of ethnic minorities by vigorously enforcing equal opportunities and weeding out racist practices.

Racism awareness training (RAT) became a key tool in this fight in conjunction with the appointment of ethnic advisers and the establishment of council committees and ethnic monitoring units. All the inner-city London boroughs and the large conurbations elsewhere set up RAT courses for their staff. There was a perfectly

*Say it Loud*

reasonable logic to their introduction. If racism was all in the mind rather than something learnt directly from a material reality that created it and constantly reinvented it, it could surely be undermined by revealing to racists the error of their ways.

The theory and practice of RAT had already been worked out in the US. In particular the writings of Judy Katz became influential. According to her racism is a "psychological problem...deeply embedded in white people from a very early age both on a conscious and an unconscious level". She wrote a pamphlet whose title tells you all you need to know about her take on fighting racism: *Systematic Handbook of Exercises for the Re-education of White People with Respect to Attitudes and Behaviourisms.*

RAT even found its way into the police force, to some extent. Multicultural studies were set up and a black lecturer was briefly employed to teach it. He didn't last long, however. He found himself suspended from Hendon Training College for overstepping the mark when he had the audacity to challenge the racism of his students. As Sivanandan put it, the police did not want to be seen as white people suffering from racism but as police suffering from blacks.

RAT was not confined to white people either. The Lewisham Racism Awareness Training Unit sought to help black people to discover their identity through "consciousness-raising" to "strengthen practices that lead to power acquisition particularly within the confines of white-dominated organisations and society in general".[27]

Theorists such as Katz see racism as something innate to "white culture", so the best one can achieve is for whites to become "anti-racist racists". It is a hopeless strategy.

This obsession with the surface appearances of racism extended to language and provided much ammunition with which the right wing press could attack the left. Stories, often lies, of left wing led councils banning books and censoring nursery rhymes were spread about by the press as examples of "political correctness" that were eating away at all things sensible and British.

Labour councils were of course right to take issue with educational materials that perpetuated racist stereotypes but they should have done so as part of a wider campaign to effect real change in educational provision. A succession of reports, notably the Swann Report, exposed the failings of the British education system in so far as African-Caribbean children were concerned. However, no meaningful reforms were introduced to overcome the institutional racism that stymied their educational opportunities. The guilt-trip frenzy that was RAT was replaced by anti-racist training and anti-racist policies used in schools to deliver equality without fundamentally challenging racism.

No matter how misguided some of the anti-racist work may have been, for the right it was always problematic. In 1988 Ian Macdonald QC led an inquiry into the killing of 13 year old Ahmed Ullah by a white schoolmate at Burnage High School in Manchester. Macdonald and his team subsequently wrote a serious, thorough and constructive report. A part of the report criticised the school's crude, top-down implementation of anti-racist policies. It rightly argued that the school had failed to fully engage its white pupils and parents, and was critical of the decision to prevent Ahmed's white classmates from attending his funeral. Unfortunately the report was leaked to the press and caused a furore. The right jumped at the chance to pillory anti-racism in general.[28] Manchester City Council, which had commissioned the report, subsequently refused to publish it for fear of being sued for defamation. It was eventually published privately under the title *Murder in the Playground* by Macdonald and his co-authors, Reena Bhavnani, Lily Khan and Gus John.

At around the same time a head teacher in Brent called Maureen McGoldrick was summarily suspended by the council for apparently making a racist comment over the phone. She was given no opportunity to defend herself or for her past record to be considered in her defence. She became another gift to the right's assault on anti-racism.[29]

The limits of top-down anti-racism were clear. Unless it was the property of the people whose interests it purported to defend and advance, then it would fall prey to the power games of middle class individuals out to achieve personal advancement under its name. It would also fall victim to a media onslaught against the "loony left".

## Miscarriages of justice

While many black councillors and middle class administrators were busy erecting the apparatus of "anti-racism", racial oppression did not disappear. On 28 September 1985 the police shot and paralysed a Jamaican woman, Cherry Groce, when they burst into her home in Brixton seeking to arrest her son. A protest at the police station descended into running battles and it would be two days before the police could bring the area back under their control. A week later the residents of Broadwater Farm estate in Tottenham, north London, rose against the police killing of Cynthia Jarrett in a raid on her home.

In the course of the fightback a police constable, Keith Blakelock, was also killed. Local council leader Bernie Grant famously commented that the police had received "a bloody good hiding" and was castigated for bravely coming to the defence of those who refused to bow to the police.

After the police regained control a relentless campaign of raids and intimidation unfolded for several months. Six people were eventually charged with the murder of Blakelock. No police officer was to be charged over the killing of Cynthia Jarrett. Three of the charged were juveniles and their cases were dropped. Despite no forensic or witness evidence against them, the remaining three, Winston Silcott, Engin Raghip and Mark Braithwaite, were convicted of murder. After years of campaigning, on 25 November 1991 all three were cleared.

Another campaign against a miscarriage of justice at the hands of the police and justice system came to prominence during this time, that of the Cardiff Three. Lynette White was murdered in Bute Town, Cardiff, in 1988. Despite the initial suspect being white, five black men were arrested and three—Tony Paris, Yusef Abdullahi and Stephen Miller—later convicted of her murder. They were finally freed on appeal in December 1992. It wasn't until 2009 that 13 serving and former South Wales police officers were charged for their mishandling of the case.

## No asylum here

Immigration as a political issue never went away in the Tory years. The recession that blighted Britain in the early 1980s eventually passed and the economy started to grow again, albeit minus a sizeable chunk of manufacturing industry. This did not mean, however, that the ruling class could now discount the need to use immigration as a weapon to divide and rule.

Primary immigration into the UK had been brought to a grinding halt by the mid-1970s, but this did not bring an end to the number of people arriving. Family members of those already here continued to come, as did asylum seekers driven from their homes by wars and economic collapse. Capitalism, as an ever more connected global system, depended on the migration of labour as a necessary partner to the competitive accumulation of capital. As this process of globalisation quickened so too did migratory responses.

In addition to the tightening of immigration controls aimed primarily at dependants coming in from the Indian subcontinent, the Tories introduced the Nationality Act in 1981 which once and for all removed the right to citizenship from New Commonwealth citizens. In order to enter the country you now had to prove that you had a grandparent born in the country. Of course many from the white old Commonwealth could meet these criteria but none from the non-white New Commonwealth could.

Labour's constant pandering to racism in the 1970s had not only emboldened the NF. The Tory right became more confident too. Conservative MP Tony Marlow made explicit what many others thought when he proclaimed in 1980, with no shame:

> People have criticised these measures because they say they are racialist, as if racialist is a word of abuse. What does racialist mean? It means tribal. After all, man is a tribal animal. We have a feeling of kith and kin for people like ourselves, with our own background and culture.[30]

Journals such as the *Salisbury Review* sprang up to provide intellectual succour to this new right. Repatriation of immigrants and their offspring born in the country was a regular theme of the publication. So too were the linking of black people to crime and claims of Pakistanis and Indians abusing the arranged marriage system to evade immigration rules. Immigration raids, now without the need to even provide the name of the person being searched for, were conducted with increasing regularity.

At the same time the UK became notorious for the way it treated asylum seekers, having one of the worst records in Europe for accepting those fleeing persecution and war. In the two years from 1984 Britain took in only 240 asylum seekers for every 1 million people in the country compared to 5,000 per million for Sweden and 4,000 per million for Switzerland. Of those who did get to the UK 60 percent were granted refugee status in 1981 but that figure dropped dramatically so that by 1988 it was down to 25 percent.

In 1987 the Tories introduced heavy fines for airlines that carried asylum seekers on their planes, effectively forcing the airlines to become immigration officers. In 1991 the fine was doubled and visa restrictions were introduced for 90 countries. This was further extended in 1992 to cover the states that made up the former Yugoslavia. Likewise when civil war broke out in Sierra Leone in 1995 restrictions were immediately imposed to prevent refugees from coming here.

Deportation became routine and brutal. Joy Gardner was a 40 year old Jamaican woman who the police arrived to arrest and deport from her home in Crouch End, north London, in July 1993. She was trussed in a body belt and 13 feet of sticking tape was wound round her head, purportedly to stop her from biting the officers. Her subsequent death ignited a firestorm of protest leading to the police officers involved facing trial on manslaughter charges. They were, of course, acquitted.

Yet another piece of immigration legislation was passed in 1993 allowing newly arrived asylum seekers to be deported from the country within days. In that year 10,530 asylum seekers were detained, often in brand new purpose-built detention centres such as Campsfield House in Oxfordshire. The inhuman treatment of prisoners who had already come through unimaginably harrowing circumstances of persecution and torture led to the outbreak of hunger strikes in 1994 and protests in their support.

John Major's government eventually produced an aptly named "White List" of countries that would no longer be considered places from which there could be any reason to flee. Entry would therefore automatically be refused to anyone arriving from said countries. Even the *Economist* magazine found the new rules baffling: "[The] policy has already reduced the inflow to a trickle. The number of successful applications for British citizenship [is] at its lowest for ten years. Nowhere in Britain is being swamped".[31]

The real reason for the legislation, as always, wasn't to do with numbers but with scapegoating.

The Tory moves in Britain were mirrored across Western Europe with the erection of a Fortress Europe to keep out people from Africa and Asia, but also from Eastern Europe. The new freedoms that Western governments were apparently glad to see those in the former Communist states enjoy did not include the freedom to travel to Western Europe.

### From confrontation to compromise

The period from the 1970s to the 1980s that this chapter has focused on shows some inspirational struggles and the potential for resistance that offers a real challenge to the state and wider racism. From the mass movements against the Nazi NF to the growing combativity of black workers in the trade unions, to the explosions of discontent in the riots of the early 1980s, we have seen that a new generation of black people were determined to insist on their place in British society and real opportunities for black and white unity were forged. Racism and fascism were both dealt some serious blows in this period, yet both have endured and repeatedly resurfaced.

We have also seen the varied anti-racist strategies of reformism, revolutionary struggle and black nationalism all put to the test. In particular the 1980s marked the ability of the state and the Labour Party to co-opt a layer of activists into attempting to change things from within—to move from confrontation to compromise with the system. Militant struggles opened up the space for a layer of individuals to advance or to find positions of "influence", yet the majority of black people were left behind—facing racism, disadvantage and exploitation alongside their white working class counterparts. These contradictions laid the basis for the battles yet to come.

# A defining struggle:
# The Stephen Lawrence campaign

**Hassan Mahamdallie**

> I USED to talk to Stephen about the dangers of being out and the dangers of the police as well, because of stories that you hear that used to frighten me. The stories that you would hear would be about walking on the street on your own or with your friends or whatever, and the police would stop you and bundle you in the back of the van and beat up the kids. That is the story that would be going round, especially with black children.
>
> Stephen's attitude towards the police was always: "Well if I'm not doing anything wrong how could they do that to me?" I used to say to him from what I am hearing you don't have to be doing anything. I didn't trust the police, I never have done, and I certainly don't now. Stephen did not have that mistrust, however, because as far as he was concerned, if he wasn't doing anything wrong he had nothing to worry about. That was his attitude.[1]
>
> — Doreen Lawrence's testimony to the Macpherson Inquiry
> 8 March 1998

In May 1997 Tony Blair's New Labour Party was swept into office with a left wing mandate from voters but a right wing reformist political programme. In the run up to the general election the Tories had in desperation tried to play the race card and appeal to bigotry. Tory strategist Andrew Lansley had advised that "immigration as an issue played well in the last election and still has the capacity to hurt our opponents".[2]

However, part of the general mood in the country for change

was the feeling that scapegoating politics wouldn't save the Tories' necks this time. Two examples from the 1997 election exemplify how voters rejected what they saw as the Tory politics of division: Wolverhampton MP Nicholas Budgen, defending Enoch Powell's old seat, took Lansley at his word, played the race card over immigration and expected to hold his seat. Instead he was soundly defeated by the Labour candidate. In Exeter the religious right Tory candidate Adrian Rogers, who considered homosexuals to be leading "deviant lifestyles", ran a vitriolic campaign against openly gay Labour opponent Ben Bradshaw. West Country voters responded by rejecting the totality of Roger's politics and beliefs and sent Bradshaw to Westminster with a healthy majority.

During the 18 years of Tory rule there had been a quickening of state racism, as described in the last chapter. The racism deployed by the Tories through the Thatcher and Major years always provoked a response by those directly under attack, who more often than not would be successful in drawing active support around them, even if they did not always succeed in their aims. For example, there was a sustained campaign to shut down the immigration detention centre at Campsfield, near Oxford, that had opened in 1993. Many hard fought, imaginative and well supported anti-deportation campaigns attempted to prevent asylum seekers being sent back to their persecutors.

Black deaths in police or prison custody continued during the Tory years. As we've heard it was the death of Cynthia Jarrett during a police raid on her house that had sparked the Broadwater Farm Riot in October 1985. Other victims included Winston Rose (1981), Colin Roach (1983), John Mikkelson (1985), Clinton McCurbin (1987), Leon Patterson (1992) Joy Gardner (1993), Shiji Lapite (1994), Brian Douglas (1995), Wayne Douglas (1995) and Ibrahima Sey (1996). All provoked family campaigns supported by their local communities that eventually gelled into a nation-wide united coordinating body.[3]

By the late 1980s the Tories' drip-drip reliance on racism had succeeded in resurrecting the far-right, with the British National Party (BNP) finally dragging itself out of the ruins of the National Front. In 1990 the BNP opened up a shop-front headquarters in

Welling, south east London, and began to provoke, encourage and organise racist sentiment against the area's relatively small black population. The BNP encouraged existing armed gangs of racist young men, linked by family ties and connected to major drug dealing, living on geographically and socially isolated estates, particularly Thamesmead, to greater violence. Police racism and far-right inspired violence fed into each other, leading to murders by gangs of youths whose racist motivation was then downplayed or denied during the subsequent police investigations. One measure of the BNP's influence was a 210 percent increase in racist attacks in the wake of the opening of their Welling "bookshop". Given the police's institutional starting point that black people were the problem, it was not surprising, although still alarming, that the police habitually failed to catch the guilty or break up the gangs. This in turn encouraged the BNP and the racists under their influence to think of themselves as untouchable and commit further atrocities.

In February 1991 15 year old Rolan Adams was murdered in Thamesmead by a gang shouting "Nigger" before stabbing him in the throat. The police treated the incident as a territorial dispute between gangs, in the face of overwhelming evidence that Rolan was the victim of a racially motivated murder. Then Rohit Duggal, another 15 year old, was stabbed to death by a gang outside a kebab shop in Eltham in July 1992. His murderer had called Rohit a "paki", yet the police again denied a racial motive, implying that Duggal was somehow to blame.[4]

### The death of Stephen Lawrence

On 22 April 1993 18 year old Stephen Lawrence and his friend Duwayne Brooks were ambushed at a bus stop in Well Hall Road, Eltham, by a gang of most likely six young white racists, one of whom shouted, "What, what, nigger". Duwayne managed to escape his attackers, all of whom were local to the area, but Stephen was caught, surrounded and knifed to death.

The failure of the police to catch the killers in the hours and days following the murder is well documented.[5] The killers were allowed to escape to their nearby houses, construct alibis, hide the murder weapon (that has never been found), destroy clothing and other evidence and set about intimidating witnesses. They also quite likely colluded through longstanding criminal connections with the drugs trade with a corrupt officer or officers, who may well have been bribed to shield the perpetrators from being caught. The behaviour of the police who initially investigated Stephen's murder was best summed up by his mother Doreen in her submission to the Stephen Lawrence Inquiry:

> We were told [by the investigating police officers] that there was a wall of silence. We couldn't understand this because people were constantly visiting us and phoning our home giving names and information... We also now know that the police received a vast amount of information, not only from the public but several police officers via their informants... These boys...were known to the police because of the other stabbings they had committed... Racism is institutionalised... It's like "Who are you to think I am racist". Well I say—how dare I think you are not, because nothing in your actions has proven to me you are not, and I see no other explanation for your attitude and behaviour.[6]

The growing realisation that the police investigation into the murder of Stephen Lawrence was heading for failure, with the fear there would now be an escalation of racist attacks and killings in that part of south east London, catalysed a campaign in support of the Lawrence family and their insistence on justice with a wider call for the BNP headquarters just up the road in Welling to be closed down. The police reacted precisely as they had done in past similar circumstances—they denied any racial motive in the killing. This led to the dismissal of vital information including intelligence. They sought to undermine the credibility of the family and attack anti-racist campaigners as criminals and the source of the problems in the area.

The sense of urgency was ratcheted up when in September 1993 the BNP's Derek Beackon narrowly won a council seat on the Isle of Dogs in Tower Hamlets, east London. The election campaign was accompanied by a wave of brazen and violent attacks on local South Asians, including an attack on 17 year old Quddus Ali, who was kicked to within an inch of his life and left permanently brain damaged.

In a significant move activists eventually pushed the TUC to call a demonstration that marched through east London in March 1994. As we will discover in chapter 6, this marked the turning point in the campaign against the BNP and fascist influence in the East End. Two months later Beackon was defeated in council elections. The success of the determined and systematic "Don't Vote Nazi" campaign was marked by a 150,000 strong Anti Nazi League carnival in Brockwell Park, south London, in May 1994.

Protests and demonstrations against the BNP headquarters had to endure police harassment, attacks and arrests, including of Duwayne Brooks at one point. These culminated in a savage assault against the 60,000 strong Unity demonstration of October 1993, which began with the truncheoning of the march's chief steward Julie Waterson and ended in a frenzied police riot against the anti-racist protesters. The next day the *Mail on Sunday* ran the headline "Masked Mob Stones Police".[7] The truth is that if the protesters had been allowed to demolish the BNP headquarters brick by brick, things would have been very different.

It was not lost on anyone that day that the police had put considerably more resources into battering anti-racist demonstrators and protecting the BNP HQ than they had done into catching the killers of Stephen Lawrence. Mass arrests took place during the march and after of individual protesters attempting to defend themselves against police attack and in September 1995 nine Welling protesters were sentenced to a total of 20 years and six months in prison. And still Stephen's killers, whose identities were widely known, walked free. Undeterred, the Lawrence family continued to gather wide support. Many organisations and individuals rallied to the family's cause, with the trade unions being some of the most consistent.

At the same time the Metropolitan Police, who were squirming under the pressure of unprecedented negative publicity, including a high profile intervention by Nelson Mandela on a visit to London that had forced them to finally round up the prime suspects, continually assured the Lawrence family and their lawyers that they were doing their best to catch Stephen's killers. They sought to marshal "evidence" to support this fiction. In November 1993 an internal police review of the investigation led by DCS John Barker (a former head of the Scotland Yard Flying Squad) concluded that "the investigation has been progressed satisfactorily and all lines of enquiry correctly pursued".[8] This review was subsequently roundly condemned by the Stephen Lawrence Inquiry five years later as "flawed and indefensible", with Barker admitting in evidence that he was told by senior officers "not to be heavy-handed" or to "undermine" officers.[9]

A second, similarly unsuccessful, police investigation was mounted in 1994. This was followed in 1997 by a Police Complaints Authority (PCA) investigation into an official complaint lodged by the Lawrence family. It was carried out by neighbouring Kent police and was therefore not an independent report. Although it criticised the first investigation (how could it not at this point) its overall thrust was to exonerate the police of the main criticisms made by the Lawrences. It found no evidence of corruption or collusion with criminals and concluded by stating:

> The complaint investigation has not produced any evidence to support the allegations of racist conduct by police officers nor has it produced any evidence to support many of the specific allegations made by the Lawrence family in relation to events on the night of the murder. The evidence shows that the police operation undertaken immediately after the assault on Stephen Lawrence was well organised and effective.[10]

As Doreen Lawrence later pointed out, the police and authorities were, above all, pursuing a strategy of containment. "By keeping us occupied they kept the black community quiet, it gave us a false sense of security and it made black people feel that justice could be achieved".[11]

In April 1995 the Lawrence family and their legal team were forced by the lack of police progress to mount a risky private prosecution against the suspects. Eventually three of them, Neil Acourt, Luke Knight and Gary Dobson, were sent for a trial beginning in April 1996, but the case collapsed after the judge ruled that Duwayne

Brooks's identification evidence could not be heard. All three were acquitted with the result that that they could not now be tried again for the same crime under existing "double jeopardy" rules. It was a terrible blow to the family and their growing body of support.

In February 1997 the inquest into Stephen's murder was marred by the reluctant appearances of the key suspects who refused to answer any questions put to them by the coroner instead repeating "I claim privilege." This incensed all who witnessed it, including the coroner, Sir Montague Levine. The inquest and the arrogant behaviour of the prime suspects were widely covered in the media. The inquest jury delivered a verdict of unlawful killing, adding the unusual and significant rider that Stephen had died "in a completely unprovoked racist attack by five white youths"—in other words pointing a finger directly at brothers Jamie and Neil Acourt and Luke Knight, Gary Dobson and David Norris as the killers. The verdict once again highlighted the failings of the police. The following day, 14 February 1997, the *Daily Mail*—following in the wake of the principled and courageous stance of the inquest jury—splashed the front page headline "Murderers: The *Mail* accuses these men of killing. If we are wrong let them sue us" with photos of the five suspects underneath.[12]

It was then that Shadow Home Secretary Jack Straw, a few months away from a general election, told the Lawrences that should New Labour get into office he would grant a public inquiry, a demand that the family campaign had been agitating for since 1993.

Despite the *Mail* retrospectively claiming a key role in the Lawrences' campaign, any honest account would recognise that the main pressure on the establishment to deliver any kind of justice was generated by ordinary people, black and white, up and down the length of the country. It was the grassroots that had supported, marched, petitioned, lobbied, fundraised and turned the screws on the powers that be, with the trade unions acting as the backbone of that movement. The Lawrences were invited to speak at many union meetings and union sponsored rallies. As Neville Lawrence recalled, speaking at the 1998 TUC conference about the dark days following his son's murder, "I thought, 'who am I going to turn to? I did not have the money. Where will I get support?' and I remember meeting a group of trade unionists who said, 'We are going to help'."[13] This base of support was reflected in the trade union solidarity days that were organised during the Lawrence inquiry. There were no equivalent *Daily Mail* days.

In June 1997 the newly installed Home Secretary Jack Straw met the Lawrences, their lawyers Imran Khan and Michael Mansfield QC and two MPs, Bernie Grant and local constituency MP John Austin-Walker. A month later Straw announced that there would be an inquiry "into the matters arising from the death of Stephen Lawrence on 22 April 1993 to date, in order particularly to identify the lessons to be learned for the investigation and prosecution of racially motivated crimes".[14] This was a wide remit. Straw appointed former high court judge Sir William Macpherson of Cluny whom he considered a safe pair of hands as the inquiry chair. Macpherson's past record as a judge looked so unpromising that the Lawrence family legal team attempted to get him replaced on the eve of the inquiry. Yet during the course of the proceedings Macpherson was clearly so horrified by the unfolding evidence that he became determined to deliver wide ranging conclusions.[15]

The inquiry began its public hearings on 16 March 1998 at Hannibal House, Elephant and Castle, south London, and ended in Birmingham on 13 November that same year. It considered 100,000 pages of written documentation, sat for 59 days in south London, 88 witnesses gave evidence and 12,000 pages of transcript were produced. The final report ran to 340 pages accompanied by appendices of similar length.[16]

Even before the final report was published in February 1999 the hearings alone had resulted in a deep crisis of legitimacy in a key organ of the British state—the Metropolitan Police. The Met had given good service to the Thatcher government particularly during the 1984-85 Miners' Strike and the union-busting dispute at Rupert Murdoch's Wapping print works the following year. The Tory years had seen an inexorable militarisation of the police, who had been showered with new weaponry and powers, ending any fantasy of Dixon of Dock Green style "policing by consent". As Audrey Farrell had pointed out in 1992:

Hatred of police action has spread far wider than the establishment would have liked it to. Resentment is no longer mainly restricted to black people, young people and the left. Large numbers of "respectable" working class people have seen their attempts to save jobs and communities dealt with by the blows of a police truncheon.[17]

Outrage at the police's failure to catch Stephen Lawrence's murderers mounted as the inquiry went on. Each new event or revelation slotted another piece of the puzzle into place, building a total picture in the minds of the public. The behaviour of the police officers called to give evidence in the trial, all of whom clearly still believed that there was little or no racial motive to Stephen's murder; the compelling narrative that the hearings had constructed of police racism, indifference and probable corruption; the blank refusal of Metropolitan Police Commissioner Sir Paul Condon to admit that his force was institutionally racist or corrupt; the repugnant strutting of the suspects whose freedom rested on the botched police investigation; the public hearings in other parts of London and other cities that were filled by accounts of relentless stop and search, police brutality and extreme racist behaviour; the growing disbelief at what was being revealed to them etched on the faces of Macpherson and his inquiry team; the detailed examination of witnesses by Michael Mansfield; the dogged determination of the Lawrences to see justice done; the aggressive cross-examination of Doreen Lawrence and Imran Khan by barristers representing the police; the huge and vocal presence of ordinary people daily packing out the public gallery; all of these factors created a political whirlwind with the Metropolitan Police at the centre. It threatened to suck in other police forces along with wider institutions of the state, and raise fundamental questions about the nature of society and the pillars it rested on. This force engulfed not only the Met Police but Jack Straw and the New Labour administration that had set the ball rolling.

There was also a wider context to the inquiry. In the very same month that the five suspects in the murder of Stephen Lawrence were forced to give testimony, celebrations took place to mark the 50th anniversary of the arrival of the *Empire Windrush* at Tilbury Docks on 22 June 1948. The *Windrush* anniversary of the first significant arrival of Caribbean immigrants after the Second World War took on a symbolism far beyond its original purpose. It was expected to be purely a celebration of post-war black presence in Britain. Now many were asking how far black people had advanced in British society in that half century and whether an end to racism would ever be in sight. The Lawrences' battle had raised a vital question for all society—how was it at the end of the 20th century, in a supposedly modern, multicultural Britain, indeed a "New Britain", that black people could still suffer the most profound and structural racial discrimination seemingly more akin to the 1950s than 1990s? When Doreen Lawrence asserted that no police officer had tended to her dying son because they did not want to get "black blood" on their hands she produced a powerful symbol of all that seemed to be wrong with British society. She exploded the self-congratulatory myth constructed by established politicians of a "tolerant" Britain. That the family had chosen to bury British-born Stephen's body in a grave in Jamaica sent an uncomfortable message. It was the *Windrush* journey reversed.

The Lawrence affair itself demonstrated the contradiction between the uneven experiences of black people in Britain in a stark way. On the one hand there were millions of people, black and white, from Aberdeen to Plymouth, who urged on the Lawrences and their supporters to push it all the way. On the other hand the most powerful forces in the land resisted this process of exposure, most notably the police.

The reputation of Metropolitan Police Commissioner Sir Paul Condon (later Baron Condon), who had declared on his appointment, just three months before Stephen Lawrence was slain, that he should be judged on his success or failure to tackle racism and police corruption, lay in ruins when his inaugural pledge came back to haunt him in ways he could never have imagined.[18]

The Lawrence team was the only element at the inquiry which sought to fully explain exactly why the police investigation into Stephen's murder had gone so horribly wrong. If police racism was staring you in the face, it was police corruption that cast a long shadow over the entire Macpherson inquiry. During the inquiry the Lawrences' legal team (led by Michael Mansfield) were prevented from fully following the leads they had uncovered particularly linking David Norris's career criminal father Clifford Norris with officers on the murder team. As the Lawrence team argued, "There is a matrix of quite exceptional coincidences and connections here which weave such a tight web around this investigation that only the ability to suspend disbelief can provide such an innocent explanation".[19]

As Neville Lawrence argued in his evidence, "I would say that both racism and corruption played a part in this investigation... As to corruption I think that some police officers investigating my son's death were connected to the murderers in some way or other".[20]

Today, given the revelations of corruption surrounding the police and Rupert Murdoch's News International, it is not difficult to imagine that some of the police officers were open to criminal influence. Yet in 1998, despite the insistence of the Lawrence family and their legal team, it was assumed that corruption had not played a part. The inquiry brought to bear a criminal standard of proof over allegations of corruption—in other words it had to be established "beyond reasonable doubt" that an officer had been corrupt, a bar set impossibly high given that the Lawrence team and the inquiry panel had no access to police intelligence or internal investigations into police corruption (which we now know to have existed). The inquiry concluded, "It is right that we should say at once that no collusion or corruption is proved to have infected the investigation into Stephen Lawrence's murder. It would be wrong and unfair to conclude otherwise".[21]

We now know that it was wrong for the inquiry to come to this conclusion. Since the report was published there has been a steady stream of information pointing to precisely the opposite conclusion to that drawn by the inquiry. It is now accepted, even by top police, that there were probably corrupt links between the police and the prime suspects. If all the evidence had come out at the Macpherson Inquiry it would have been a hammer blow to the Metropolitan Police in its guise as a legitimate state institution. The repercussions would have been immense.

## Institutional racism

The most significant finding of the Macpherson Inquiry was that "institutional racism" was the main reason for the police's failure. Although Condon fought a rearguard action against its inclusion in the report, it represented an advance from the Scarman Report which had put police racism down to the "bad apples" theory of prejudiced individual officers acting in extreme "frontline" circumstances. It was a combination of the arguments of the Lawrences and their team, hardening public opinion against the police, and officers' performance in the witness box, that drove the inquiry team to probe a deeper understanding of the nature of the problem confronting them.

Condon's wretched performance in front of the Macpherson Inquiry when he appeared in October 1998 centred on his refusal to admit that his force was institutionally racist. Questioned by Macpherson as to whether he thought that the Lawrence scandal added up to "a collective failure" and "general malaise" (in other words institutional racism) Condon sought to cloud the issue: "The notion of a mysterious collective will is a difficult definition to acknowledge," he replied. Condon defended his force by raising the canard that no serious critic had advanced—that institutional racism meant that all officers under his command were hardened racists who went to work to "play out a racist agenda", as he put it. Macpherson retorted testily, "How can that [collective failure] be dealt with if it isn't accepted that it exists?" But Condon refused to be "hung up on the words". Condon begged of Macpherson that he should not be forced to utter the words "institutional racism". For him even an acknowledgement that racism was "widespread" in the police was beyond the pale. "I'm not in denial," Condon protested during questioning by inquiry member Tom Cook, himself a former West Yorkshire top officer. "Just say yes," pleaded inquiry member Dr Richard Stone, to no avail.[22]

Despite Condon's efforts, there was no doubt that the inquiry would identify the police as institutionally racist. This was a crushing blow, particularly to the Met.

However, in the final reckoning the Macpherson report was to throw the police and the wider establishment a lifeline. The final

*Say it Loud*

report cited but passed over the definition given by 1960s US Black Power theorists Stokely Carmichael and Charles V Hamilton that institutional racism "originates in the operation of established and respected forces in society".[23]

Carmichael and Hamilton had explained that "institutional racism relies on the active and pervasive operation of anti-black attitudes and practices". The police, operating as an established and respected force, has a particular role to play in fomenting and reinforcing racist ideas and actions by cementing in people's minds notions of criminality, difference and inferiority imputed to black people (or Asians, Gypsies and Travellers, Muslims) as a group. Each contact that the police have with black people—from stop and search, excessive force, heavy policing or "swamping" areas perceived as "black", disproportionate arrests and incarceration, the construction of stereotype "black" crimes such as mugging, drug dealing, rioting and gang culture and refusing to protect them against racist attacks—confirms these notions. For example the infamous "sus" laws were deployed to stigmatise black people as inherently criminal by arresting innocent individuals and dragging them before the courts.

As criminologists Ben Bowling and Coretta Phillips have documented.

> Research evidence over the past three decades has found that specific stereotypes are commonly used by police officers to classify people on the basis of their ethnic origin. Studies found that Asians tended to be regarded as devious, liars and potential illegal immigrants... The pliability of stereotypes of Asian and particularly Muslim people has been documented in recent research, which has suggested that perceptions of Asian and particularly Muslim people have undergone a transformation. Stereotypes, which assumed that Asian people were conformist, are now thought to be less applicable and, rather, the very stereotypes assumed to explain law-abiding behaviour (eg family pressures, tight knit communities and high levels of social control) are now thought to promote criminal and deviant activity among Asian youth... The shift in the perception

of such groups has been located in both local and global notions of Asian youth as increasingly involved in gangs, violent, disorderly, riotous and, more recently, as potential terrorists. Stereotypes of black people have been more consistent in that they are thought to be more prone to violent crime and drug abuse, to be incomprehensible, suspicious, hard to handle, naturally excitable, aggressive, lacking brainpower, troublesome and "tooled up"... These findings have not been restricted to constables but have been found throughout the ranks.[14]

If we look wider we can see that this phenomenon is not confined to Britain, but is global and historic. As Audrey Farrell argued:

Across the world, police racism is best understood by looking at the function performed by the police within capitalism rather than by looking at the composition of the police force or the characteristics of individual policemen. It is certainly not explicable in terms of the behaviour of those they police.[15]

The treatment of black people by the police was raised on numerous occasions during the Macpherson Inquiry. It was revealed to be deep-rooted and systematic. For example, at the west London public hearing the Southall based civil rights Monitoring Group told the inquiry that:

From our experience we've identified two key trends; firstly, victims of racial harassment do not receive a fair, just and acceptable service from the police and secondly, when victims call upon the police it is they who are treated as perpetrators and criminalised.

A local vicar, the Reverend David Wise, drove the point home saying that as far as his Baptist congregation was concerned, "the experience they have of the local police is more like the Monitoring Group picture than the police presentation [which had started the hearing]". Wise recounted how one of his congregation, originally from Barbados:

was returning from college on a Saturday evening when he was pulled over by a police car. He was asked to get out of his car. He

*Say it Loud*

asked why. A police officer said, "We've got a call. You're a fuck-ing druggie. You black people are all fucking druggies." He was searched and sent on his way frightened and intimidated.

The man refused to lodge a complaint: "He was afraid that the police would target him, or if he needed the police in the future, they wouldn't come".[26]

What Carmichael and Hamilton did not argue was that anti-black attitudes and practices "infected" otherwise legitimate institutions expressing themselves in "unwitting" acts of discrimina-tion. But this was the notion that Macpherson and his team settled upon. This led the report to the coining of the wholly inadequate formulations "unwitting racism" leading to a "collective failure" to describe the behaviour of the police over the Lawrence affair. This was in one sense a collapse back to an aspect of the findings of the Scarman Report. It was Scarman who had rejected any idea that the police were a racist institution, but accepted that it might possibly "unwittingly discriminate against black people".

The report quoted Lord Scarman:

> In that seminal report Lord Scarman responded to the suggestion that "Britain is an institutionally racist society," in this way:
>
> "If, by [institutionally racist] it is meant that [Britain] is a soci-ety which knowingly, as a matter of policy, discriminates against black people, I reject the allegation. If, however, the suggestion being made is that practices may be adopted by public bodies as well as pri-vate individuals which are *unwittingly discriminatory* [my emphasis] against black people, then this is an allegation which deserves seri-ous consideration, and, where proved, swift remedy."

Macpherson then went onto argue that "Lord Scarman accepted the existence of what he termed 'unwitting' or 'unconscious' racism. To those adjectives can be added a third, namely 'unintentional'." The report then sought to employ these definitions to build a linguis-tic bridge between the inquiry team and Paul Condon:

> All three words are familiar in the context of any discussion in this field. The Commissioner used all three in his letter written to the

Inquiry on 2 October 1998, after his appearance at Hannibal House during our hearings.

Unwitting racism can arise because of lack of understanding, ignorance or mistaken beliefs. It can arise from well-intentioned but patronising words or actions. It can arise from unfamiliarity with the behaviour or cultural traditions of people or families from minority ethnic communities. It can arise from racist stereotyping of black people as potential criminals or troublemakers. Often this arises out of uncritical self-understanding born out of an inflexible police ethos of the "traditional" way of doing things. Furthermore such attitudes can thrive in a tightly knit community, so that there can be a collective failure to detect and to outlaw this breed of racism. The police canteen can too easily be its breeding ground.[27]

In the final analysis the definition of institutional racism adopted by the inquiry amounted to a compromise with the state. Not only did it not satisfactorily explain the origin and purpose of institutional racism as Carmichael and Hamilton had, but it held out to the police the possibility that if it pledged to reform itself, by recruiting more black officers for example, it could eventually dig itself out the hole the Lawrence scandal had dropped it into. However, there was another powerful factor at play that did not hold out the prospect of easy containment—the changing attitudes of the population towards the police.

A Gallup poll taken on the eve of the publication of the inquiry report in February 1999 found that those "satisfied" with the police had fallen sharply from 74 percent in 1989 to 58 percent in 1999. Those who said they were "very satisfied" with the police had fallen from 26 percent in 1989 to 8 percent a decade later—38 percent considered police officers "racist" with 31 percent regarding officers as "dishonest".[28]

An ICM poll produced at the same time found that a quarter of the population believed that "most police were racist". In a figure that shows that the general public had an understanding of the concept of institutional racism, one in three people believed that, whatever the personal intentions of the officers involved, the way the police work led to discrimination against black people.[29]

This shift in attitudes was partly to do with people's individual experience of the police, the role of the police in major events such as the Miners' Strike and the Hillsborough football disaster, but also increasingly a recognition that the police singled out black people for "special treatment". The willingness of people to sign petitions in support of the Lawrences' demand that Condon be sacked was as strong in small towns in Scotland as it was in inner London.

The inquiry itself demonstrated that racism was not confined to the capital. The Macpherson team mounted a short tour round England as Part Two of their inquiries, holding one-day public hearings in Manchester, Bradford, Bristol and Birmingham, as well as west and east London. All top police officers who came before the inquiry team sought to head off criticism, attempting to persuade the panel, usually with the silent or near silent presence of a black or Asian junior officer by their side, how eager they were to embrace change and to lay out the race initiatives they were engaged in or planned in the future. In Manchester on 13 October 1998 the city's chief constable, David Wilmot, even went so far as to jump before he was pushed and declare that he accepted his force was "institutionally racist", thus effectively undermining the stance taken two weeks earlier by his London counterpart.[30]

At the hearing in Birmingham a month later West Midlands police officers boasted that their practices represented a return to policing by consent and sought to give a sparkling view of policing in the region. Unfortunately for them their testimony was followed by a number of speakers who accused the police of gross racism, violence towards the black community and a failure to protect the city's black citizens from racist violence.

The hearing heard from local young black man Carl Joseph who had been stopped in his car by the police 34 times in two years. So weary was he of having to hand in his documents at the police station after each search that he eventually lodged his driving documents permanently with West Midlands Police (they were somewhat ungratefully reluctant to acknowledge this helpful gesture). At the end of the day's hearing a sombre and rather depressed inquiry member, west London GP Dr Richard Stone, declared, "I feel very sad after today—this visit is the most sad of our visits so far." In a rare public expression of his troubled mind Neville Lawrence stood up in front of the public gallery and turning to the police said, "I'm really a little bit disappointed. We need to accept the inevitable—that things are wrong before people can go ahead. To make changes people have to admit what's wrong".[31]

## The aftermath

In the wake of the inquiry came a whole number of other widely supported campaigns—for example supporting the family of East African Indian student Ricky Reel who was found drowned in the river Thames after being chased by racists, and vigorous and very political campaigns against deaths at the hands of the police (which united black families such as the relatives of Roger Sylvester in Tottenham and Christopher Alder in Hull with the Scottish Harry Stanley family in Hackney). In every town in Britain any one of these campaigns could pack a community hall and be the subject of a successful trade union resolution.

In September 1998 a black man stepped forward to address a public meeting against police racism held in south London's Brixton. The audience fell silent as Kwesi Menson proceeded to lay out in understated tones the truly shocking account of his brother Michael's death and the events that followed.

Kwesi explained how at 2am on the morning of 28 January 1997 he had been woken by the police. Officers told him that his 30 year old brother Michael, a former musician with prominent 1980s band Double Trouble, had been found by motorists staggering along the North Circular Road, Edmonton, north London, flames leaping from his back. By the time police arrived the horribly injured Michael was almost naked, his clothes leaving a burning trail across the road as they melted and dropped off him. Michael had massive burns to his back, torso and buttocks. Kwesi then told how, when he rushed to see his brother in hospital Michael had been lucid: "When we saw him he was lying on his back, he was alert and the hospital staff had done a good job minimising the pain and he was able to talk to us." Michael spoke to his brother, saying that "four white lads, they set my back on fire—why did they do this to me?" Kwesi recounted how "I was shocked and urged them [the police] to come and take statements". He then explained how the family had "told everybody" at the hospital what Michael had said and asked why the police had not even taken a statement. Kwesi recalled that "one of the sisters said she would be contacting the police and urge them to come down directly. She was shocked and angry." He explained how subsequently a police officer had come to the hospital, but had "indicated he wasn't going to ask any questions and he left the room". Michael slipped into a coma and two weeks later died of what a pathologist would describe at his inquest as "multi-organ failure as a result of severe burns". No statement had been taken from the dying, but initially conscious, man.[32]

Of the police Kwesi told the shocked Brixton audience, "From the outset I asked for a thorough investigation and I was assured that was the case." Kwesi's Brixton speech came just days before the inquest into his brother's death opened at Hornsey Coroners Court in north London. The questions that would be implicitly raised during the inquest and explicitly by the Menson family in their campaign that followed were: had Michael Menson been failed by the police because of racist "assumptions" that officers had made about him from the moment of their first contact with him? Had the officers approached Michael in the same way as the officers involved in the Lawrence case had done? What if Michael Menson had been white and smartly turned out—would he have been treated any differently?

The inquest opened in north London on 7 September 1998. The police argued that there was no evidence of a crime and therefore no crime scene had been established, and no forensics had taken place, and that Michael Menson had most likely set fire to himself in a suicide attempt.

This was the view of WPC Johanna Walsh in her evidence to the inquest. She was on night duty in an unmarked car when she heard the call for an ambulance to attend Michael. When she arrived she found a black man "burnt all over his shoulders, down his back, side of the body and the top of his buttocks". Walsh said that Michael "behaved as if he were in a trance. When I arrived at the scene I had an open mind," she testified, but then she began to believe he was mentally ill—"I came to that conclusion." Walshe added, "I didn't believe at the time he knew what he was saying."

However, this was not the assumption of others who went to Michael's aid. David James, an off-duty firefighter based in the West Midlands, was driving along the North Circular when he spotted flames. He was shocked to see that they were emanating from a man, who, by the time he saw him, was naked apart from his socks. James helped the police who arrived first and assisted the paramedics. James under questioning from the police legal team was firm that "it didn't cross my mind that he [Michael] was mentally ill".

A forensic scientist and fire investigator called to give evidence to the inquest utterly destroyed the police's chain of assumptions. James Munday testified that the nature of the spread of the flames consistent with the burns found on Michael meant that:

> Michael Menson's jacket was ignited by a naked flame while he was lying down—the fire consuming most of the coat—before walking away... While I can't eliminate Michael Menson lit the back of his own clothes while lying down, that method would have been unique by my experience.

In other words Michael had been deliberately set on fire by an attacker or attackers. The inquest jury returned a verdict of unlawful killing.[33]

The police were forced to belatedly open a high level murder investigation and in December 1999 three men were found guilty of murder. They had come across Michael, robbed and assaulted him, taunted him, poured an accelerant on the back of his coat and set him on fire. One of the killers, Mario Pereira, under questioning about the murder had replied, "So what? He was black".[34]

Each time another example of the police's treatment of black people became known, it served as another blow to the police and their claim to be a legitimate force for law and order. For the powers that be a line had to be drawn in the sand. Jack Straw had refused to sack Metropolitan Police Commissioner Paul Condon, upon whose watch the Lawrence debacle had taken place. Instead he was allowed to retire shortly afterwards with his pension intact.

In parliament Bernie Grant was a lone voice in his call for the resignation of Condon. The following year Straw appointed Condon's deputy John (later Baron) Stevens, a so-called "copper's cop", to the post of commissioner in a move to reassure the ranks that there would be no fundamental change.

During the inquiry a mooted national demonstration in support of the Lawrences and against the police did not materialise. If the march had taken place it would have not only have been huge in numbers but would have set an agenda that could have seen the police and the government's room for manoeuvre all but disappear.

## The backlash
The police, particularly the lower ranks, instinctively understood the fundamental nature of the attack that the Lawrence affair represented on their hitherto unbridled right to be racist and abuse their powers.

On the morning of 19 May 1999[35] hundreds of burly suited and booted men streamed into Blackpool's Winter Gardens conference centre. Among the square shoulders it was possible to glimpse a handful of women and if you were sharp-eyed the one or two black people present.

It was the annual trade union general meetings season—but this was a trade union gathering with a difference. The Police Federation was Britain's only union to have been set up by an act of parliament. It had come into being in 1919, as an outlet for rank and file officers' grievances after the ruling class had been scared rigid by police strikes during the revolutionary upheavals of that year. At its inception it had been nicknamed the "goose club" because its members were expected to march closely in step with the authorities. But 80 years after it was set up a battered federation was feeling out of step with widening sections of society, which it knew held its members in deepening contempt.

The rank and file of Britain's police were gathering together by the seaside just three months after the release by the Home Office of the most damaging document in their entire history. The Federation itself had to admit that "the Macpherson Report is the most searing indictment of policing ever published".

Fred Broughton, the then chairman of the federation, moved quickly to reflect the defiance that dominated the conference—he had the officers stand in silence not for Stephen Lawrence or even the many other recent victims of racist violence as one may have expected him to do, but for TV presenter and police heroine, the recently murdered Jill Dando and two officers who had lost their lives on duty in the previous 12 months. (The Dando example later took on an unfortunate significance for the police—Barry George, the man convicted in 2001 of the murder, was cleared of the killing eight years later, after a jury found that he had been wrongly convicted and had suffered a gross miscarriage of justice as a result of the police fitting evidence around him.)

An indication of rank and file officers' attitudes in the wake of Macpherson could be gleaned from an anonymous letter printed in the question and answer column of the *Police Review* in-house magazine available at the conference: "I am thinking about trying to start up a police association for white male heterosexual officers. Is there anything in the Police Regulations to prevent me from doing so?" The officers' query was replied to by the magazine's legal editor thus: "Sadly I learn that there are perceptions within the service that such an association is needed."

However, Broughton did not attempt to hide the problems his besieged members faced: "The 12 months which have passed has been the worst the police service had ever seen—wherever we look there are problems." But Broughton, in tune with the mood of the conference, was not about to give an inch to the critics. Yes, the Lawrence murder had been an "outrageous crime", yes, the investigation had been "flawed", but that was as far as he was prepared to go. To huge applause he defended the "one humble inspector [who] faces the full might of disciplinary procedure" before condemning the public inquiry as "more like a kangaroo court than a judicial inquiry". The aspect the police most hated about the inquiry had been the mostly black people in the public gallery who had made their views known especially when police officers in the dock came out with what they saw as outrageous personal opinions, racist attitudes or obfuscations.

Broughton refused to contemplate that the officers involved in the investigation had been racist. But he was also looking to a longer strategy and turned his mind to what he saw as a pressing matter—the need to get more black faces in the ranks. He was articulating the argument put by sections of the police and the government that black recruitment would be the only way to put off charges of racism in the future—after all if a black man was stopped by a black officer, how could that be a racist act?

So Broughton used to opportunity of the conference's opening to unveil a new set of recruitment posters under the banner "Fairness...Equality...Diversity" which in a ham-fisted way sought to upend racist stereotypes, for example showing a picture of a black man with the words, "What Do You Call a Black Man in a BMW?" (the answer being a police officer). Unfortunately for the police the ironic play on stereotypes fell flat; the poster only reminded people how racist they were—stopping black men in posh cars being well known as the historically favoured "sport" of racist police officers. The tensions in Broughton's "anti-racist" approach were revealed when, having unveiled the posters, he railed against the small Black Police Association (BPA) who had in his eyes tried to "sabotage" the campaign by telling the press that the federation lacked "credibility" when it came to issues of racism.

Later on in the day the federation's delegates were treated to a stock pro-police speech by the then Shadow Home Secretary, Tory MP Sir Norman Fowler. Fowler described himself as "a long-term admirer of the Police Federation". He clearly held to the conspiracy theory much favoured by delegates that sinister left wing forces had used the Lawrence Inquiry to undermine the rule of law and order. This belief had manifested itself during the inquiry in a lame and aborted attempt by police lawyers to put Lawrence lawyer Imran Khan's political beliefs under the spotlight. "We do not have a racist police service in this country," Fowler smoothed—"The enemies of the police should not pervert the message of the police."

A day later, despite being by far the most right wing Labour home secretary in history up to that point, Jack Straw got a very different reception than Fowler's from the Blackpool delegates.

Before Straw mounted the podium to deliver his speech he had to endure a lecture by Broughton:

I want to make it clear that this Federation does not accept that the police service is, in Macpherson's words, "riven with racism". Our point of departure with the Macpherson report is in its blanket condemnation of the police service, which it expresses in such a way as to place the whole of the blame for the problems that police face, in dealing with ethnic minorities, on the shoulders of police officers.

Quite what Broughton meant by the curious and revealing phrase "dealing with ethnic minorities" was clear in his next point—one which would be amplified by other police officers, the right wing press and politicians of all stripes in the months to follow.

For the right wing Macpherson had opened the floodgates to what was defined in the media as "black crime", principally street crime or "mugging". Broughton asserted that:

Macpherson makes no attempt to understand, and shows no attempt of wanting to understand, just what it is like to be a police officer in the inner cities of Britain today. As a result, we fear that his report may add to, rather than solve, some of the problems that exist in those areas. In particular, it has been noted that there has been a sharp fall in the number of stops made by police officers, accompanied by a sharp rise in the number of street offences, including robbery and personal violence... There is a real danger that our officers, working in the high tension areas, may in the light of Macpherson, decide that discretion is the better part of valour.

A somewhat chastened Jack Straw now took the platform to nil applause. He started by attempting to ingratiate himself with the audience by heaping praise on the police and their "bravery, loyalty and devotion", assuring them that "the British people are forever in your debt". Straw dismissed any notion that the police were riven with racism and repeated what was becoming a deeply cynical

*Say it Loud*

establishment mantra that the police were no more or less racist than the rest of society. Straw, replying to Broughton's worries, pledged that "the powers of stop and search are going to stay—we have to work to ensure they are not used in a discriminatory way—be under no doubt you and your members should continue to exercise your powers...you have our backing." Straw threw another bone to the police by announcing plans to curb the right of defendants to trial by jury. His Herculean efforts at grovelling were rewarded at the end of his speech by a modicum of polite applause.

As soon as the Macpherson report was published powerful forces in British society moved quickly to undermine and dismiss its findings. The Tory press attacked it in a ferocious and concerted effort to protect the status quo. The *Mail* condemned its rather mild recommendations as written by extremists (a retired judge, a bishop, a retired policeman and a GP) and for going much too far in the other direction (as though the seeking of equality had its limits).

Hysterical descriptions by the *Daily Telegraph* and the *Sun* of the Macpherson report included Stalinist, Hitlerite, totalitarian, McCarthyite, Orwellian, and even "one of the worst things that has ever happened to race relations in this country". *Sun* columnist Richard Littlejohn attacked Tony Blair's "political correctness" in the newspaper, writing, "Has Tony Blair become our first black prime minster? I'm surprised Blair didn't mention that his childhood hero was Malcolm X, that his favourite food was goat curry and yams, or that he changed his middle name to Linton as a tribute to Rastafarian dub poet Linton Kwesi Johnson", and that "no one ever voted for a multicultural society. It was imposed upon them".[36]

The day after the report was published *Daily Telegraph* editor Charles Moore wrote an editorial called "A misguided and Unfair Report", rejecting the findings of the police being institutionally racist. Moore labelled Stephen Lawrence's friend and murder witness Duwayne Brooks "obviously a difficult man" and said that the report and the family's "attitude" "inflames racial feelings". The *Mail*, having championed the Lawrences, did a U-turn, branding the report a "witch hunt" and arguing that enacting its recommendations would "irrevocably change the British way of life".[37]

The press, encouraged by politicians and the Police Federation, tried to re-link the idea in the public's consciousness that black man equals criminal, perpetrator rather than victim. It was an attempt to replace the face of Stephen Lawrence with that of a stereotypical black "mugger". The right wing were encouraged by black activist turned New Labour minister Paul Boateng who assured the *London Evening Standard* that:

> No one should believe that they can use Sir William Macpherson's report as some sort of cloak for their criminal activities. We don't intend to allow that to happen. We back the police four-square in cracking down on street robberies. Stop and search is there to be used as part of the police's armoury. We expect the police to use it. There's no softly-softly policy, there's no hands off policy.[38]

This establishment response, to protect the police and re-label black people as the problem, was therefore a carbon copy of what happened after the Scarman Report. Following that report the then Metropolitan Police Deputy Assistant Commissioner Leslie Walker went on television to claim that 80 percent of all street crime in London was carried out by black people. This was then picked up by the national press who portrayed a "black crime explosion" as a consequence of Scarman. As Paul Gordon and David Rosenberg have written:

> The release of the 1982 crime statistics and the way in which they were reported by the press amounted to an attempt by the police and the press to criminalise black people, especially young black men, and to blame them for violent crime in the inner city.[39]

The five-hour debate in the House of Commons on the Macpherson report was marred by Tory MPs who lined up to attack it, including Woking MP Humfrey Malins who said, "When I hear it said by politicians that our Metropolitan Police are institutionally corrupt, institutionally racist and institutionally incompetent, I think that the world has sometimes gone completely mad", and that "the Macpherson report is another example of 5 percent of the population making 95 percent of the laws". Another Tory, Gerald

Howarth, said that as far as he was concerned, "the report is driven by a desire to be seen to be politically correct". Howarth then went on to say that:

> It is fair to say that some unpalatable truths have to be faced, one of which is the fact that no government have ever received a mandate to turn the United Kingdom into a multiracial society. Despite the warnings given in the 1960s and 1970s about the inevitable social consequences of large scale immigration to Britain, successive governments have ploughed on regardless... I regret that some who have come here freely and others who have sought refuge in this county appear no longer content to learn and accept our native customs and traditions, but wish to assert their own.[40]

The police's predilection for criminalising black people was not curbed by the Macpherson report. If anything, they were out for revenge. This was shown when Andrew Wilson, a black man, made history when he was charged and found guilty of "racially aggravated harassment" under new "race hate" provisions in the Crime and Disorder Act 1998, which were supposed to deter racist attacks against black people, not be used against them. Who brought the charge against Wilson? The answer is the police. His "crime" was to have called officers searching him "white trash".[41]

At the very same time as the Macpherson report was being debated New Labour sought to shore up another plank of state racism by introducing a new anti-immigrant measure, an Asylum and Immigration Bill. The man Jack Straw appointed to oversee the Macpherson inquiry, Mike O'Brien, was the same man empowered to drive the legislation through. In the bill's White Paper the government, without a hint of irony, praised the contribution of the *Windrush* generation before laying out draconian rules designed to deter asylum seekers.

New Labour did its best to pull the mood against asylum seekers further to the right than it had been before the 1997 general election. A poll taken in February 1997 found that although half of whites thought refugees "cause problems for Britain" "a majority (75 percent) agreed that most refugees arriving in Britain are in need of our help and support, with women and the young being particularly sympathetic".[42]

Within black communities warning bells soon began to ring that the brakes were being applied on the report's recommendations by the New Labour government. As Vikram Dodd reported in the *Guardian* six months after publication:

Black and Asian unease is growing. The Home Office says that work on Macpherson's 70 proposals has begun, with most under review or out to consultation. Just a few have so far been implemented and, to some within the black community, this is the first sign of betrayal... Labour asked for time, but there are fears that it is quietly shelving the tackling of racism until its second term. The concern is if a consensus for reform cannot be forged now and acted upon, when the white heat of outrage at the scandal is at its utmost, it is never going to be.[43]

The ongoing danger of murderous far-right violence then literally exploded onto the streets of London. David Copeland joined the BNP in 1997 and the National Socialist Movement in 1999 and had been photographed guarding BNP leader John Tyndall. In the spring of 1999 Copeland set off three nail bombs in central London. The first, on Saturday 17 April, went off in Brixton, injuring 50 people including a baby who had a lengthy nail embedded in its skull. A week later a second bomb detonated in Hanbury Street, off Brick Lane in the East End, injuring 13 people. Another bomb went off on Friday 30 April 1999, destroying the Admiral Duncan pub in Soho, killing three people and injuring over 80 others, 30 seriously. Copeland had targeted a black area, a South Asian area and a gay pub. If he had not been caught he would have gone on to other targets. Copeland later confessed, "I bomb the blacks, the Pakis, degenerates. I would have bombed the Jews as well if I got the chance".[44]

Copeland testified that he had been a lone bomber, but serious commentators, who had knowledge of Britain's fascist groupings with their long history of terrorist links, doubted very much that this was the case.

Yet barely had the dust settled on Copeland's murderous

*Say it Loud*

campaign when the establishment was convulsed by another frenzy of bigotry on the publication of a report, *The Future of Multi-Ethnic Britain,* by the Runnymede Trust in 2000. The report was an analysis of the state of race relations in Britain, accompanied by a checklist of recommendations. It was not particularly well received by anti-racist commentators. However, instead of debating the issues raised in the report the press picked out one passage in the 400-page publication which said, "Britishness, as much as Englishness, has systematic, largely unspoken, racial connotations."

The report was dismissed as "rubbish", "balderdash", "sub-Marxist gibberish", "PC crap", "ludicrous", "offensive" and "garbage". The Tories demanded that it should be "binned", and one journalist even called for its authors to be prosecuted under the Race Relations Act. The then Tory leader William Hague wrote in the *Daily Telegraph* that if the report's recommendations were implemented "then our police would be paralysed, school exams would be fiddled, classroom discipline would collapse and our political institutions would be stuffed with people on the basis of their colour rather than on whether they could do the job". Hague went on to say that in the 1970s the "threat" to British society came from "militant trade unions". The "danger" today was from "anti-British" campaigners against racism. New Labour ran away from the argument. Home Secretary Jack Straw distanced himself from the report, saying that he was "proud to be British".[45]

Those attacking the Runnymede report were the same people who attacked Macpherson. One of the first Tories to condemn it was Gerald Howarth. Howarth said, "It is an extraordinary affront to the 94 percent of the population which is not from ethnic minorities. The native British must stand up for ourselves".[46]

In 2001 Jack Straw was succeeded by David Blunkett as home secretary with responsibility for discharging the inquiry's recommendations. By 2003 Doreen Lawrence was warning that Blunkett had lost interest in the issue. He was usually absent from the Home Office steering group charged with implementing Macpherson he was meant to chair. Doreen's warning had been prompted by Blunkett's publicly stated opinion that "the slogan created a year or two ago about institutional racism missed the point".[47]

Doreen's declaration that Blunkett had lost interest in Macpherson and combating institutional racism was made in the aftermath of the rioting by Asian youth that took place in the northern towns of Oldham, Burnley and Bradford in the summer of 2001. This was of course followed by 9/11 which triggered a new era of racism, this time directed at Muslims.

Blunkett was succeeded as home secretary by Charles Clarke. In October 2005 Clarke announced in a cursory written statement to parliament:

> I asked my officials to carry out a review of race advisory panels within the Home Office to ensure that we are getting the most effective advice. The review recommended we move away from Standing Committees to a project-based approach, in which groups with relevant perspectives, community links and expertise are brought together to offer advice on specific issues within timescales that help us to deliver change quickly.
>
> I have therefore stood down the Stephen Lawrence Steering Group.[48]

The disbanding of the steering group sidelined Doreen and the other independent members, with the recommendations of Macpherson kicked into the long grass. Doreen, once again, was forced to speak out publicly:

> I cannot believe we have achieved anything near what we should have done on the steering group. For the first time in British history we had independent people sitting around a table with the Home Secretary, acting as advisers to him as to how the community was feeling. The government should be applauded for that...but why have they dropped it?[49]

It was to be nearly 19 years after Stephen's murder before the Lawrence family were to achieve partial justice, when in January 2012, due to advances in forensic science, Gary Dobson and David Norris were convicted of his murder.

However, there was no sense that the final chapter had been written in the case of Stephen Lawrence, or that institutional racism was a thing of the past. In a newspaper interview published after Dobson and Norris had been convicted Doreen Lawrence declared:

> After the inquiry there was a sense that all the institutions wanted to do the right thing, they wanted to change. But I don't hear people talking like that anymore. I don't know whether they believe that it's been accomplished, that racism has been eradicated, but the reality is that it hasn't. What's happened is that racism still exists but it is not so overt, that doesn't mean it is not still there and in some ways it is worse having it underground.
>
> The inquiry gave an opportunity; there was a chance to change and things have changed but it's not gone far enough... People worry that it is out of their power to do something, but it is in all of our realms to change things.[50]

A new chapter seemed likely to open up in June 2012, when the Tory Home Secretary Teresa May, under pressure in the aftermath of the convictions of Dobson and Norris, ordered an independent review into the previous police inquiry into allegations of corruption in the Stephen Lawrence murder case.[51]

The Stephen Lawrence scandal was a watershed in British history and continues to dog the police and the establishment, two decades after the murder in Well Hall Road. All in all, this is very much unfinished business and there are serious lessons to be learned. It is critically important for campaigners and activists to have a thorough and sophisticated understanding of the nature and extent of institutional racism in our society. The Stephen Lawrence Family Campaign helped to expose that reality but it also did much more. It demonstrated how a dogged, determined and indefatigable family could take on the establishment and, in so doing, call upon the concrete and practical support of black and white working class people across the land.

## CHAPTER 4

# A promise betrayed:
# Racism after Macpherson

**Brian Richardson**

THERE CAN be little doubt then, that despite the passage of more than a decade since the publication of the Macpherson report, institutional racism remains deeply embedded in British society.

As the preceding chapter has shown, New Labour's rhetorical commitment to change barely lasted the length of time it took Home Secretary Jack Straw to present *The Stephen Lawrence Inquiry Report* to parliament. By the following weekend the government was in headlong retreat in the face of a vicious media backlash led by the *Daily Telegraph, Daily Mail* and *Sun*. It remained to be seen though how quickly and how far the government would abandon its commitment to deliver a "step change in our attitudes to race relations" and whether others would pick up the gauntlet.[']

In this chapter we examine what progress was made in implementing the key recommendations of Macpherson's report. The hope among anti-racist activists was that the home secretary's failure to sack Paul Condon was simply a false start. The New Labour government which had nailed its anti-racist credentials to the mast by initiating the inquiry would surely recover its stride and make good on the promise to deliver far-reaching reforms. In any event many campaigners felt that, regardless of the government's attitude, it would be impossible to hold back lasting change now that institutional racism had finally been exposed and acknowledged.

Our particular focus in this chapter will be upon the two main areas that Macpherson addressed in his conclusions and recommendations, education and policing. There is a direct correlation between educational exclusion and underachievement and the criminalisation of those affected. Those who are marginalised and excluded are more likely to leave with few, if any qualifications, and remain or sink into poverty which may lead them into a life of despair and crime. Hence Martin Narey, at one time the Director-General of the Prison Service, observed, "The 13,000 young people excluded from school each year might as well be given a date by which to join the prison service some time down the line".[2] Narey's warning was included in a report commissioned and published by the then Department for Education and Skills itself.

Before capitulating to the press, Home Secretary Jack Straw had in fact welcomed all 70 of Macpherson's recommendations and promised to publish an action plan setting out how the government proposed to implement them. The legislative response was to be the passage of the Race Relations (Amendment) Act 2000, which extended pre-existing legislation so that it now covered, among others, the police and placed a "positive duty" on all public bodies to promote race equality. In addition, Straw pledged that the report's simplified definition of a racist incident would be adopted by all public bodies and that such incidents must be investigated and satisfactorily resolved.[3]

Taken at face value the act and the action plan seemed perfectly acceptable, though the obsession with targets and "key performance indicators" was typical of New Labour under Tony Blair and Gordon Brown. In itself, however, there was no guarantee that this bureaucratic approach would deliver fundamental change. What mattered more was whether a rhetorical commitment to hold institutions to account was augmented by the kind of personal responsibility and leadership that Straw had promised.

Many campaigners were convinced that the government's commitment was genuine, that the legislative reforms were robust and that lasting change was on the horizon. Moreover they were confident that they themselves could play a leading role in delivering it. In a repeat of the process that occurred in the 1980s, a number of activists readily accepted positions as consultants, race advisers and "equality and diversity trainers".

The efforts of these individuals was, largely, well intentioned and it would be wrong to suggest that nothing was achieved. For example, it is unlikely that there would have been serious investigations into the murders of Zahid Mubarak or Anthony Walker had it not been for the Stephen Lawrence Inquiry.[4] More than a decade after Straw made his promise, however, few of the people who accepted these consultancies can look back on their achievements with any great satisfaction.

In reality these top-down efforts at reform were hamstrung from the very beginning by a lack of commitment and weak leadership. The role of the Commission for Racial Equality (CRE) as the statutory body responsible for monitoring progress and, if necessary, taking action against those institutions that failed or lagged behind was supposedly pivotal.

Following the retirement of Sir Herman Ouseley, the CRE was initially led from May 2000 by Gurbux Singh, a hapless former local authority bureaucrat. Few campaigners had ever heard of him, much less encountered him in any anti-racist struggles. Within a couple of years he had been forced to resign in disgrace after being convicted of threatening behaviour after a boozy afternoon watching cricket at Lord's. He learnt the hard way what his brethren understand intuitively, that it rarely pays to mess with police officers. His tenure had been marked by capitulation and compromise in the face of inertia and intransigence from those public bodies he was supposed to be challenging. The impetus for change was already being lost.

Singh was succeeded in 2003 by Trevor Phillips, a man with a far higher profile, and a personal friend of Jack Straw who had preceded him as president of the National Union of Students. Subsequently he had forged a successful career as a television presenter and executive. Phillips was therefore a man with connections who understood the media. He had also remained extremely close to New Labour, so much so that in 1999 he had sought the party's nomination for the newly established and potentially powerful post of London mayor. During the campaign he launched a blistering attack on his main rival Ken Livingstone when the latter invited him to step aside and instead run as his deputy on a so-called "dream ticket". Phillips boasted proudly about his numerous achievements as a broadcaster, businessman and trustee of various arts and voluntary sector bodies and suggested that, "All of us who come from minority communities get rather used to and fed up of, any time we emerge on the public scene, people treating us as apprentices, you know".[5]

Far from being patronising or opportunist, Livingstone's record on race matters as the leader of the Greater London Council, as MP for Brent East and subsequently as Mayor of London bears positive comparison with most. Nevertheless, Phillips was entitled to highlight the fact that black people made up a third of the capital's population and that, as such, we should receive proportionate political representation. It was also therefore fair enough for him to insist that there should be a black candidate in the race. Nevertheless, by October of that year Phillips had decided to abandon his own bid for the mayoralty and, instead, accept the position of running mate to New Labour's preferred candidate, the white, male, former health secretary Frank Dobson.

Livingstone was to have the last laugh in this matter. After losing New Labour's nomination, he stood as an independent and crushed Dobson, gaining three times as many first preference votes. He stormed to victory and one of his first appointments was that of the radical black activist Lee Jasper to be his Director for Equalities and Policing. Meanwhile until he was rescued and offered the CRE post as his consolation prize, Phillips languished on the London Assembly, a powerless "watchdog" that contributes little to the governance of London and is largely ignored.

In October 2007 the CRE was subsumed into a new body, the Equality and Human Rights Commission (EHRC), which also took over the functions of the Disability Rights Commission and Equal Opportunities Commission. As a reward for his continuing loyalty to New Labour, Phillips was appointed its first chair and remained in the post until 2012. This was despite fierce criticism from other commissioners and widespread opposition from a dedicated staff team who became increasingly frustrated at his failure to promote positive change and protect the commission from swingeing cuts.

Given his media contacts and eye for a story it was no coincidence that Phillips chose to mark the tenth anniversary of the publication of the *Stephen Lawrence Inquiry Report* in 2009 by giving an exclusive interview to the *Daily Mail*. The EHRC had just launched its own report entitled *Race in Britain*. This report is a thorough and comprehensive survey and many of its findings are to be welcomed. Phillips was right to suggest for example that "Britain is now the least racist country in Europe".[6] He was also right to illustrate this point by highlighting the growing the number of children with mixed heritage.

It must be stressed, however, that the progress Phillips described had occurred largely despite, not because of, the actions of government or public institutions. In football for example, it was grassroots anti-racist fans who initiated the campaign to drive fascists off the terraces. Self-evidently, mixed race children exist as a result of their parents meeting and falling in love with each other, not because they were forced together by race relations legislation. In fact, in the decades after the Second World War, official policy, as well as the actions of factory owners and landlords, frequently institutionalised and reinforced divisions between British born workers and those who had recently arrived.

It was also dangerously myopic of Phillips to assert that, "The police have shown a much better understanding of how to deliver a public service that doesn't discriminate just because of the colour of your skin".[7] Though he acknowledged that there remained much work to do, his conclusion was that it was no longer "valid" to label the police institutionally racist. As he must surely have anticipated, it was this claim that captured the headlines.

A whole generation of black people who have grown up in Britain in the new millennium can tell a different story. One such person is Edric Kennedy-Macfoy, an off-duty firefighter who went to assist the police in the early hours of a Sunday morning in 2011 when he saw them coming under attack from a group of partygoers in north London. For his troubles, Kennedy-Macfoy was told, "Fuck off, you prick", dragged from his car, shot with a stun gun and prosecuted for obstructing the police. Fortunately the tribunal at Brent Magistrates court believed his account and Kennedy-Macfoy was acquitted.[8]

*Say it Loud*

Countless others charged with assaulting or obstructing police officers have been less fortunate. Instead they have been routinely convicted by magistrates who refuse to believe that a constable is capable of lying and invariably conclude that the evidence of police officers is "consistent and compelling". It was a rage against such oppression, brutality and injustice that burst out on the streets of England following the police shooting of Mark Duggan in the summer of 2011.

At the same time that he was exonerating the police, Phillips was also highlighting the fact that Britain's anti-discrimination laws were derived from a multitude of sources amounting to approximately 4,000 pages of legislation. His main point was that these laws were too complex and that what was required was their amalgamation into a single equality law addressing all areas of discrimination.[9] He also argued that existing laws had created what he categorised as an unhelpful hierarchy of oppression with race at the top.

How true this is, and where different groups are placed in the pecking order is something of a moot point. It cannot be disputed, however, that there is no automatic unity of the oppressed. To take just one example, there can be little doubt that some violent and reactionary homophobia can be found among certain sections of the black community. What is equally true, however, is that such discord is by no means natural or inevitable. As we have argued throughout this book, it is manufactured and maintained by a ruling class that relies upon the division of the workers in order to retain its dominance.

The hierarchy that Phillips referred to is indicative of the fact that even where we have wrenched concessions out of the system, the outcome has frequently been to reinforce division. As chapter 2 demonstrates, oppressed groups have been played off against each other in competition for the state funding that was fought for in order to challenge discrimination. In theory, the passage of an all-embracing equality act and the establishment of a commission that encouraged a broad-based focus on human rights were good things. In reality they represented a con trick by New Labour. There was no commensurate increase in funding for this new body. Instead with the onset of austerity the EHRC became increasingly emasculated and impotent.

The fundamental problem is not that there is too much legislation or that before the passage of the Equality Act people simply did not know where to find and how to implement their rights. The very fact that this vast array of laws has not delivered equality is indicative of their ultimate impotence. The plain truth is that these laws fail because, in the final analysis, under capitalism, it is the interests of the ruling class that prevail. It was struggle that won the improvements we have experienced in the first place. It is struggle that is required to defend them in the face of backlashes and cuts and it is struggle that will be required to finally banish oppression in all its forms.

## Asylum

A country's treatment of those people that seek asylum within its borders is a key measure of its humanity. Under international law anyone with a well-founded fear of persecution is entitled to seek refuge outside the country of their birth. The Refugee Convention that established this was ratified in 1951 as a direct response to the Nazi Holocaust. Wars and other conflicts have continued to ravage people's lives since then but only a very small minority have ever sought refuge on these shores. The percentage of displaced people seeking asylum who come to Britain or Europe in general is hugely exaggerated. A Red Cross survey in 2009 revealed that the public perceived that over 100,000 people had applied for asylum that year. The actual figure was 24,485, while the total number of people seeking asylum worldwide was 923,400.[10]

Many of those who do arrive are understandably traumatised and vulnerable. Instead of treating them with compassion, however, successive governments have stigmatised and excluded them. Those governments' primary concern has been to avoid the perception that they are "soft" on "bogus applicants". One of the most disgraceful examples of New Labour's shameful record in this regard came just a year after Macpherson had reported. Under proposals introduced by the Immigration and Asylum Act 2000 asylum seekers were to be dispersed around the country away from settled networks of support and given vouchers instead of money to buy food and clothing.

In the face of this onslaught, the response of ordinary working class communities has often been admirable. Many thousands of people have defied media scare stories about bogus claimants, welcomed new arrivals into their schools and localities and set up campaigns to prevent their deportation. Far from simply swallowing popular myths, people's ideas and attitudes are also shaped by the day to day experience of living, learning, working and struggling together.

One of the most inspiring examples of this was provided by the girls of Drumchapel High School in Glasgow. There a group of students and teachers came together in 2005 to challenge the UK Border Agency's decision to deport their classmates from Kosovo. Their campaign played a key role in forcing the government to end the policy of detaining children for immigration purposes in 2010 and inspired an award winning play, *The Glasgow Girls*.

## Educational exclusion and underachievement

Education has the potential to have a profound impact upon a young person's life chances. One of the more pernicious stereotypes about black families, and one which was oft repeated in the aftermath of the riots, is that they are simply not interested in their children's schooling. Instead of making sure that their kids turn up and achieve good grades, these feckless parents supposedly allow their children to drift and roam the streets.

On the contrary, far from being indifferent and disengaged, black parents have frequently been deeply concerned. Macpherson himself recognised that education was an iconic issue that has exercised black people down the decades. When he expanded his inquiry to consider what wider lessons could be learned about race relations Macpherson observed that:

> There was a weight of opinion and concern in relation to two specific aspects of education. First the failure of the National Curriculum to reflect adequately the needs of a diverse multicultural and multi-ethnic society. Secondly the number of exclusions from schools which were apparently disproportionate to the ethnic mix of the pupils.[11]

Such concern about their children's education among black parents is nothing new. By the mid-1960s the first wave of children born to the *Windrush* generation were completing their journey through the education system. Many were doing so with depressingly low levels of achievement. Alarmed by this, a group of black parents and activists commissioned a report by one of their number, Bernard Coard, which was eventually published under the title *How the West Indian Child is made Educationally Subnormal in the British Education System*.[12] The report's core message is clear and direct. Too many children were failing not because of their own inherent inadequacies and shortcomings, but because the system discriminated against them. They were not born with deficiencies, but were made "subnormal" by a system that treated them as inferior.

Coard's pamphlet and the Black Parents Movement that commissioned it were the foundations of a campaign that helped to transform education in the 1970s and 1980s. We should not exaggerate its impact and it would be wrong to suggest that this period was some sort of golden age. Far too many children continued to leave school with little to show for it, but for some there were real benefits. We were respected, nurtured and encouraged to pass our public exams, go to university and move into responsible jobs. More broadly, the advent of initiatives such as Black History Month helped to create a more diverse and progressive school experience, with multicultural texts replacing the likes of *Little Black Sambo* and Enid Blyton's Noddy books in school libraries. We were also taught about other religions, not just Christianity, wider history, not just that of British kings and queens, and samosas took their place on the lunchtime menu alongside liver and mashed potatoes.

Continual forward progress is never guaranteed, however. As we have already noted, comprehensive and multicultural education was always under attack from a right wing that derided it as "politically correct" and loony left nonsense which debased traditional British values. The gains that were made were steadily eroded and by the turn of the millennium many of the issues that first exercised parents in the 1960s were re-emerging.

In the face of this Diane Abbott MP used her parliamentary base to host an annual conference from 1999 onwards aimed at addressing the exclusion and underachievement of black children. The first was entitled "Hackney Schools and the Black Child" and was attended by an audience of around 200. Subsequent events attracted people from across the capital and the gatherings were renamed "London Schools and the Black Child". By 2009 the assemblies were undeniably national, drawing over 2,000 to the Queen Elizabeth II Conference Centre in Westminster.

The agenda of those who attended the conferences was not simply to snipe at the government. As well as the political activists there were writers, performers and small entrepreneurs who brought books, puzzles, musical instruments and other material which sought to promote self-organisation and sufficiency as well as equality, diversity and multiculturalism.

These were serious events at which the participants engaged in earnest debate about how to address and overcome the crisis. Indeed, one of the frustrations that attendees felt was that more was not made of them. Impressive though the conferences were, as the years passed there was also a growing sense of disillusionment at Abbott's resistance to calls for her to launch and lead a movement similar to that which the likes of John Le Rose, Eric and Jessica Huntley and Gus John had initiated after the publication of Coard's pamphlet.

Few of those who attended sought to portray their children as angels or themselves as perfect parents. Indeed one matter that was frequently raised—and which resurfaced in controversial circumstances in 2012—was a concern about the government's restriction on the right of parents to discipline unruly children.[13] In short therefore, these parents were taking responsibility for their children's upbringing and they were not afraid to take a long hard look at themselves and engage in self-criticism. What most wanted was not for the government to take full responsibility for their children's welfare; these were not adherents of the "nanny state". Rather they simply wanted the government to keep its side of the bargain and provide their children with a decent education.

For many years black parents and community activists responded to the crisis in their children's education by intervening themselves.

They had set up and run supplementary schools which ran on Saturdays and Sundays with the aim of ensuring that their children retained a sense of their heritage and also sought to rescue those who were struggling.[14]

One other less collective phenomenon which continues today is also worth mentioning. Many black parents, impatient with the failings of the state sector, have scrimped, saved and worked at multiple jobs in order to send their children to public schools. Both David Lammy and Diane Abbott have a tale to tell in this respect. Lammy is full of admiration for the dedication and sacrifices his mother made to pay for him to attend the Kings School in Peterborough. Meanwhile after doing so much to demand better state provision, Diane Abbott was dismissive of the criticism she received when she chose to send her own son to the City of London School rather than a state one in her own constituency. She justified her decision on the basis that it would be wrong for her to allow her politics to jeopardise her son's best chance in life.

This sentiment is perhaps understandable. The reality is, however, that most of those living in inner city areas such as Hackney simply do not have the money to afford such an alternative. Nor should they be expected to when they contribute taxes that are meant to pay for state services. It should be clear, therefore, that many parents, perhaps most notably an unquantifiable number of single working class mothers, who are so often maligned, have struggled to do what they can to support their children and give them the best start in life. Moreover, there is some evidence to suggest that these efforts achieved impressive results. Professors David Gillborn and Heidi Safia Mirza conducted research in 2000 which highlighted the fact that, "according to government figures, black pupils start primary school with some of the highest scores in baseline assessments of initial ability".[15]

This suggests therefore that before sending them off to primary school, those parents have made a genuine investment of time, energy and commitment in their children's future. What that research went on to show, however, was that after two years those same pupils had begun to "slip behind other pupils".[16] By the time they completed their compulsory schooling there had been what Diane Abbott described as a dramatic "collapse". If these findings were true, it would seem to suggest that it is not their parents' apathy and indifference, or their own fecklessness and stupidity that are to blame for black children's educational failure. Rather there must be something profoundly wrong with the school system. The terminology may have changed from "subnormality" to "underachievement", but the fundamental issue is the same as that which was first identified by Coard in the 1960s.

Gillborn proceeds to suggest that such a conclusion about baseline assessments could not be tolerated by the then Department for Education and Skills (DfES). Thus a new "Foundation Stage Profile" (FSP) was introduced to assess children from their third birthday to the end of their reception year in primary school. By the time the department came to publish and present data about the FSP in 2005, "black children had moved from being over-achievers to under-achievers".[17] The myth that black parents are not interested in their children's education could therefore be reinstated. The parents who contributed conscientiously to Macpherson's inquiry give the lie to this vile assertion. It was precisely because they were so passionate that he felt compelled to make the observations and recommendations that we have highlighted.

In addition to its promises to hold the police to account therefore, when the government adopted Macpherson's report, it had to commit itself to reforming the education system. An Ethnic Minority Achievement Grant initially amounting to £4 million was established and the DfES also sought to jump on the bandwagon of the supplementary schools movement with £1 million worth of funds. These offerings were far too little and in the backlash against anti-racism were soon laid open to criticism that New Labour was simply robbing poor working class white Peter to pay black Paul. Nevertheless they are an indication of the trickle of concessions that were wrought as a result of struggle.

Black parents have been right to demand fairness and equality in schools. There are very obvious and specific ways in which exclusion and its corollary underachievement manifest themselves in the education system. At the heart of that system is a competitive struggle between schools for limited resources. Every year there is a desperate scramble by parents striving to get their children into the most prestigious local schools. For the schools themselves the number of pupils they attract is crucial because with each child comes cash from the local authority. The key to assessing which are the most attractive schools is a series of "league tables" which set out each school's exam results. These statistics are published in the national and local press, so every school's shame or glory is laid bare for all to see.

For schools therefore the challenge is to move up or retain a place at the top of the league tables. The Holy Grail is the number of pupils who achieve the coveted A*-C grades in the external GCSE examinations. These represent the "Gold Standard": the passport to further and higher education and the wider opportunities that such access is supposed to offer. The problem for any school is that if too few pupils are achieving these grades it will be labelled as "failing" and thereby it becomes unattractive to local parents. If insufficient pupils are enrolling, the school will be deprived of the resources it needs to improve. Consequently it finds itself trapped in a vicious cycle of decline.

Instead of having the time, confidence and resources to improve—or more importantly, the freedom to genuinely encourage and nurture the talents of young people—the urgent priority is to get the statistics up. There is, therefore, an in-built incentive to simply "teach to the test" and, crucially, to marginalise and exclude those pupils who won't guarantee exam success, and who might drag down the school's rating. Invariably in such circumstances, it is the black and working class white children who are the ones who are excluded. Schools simply do not have the time to deal with them if they are unruly, so instead they are excluded or shunted off into Pupil Referral Units. Elsewhere pupils who are expected to fail are discouraged from turning up for their exams or simply not entered for them at all.

Gillborn's research illustrates how the decision making about exams leads to the racial stereotyping that damns black pupils. The assessment of pupils must occur at a relatively early stage in order for schools to allocate resources. What he identified in the allocation process was a phenomenon similar to that which occurs in the emergency rooms of hospitals which is labelled "triage". In short, pupils are divided into three distinct groups: those who can confidently be expected to flourish, those who are bound to fail and those "either way" students who fall somewhere between the two.

The high fliers are streamed in the top sets and, while care must be taken to ensure that their standards don't slip, teachers need not worry about them too much. Instead most attention—and therefore the most experienced teachers—must be focused on the students in the middle. These are the ones who can make the difference to the school's position. The "no-hopers" in the bottom sets are all but abandoned. Indeed Gillborn observed that at one stage many bottom stream children were entered for exams where it was not even possible to achieve the all-important Grade C at GCSE in mathematics. He recalls how the audience reacted with gasps of horror and chants of "Bernard Coard" when he described this "three tier system" during a session at one of the "London Schools" conferences.[18]

The fundamental problem with schools then is not, as some activists would argue, that white teachers are simply prejudiced and determined to discriminate against black pupils. Rather the real issue is that the system is structured in such a way that it encourages and reinforces stereotyping and exclusion, in short institutional racism restructured and maintained. Despite the words of warning from Martin Narey and a whole host of learned researchers little has been done to reverse the discrimination. Hence "Black Caribbean" pupils were "almost four times" more likely to be permanently excluded than the school population as a whole".[19]

The story is not one of unremitting gloom. The fight for better monitoring, again a legacy of anti-racist struggles, has meant that more sophisticated data is now held by the Department for Education. Those statistics have revealed that some "Minority Ethnic" children, notably from Indian and Chinese backgrounds have consistently been the highest achievers in school.[20] Overall however, this is a reflection of the fact that those who had been schooled in Britain had traditionally come from relatively affluent backgrounds where additional support could be provided at home. As the authors of that paper observed, "There is a strong direct association between social class background and success in education: put simply, the higher a child's social class, the greater are their attainments on average".[21]

Importantly, the figures for GCSEs and equivalent qualifications record an increase in attainment across all ethnic groups. It is also possible to point to specific schools and local authority areas where each different ethnic group whether African-Caribbean, Pakistani or Bangladeshi is the highest achieving.[22] This is encouraging and is an indication of what can be achieved when young people are cherished and nurtured by dedicated teachers. However, those same statistics continued to reveal that, overall, pupils from "any black background achieved below the national level".[23] The relative decline in achievement among white working class boys that researchers have observed since the turn of the millennium has been a consequence of this widening social inequality rather than because schools have disproportionately prioritised black students.

The figures also need to be scrutinised. Both David Gillborn and Diane Abbott observed that in the rush to improve their school's standing, many black children, alongside those from white working class backgrounds, were nudged towards vocational as opposed to academic subjects. Though these were supposed to be equivalent to "good" GCSE passes, they are rarely regarded as such by universities and employers. Up to 2007 an alternative to GCSEs and "A" Levels was the General National Vocational Qualification (GNVQ). It has been suggested that in reality these initials stood for "Going Nowhere Very Quickly". A set of results that do not include A to C grades in maths and English are regarded as virtually worthless.

### Higher education
Clearly it is not the case that all black pupils "fail". Indeed, it has been suggested that a disproportionate number of young black people, particularly women, actually go on to higher education.[24] It is important to acknowledge these developments, but once more the bare figures must be scrutinised with some scepticism.

As recently as 2010 it was discovered that 21 Oxbridge colleges had not admitted a single black undergraduate student in 2009. Indeed, one such institution, Merton College, Oxford, had not offered a black student a place for five years, and only three in the entire decade. The plain truth is that those black students who have made it into higher education are far more likely to be seen in the lecture theatres of the less prestigious "new" universities than those of the elite Oxbridge or Russell Group universities.[25]

By comparison with the disgraceful record of the older, traditional institutions, London Metropolitan University is a model of progress when it comes to admission. Formed by a merger of several former polytechnics it teaches more black students than the entire 20 institutions of the Russell Group. Given the rhetorical commitment of successive governments to "equal access to education" and "lifelong learning", London Met should be cherished for the way it caters for "non-traditional learners" and those whose lives and work patterns do not fit neatly into college terms and timetables. Instead, and as a direct consequence of the flexible approach it has pioneered, London Met found itself facing a major funding crisis and huge cuts in 2009. Two years later its problems multiplied when the government announced that it was revoking the university's licence to admit foreign students. The university had fallen victim to the government's crackdown on immigration.

### Crime and punishment

The propensity of police officers to stop and search black people was one of the key issues at the Stephen Lawrence Inquiry. Macpherson observed that:

> If there was one area of complaint which was universal it was the issue of "stop and search". Nobody in the minority ethnic communities believes that the complex arguments which are sometimes used to explain the figures as to stop and search are valid.[26]

A measure of the ineffectiveness of stop and search is the fact that it so rarely results in an arrest let alone a conviction. The power to stop and search people is enshrined in a whole range of statutes including the Police and Criminal Evidence Act 1984 ("PACE

1984"), the Misuse of Drugs Act 1971 and the Terrorism Act 2000 ("TA 2000"), a law specifically introduced in the aftermath of 9/11. Meanwhile, Section 60 of the Criminal Justice and Public Order Act 1994 has been increasingly used to target those supposedly intent on serious violence.

According to the government's own statistics, just over 9 percent of such encounters under section 1 of PACE across England and Wales in 2009/10 led to an arrest. Meanwhile less than 1 percent of those conducted under section 44 of the TA 2000 resulted in an arrest.[27]

By comparison with their effectiveness in detecting crime, the capacity of stops and searches to stir up resentment among those who are targeted is huge. Despite this, though not surprisingly, the police fought tooth and nail at the Stephen Lawrence Inquiry to justify and defend the use of the tactic. Macpherson duly accepted the police submissions and recommended that stop and search powers should remain unchanged. He did nevertheless demand that it should be less arbitrary and in the wake of his recommendations police commissioners and chief constables promised that their operations would be more "intelligence led". The reality is that harassment of youths seen to be hanging out in the street continues irrespective of whether they are actually doing anything to justify it. As Peter Ackroyd observed in his magisterial study of London:

> [London] has always been a centre of panic, and of rumour. At the end of the 20th century for example, an official survey reported that "fear of crime is a social problem in itself" with a significant proportion of Londoners...feeling unsafe both in their dwellings and in the streets.[28]

This concern did not, in fact, coincide with an actual increase in crime as recorded in official statistics.[29] Nevertheless, a New Labour government determined to show that it was "tough on crime and tough on the causes of crime" was keen establish its credentials. It did so by creating the Anti-Social Behaviour Order (ASBO), a form of punishment that was primarily targeted at young people for irritating but non-criminal activity.[30] Although the ASBO itself is a civil

*Say it Loud*

Hundreds of bus workers outside the African Methodist Church in Battersea on 30 January 1975, joining a memorial service for Jamaican-born bus conductor Ronald Jones, who was killed on duty in an argument over a fare

*(above)* Thousands of trade unionists joined a mass picket at Grunwick film processing plant in west London on 11 July 1977 in solidarity with a group of mainly Asian women strikers
*Picture: Andrew Wiard*

*(left)* Postal workers at nearby Cricklewood sorting office were locked out by their bosses for refusing to handle Grunwick's mail. The postal workers played a pivotal role in delivering solidarity to the strikers
*Picture: Andrew Wiard*

*(right)* Jayaben Desai, the formidable leader of the Grunwick dispute, addressing pickets at the Chix bubblegum factory in Slough. The Chix workers struck for over eight months in 1979-80, successfully winning union recognition

*(above)* The moment in the Battle of Lewisham, 13 August 1977, when anti-fascists split the fascist National Front march in two. Socialist Worker described this at the time as "the most humiliating moment in the history of the Nazi Front"
*Picture: Phil McGowan*

*(right)* Pickets at Bulmer and Lumb textile factory in Bolton in May 1978 during a strike over working conditions and against the sacking of a key activist
*Picture: John Sturrock*

*(left)* Ford workers struck for nine weeks in the autumn of 1978 to demand better pay and a shorter working week

*(below)* The Specials concert against racism in Coventry June 1981

*(below, opposite)* Local residents and Anti Nazi League supporters occupied Brick Lane, east London, in July 1978, successfully driving the fascist National Front off the street. The following day 8,000 workers in the area struck unofficially against racism
*Pictures: John Sturrock*

*(top)* A mighty 10,000-strong funeral procession for Blair Peach in Southall, west London. Blair *(above)* was a teacher and member of the Socialist Workers Party (SWP) killed by police during a protest against the National Front. TUC president Ken Gill spoke at the graveside alongside SWP founder Tony Cliff. The day before he was buried, 4,000 locals filed past Blair's coffin as he lay in Southall's Dominion Cinema. Throughout that night Southall youth maintained a guard of honour over him. April 1979
*Picture John Sturrock*

*(above)* Thousands march in March 1981 to demand answers about the fire at a birthday party in New Cross, south London, that killed 14 young black people

*(left)* Demonstration against the Tories' racist Nationality Bill in April 1981

*(below)* A passerby shows National Front paper sellers in Lewisham what she thinks of their Nazi propaganda, March 1981

*Pictures: John Sturrock*

*(top)* Brixton High Street during
the riot of July 1981

*(above)* Brixton riot, July 1981
*Picture: John Sturrock*

*(left)* Police attempt to regain
control during the Brixton riot
of September 1985
*Picture: John Sturrock*

*(above)* Protest against Liverpool police chief Kenneth Oxford following his brutal tactics during the 1981 Toxteth riots and his inflammatory statements in the days that followed. One man died after being hit by a police van during the riots

*Picture: John Sturrock*

*(above)* A group of anti-racist white skinheads join a march against police harassment organised by the Sheffield Asian Youth Movement in February 1983

*(below)* Demonstration against racist headteacher Ray Honeyford outside his school in Bradford, October 1985  *Picture: John Sturrock*

*(above)* Nurses join a TUC demonstation for the NHS in September 1982
*Picture: John Sturrock*

*(left)* Striking bus drivers at Shepherds Bush depot in west London, April 1993
*Picture: Mark Campbell*

*(left)* Picket line at Gatwick airport as 17,000 British Airways workers struck in June 1993
*Picture: Mark Campbell*

*(above)* Funeral of Stephen Lawrence, 18 June 1993 *Picture: Mark Campbell*

*(above)* Around 60,000 people joined the Unity demo to shut down the British National Party headquarters in Welling in October 1993
*Picture: Mark Campbell*

*(right)* Anti Nazi League organiser Julie Waterson (front, left) celebrating as BNP councillor Derek Beackon loses his seat in the Isle of Dogs, east London in May 1994

*(above)* Some 150,000 people joined the Anti Nazi League carnival in south London's Brockwell Park in May 1994 to celebrate the defeat of BNP councillor Derek Beackon

*(left)* Protest against the desecration of Jewish graves outside East Ham cemetery in east London, June 1995
*Pictures: Mark Campbell*

*(left)* Protest outside a meeting called by the Metropolitan Police to try to get "community leaders" to back a crack down on "street crime". The meeting took place on the second anniversary of the death of Joy Gardner, who died after a forced deportation by members of the police's Alien Deportation Squad.
*Picture: Mark Campbell*

*(above)* The Onibiyo Family Campaign join the national demonstration against the Asylum Bill in April 1996          *Picture: Steve Eason*

*(right)* Abdul Onibiyo being greeted by friends and family on his return to London in 1997. He and his son Ade were deported in 1995. A major campaign involving Abdul's Unison union branch helped to overturn the decision and win his right to return
*Picture: Jess Hurd*

*(left)* Protest outside Dungavel detention centre in South Lanarkshire in August 2004, shortly after the suicide of Tung Wang, a 23 year old Vietnamese asylum seeker detained at the centre
*Picture: Duncan Brown*

*(above)* Protest in October 2010 to mark ten years since the invasion of Afghanistan. The Stop the War Coalition has brought together people of all backgrounds in a common struggle

*(left)* Sacked Gate Gourmet workers marching in September 2005. The workers, mostly Asian women, have been part of a long struggle for justice
*Pictures: Guy Smalllman*

*(above)* Striking together for decent pensions on 30 June 2011

*(above)* Marching on New Scotland Yard in April 2011 to demand justice for David Emmanuel, better known as reggae artist Smiley Culture, who died during a police raid on his home on 15 March 2011

*(below)* Riot police attempt to regain control of the streets in Hackney, east London, on the third night of rioting in London in August 2011
*Pictures: Guy Smallman*

*(above)* Thousands of anti-fascists scored a crucial victory in Tower Hamlets, east London, when they united to stop a planned march by racist thugs of the English Defence League in September 2011

*(below)* Unite Against Fascism protest vigil in Muswell Hill, north London, following an arson attack on the Bravanese Islamic Centre and mosque in June 2013. The letters "EDL" were found spray-painted on a wall of the gutted building

*Pictures: Guy Smallman*

order, breach of one is a criminal offence punishable by up to five years in prison. The introduction of ASBOs therefore gave the police and authorities another means by which they could bully and harass local youth.

A thoroughgoing, holistic and determined commitment by the government to promoting race equality would surely have helped to allay concerns about crime and anti-social behaviour. If more young black people had been in school, college, university or employment they would not have been out on the street, apparently doing nothing or supposedly menacing local communities. In turn they would not have been prey to the local constabulary. As we have noted, however, what we have witnessed instead has been the ever present pressure on schools to exclude, and, as we will see, a renewed and intensified focus on stop and search to tackle "Islamic extremists" and later an obsession with youth gangs. This has meant that the initiatives that were introduced after Macpherson were virtually strangled at birth.

As part of its remit, the EHRC conducted some research into the use of stop and search. Its report, *Stop and Think,* concedes at the very outset that:

> Since 1995, per head of population in England and Wales, recorded stops and searches of Asian people have remained between 1.5 and 2.5 times the rate for white people and for black people always between 4 and 8 times the rate for white people.[31]

One whole decade after the *Stephen Lawrence Inquiry Report* one could be forgiven for thinking that Macpherson must never have addressed the issue. As the new millennium progressed, there was an exponential rise in stop and search. In 2009/10 the Ministry of Justice's own publication *Statistics on Race and the Criminal Justice System 2010* recorded 1,141,839 encounters, a 20 percent increase on four years previously.[32] In terms of the racial profile of the stops the EHRC report acknowledged that they "remained stubbornly high" and the police have "still not achieved any significant improvement in their record on race disproportionality in stop and search".[33]

The sight of walkthrough arches to detect knives, guns and other weapons became a familiar sight outside schools, train and London

Underground stations. Under these powers, black people were up to 27 times more likely to be stopped than their white counterparts. The number that resulted in arrests was 2 percent.[34] When we consider that not all arrests lead to successful prosecutions, it can be seen that the effectiveness of stop and search under these powers is minimal. Despite this breathtaking ineffectiveness and the continuing racial disparity, the Home Office announced in 2011 that it was removing the requirement for police officers to record "stop and accounts" in order to "reduce police bureaucracy".

Clearly then there was a huge increase in the number of black people subjected to such harassment, yet no commensurate improvement in the detection of crime and in clear up rates. So it was that in January 2012 the tough talking new Metropolitan Police Commissioner Bernard Hogan-Howe, a man who was appointed because of his reputation for "zero tolerance", was forced into making exactly the same promise that his predecessor had made back in February 1999. The use of the tactic would, he promised, be "less blunt" and more "intelligence led".

This constant harassment of black youth does not happen simply because a handful of police officers fail to "stop and think" or because a minority of rotten apples act in a manner which is unrepresentative of the force as a whole. The racism of the police is endemic because their very role is to enforce the law and order of a ruling class that promotes and relies upon such oppression. However, precisely because of this structural role, the police attract the most reactionary people into their ranks and so it is no coincidence that those people behave in the way that they do.

A sharp reminder of this was provided in March 2012 when the *Guardian* ran a story about a police officer abusing a black youth while arresting him. Later the same day the same youth saw another younger black male being assaulted in the station that they were taken to. The custody suite of a police station is an area awash with cameras, other officers and civilian staff. These officers must therefore have known that they were being observed by others and potentially recorded yet still felt able to act with impunity, confident in the belief that this was simply business as usual.

*Say it Loud*

The revelations about such behaviour apparently came as a surprise to Keith Vaz, that veteran of the 1987 parliamentary breakthrough who was by now the chair of parliament's Home Affairs Select Committee. One wonders what he must have been doing in 25 years since he first sat alongside Bernie Grant, Diane Abbott and Paul Boateng in the House of Commons. In black communities such treatment is regarded as so routine and the likelihood of sanctions against the police so slim that few people bother to report it. The atrocities reported by the *Guardian* only came to light because the youth who was initially abused had recorded the officer calling him "nigger" and "cunt" on his mobile phone. He then went to the press after receiving short shrift when he approached the Crown Prosecution Service.

Just a couple of months after making his promise to improve the use of stop and search, therefore, Hogan-Howe was forced into another grovelling public declaration. This time he issued a videotaped directive to his staff and made an apologetic appearance before Vaz's committee. In the video he sternly announced that he would "not stand for any racism or racists in the Met" while claiming that "it is a small few that tarnish the vast majority".[35]

Police commissioners come and go, from Condon through John Stevens, Ian Blair, and Paul Stephenson to Hogan Howe. The same promises are made in more or less strident terms, but the reality of deeply entrenched institutional racism remains the same. Such bigotry is simply part of the everyday "canteen culture" that black officers had to endure and which they talked about during the inquiry.

It is worth recalling that the recruitment, retention and promotion of black officers were among the key recommendations of Macpherson's inquiry. This is another area where the outcome has been an abject failure. Following the Stephen Lawrence Inquiry, the home secretary set the police a target to increase their proportion of "ethnic minority" officers to 7 percent by 2009. This was a major proposal announced with much fanfare.

Three years after the due date a note quietly posted in the House of Commons Library reported, "The proportion of police officers that consider themselves to be from a minority background has risen from

2 percent in 1997 to approaching 5 percent in 2011." It also noted that "the only Chief Constable from a minority ethnic background took up his post in the Kent police force in January 2004. Mike Fuller held the position until April 2010".[36] Elsewhere the EHRC noted that there is a much higher resignation rate among black recruits than whites.[37] Not surprisingly, black people do not want to join or remain within an organisation that is riddled with racism.

The injustice suffered by black people in the criminal justice system is not limited to their treatment at the hands of the police. If convicted of a crime, black people are far more likely to be sentenced to a term of immediate custody if convicted of an indictable offence and can expect to spend longer in prison than a white counterpart.[38] In sum black people are disproportionately the victims of crime, yet more likely to be criminalised, convicted and incarcerated.

### Gangs

The obsession with black youth is not simply about low level anti-social behaviour. Increasingly the real concern is crime and, in particular, violent crime perpetrated by gangs and supposedly involving knives and guns. In London a specialist unit, Operation Trident, was established in 1998 specifically to deal with what was termed "black on black violence". It was in fact Trident officers who were involved in the fatal interaction with Mark Duggan in August 2011. Despite the controversy surrounding that incident, Hogan-Howe announced that the remit of Trident would be extended to deal with the gangs who were said to have played such a central role in the disturbances.

In the immediate aftermath of the 2011 riots, politicians were quick to assert that the disorder had been orchestrated by gangs. For example Welfare Secretary Ian Duncan Smith told the *Spectator* magazine that there was "pretty good evidence" that gangs were at the centre of the disturbances.[39] Meanwhile David Cameron promised an "all-out war on gangs and gang culture".[40] Within a couple weeks, however, Home Secretary Theresa May was forced into a humiliating retreat and an admission that gang involvement was "not as high as people first thought".[41]

Official reports suggested that the percentage of those arrested who were involved in gangs in London was 19 percent. Though considerably smaller than those original hysterical claims, this is clearly not an insignificant proportion. The influence of gangs does therefore demand our attention.

David Lammy homed in on the subject at length in his book *Out of the Ashes*. He seethed with righteous anger at a culture in which "traditional measures of success are devalued as being unreachable or a betrayal of your true identity. The only honourable and sensible means to riches and success is the fraternity of gangs".[42]

He continued remarking that, for those involved, "gang life has bastardised their notion of civic pride by dictating that they will always be at war. They will always need to threaten violence, if not employ it".[43]

Many people will share that sense of fury, not simply because it is one of the matters about which the media, politicians and police obsess. The lives of too many families have been blighted by the premature deaths, maiming or incarceration of loved ones who have been caught up in the activities of gangs. It is necessary to examine this phenomenon with a clear head though. In so doing, a number of points must be made.

Firstly it should be remembered that the existence of gangs is nothing new. In *London: The Biography*, Peter Ackroyd chronicled the changing nature of gangs, noting how "Dick Turpin led the Essex gang of thieves and smugglers in the 1730s; while a decade earlier such gifted individuals as Jonathan Wild could dominate the general course of London crime".[44] By the early 19th century the renowned Bartholomew Fair held in the Smithfield district "had...become a place of danger and lawlessness with gangs of thieves known as 'Lady Holland's Mob', who robbed visitors, beat inoffensive passers-by with bludgeons and pelted harmless persons".[45]

Later, "rival gangs vied for territory and influence"[46] and in the mid-20th century, the Kray brothers and Richardsons became notorious and much feted in the East End and south London.

Ackroyd concluded by noting that as the new millennium dawned "the Krays and Richardsons have now been displaced by those with other ethnic origins, the Jamaican 'Yardie' and Chinese triads for example, working their own particular area".[47]

It follows from this that gangs are by no means a peculiarly black thing. Both in London and beyond, the gangs that operate simply reflect the different ethnic groups and territorial disputes that exist in those areas. Thus, for example in Glasgow, the UK city where knife crime is most prevalent, the overwhelming majority of gangs and gang members are white.

Before going on to consider those that do exist, it is important to be clear what is meant by "gangs". Much of the talk about such associations is astonishingly loose and often what people perceive to be gangs are nothing of the sort. Thus any group of three or more young people hanging around together is habitually regarded as a gang. These people may be—and usually are—doing nothing more than that, hanging around. Nevertheless the suspicion that this generates leaves them open to police harassment and wider suspicion and hostility.

For example, shopping centres routinely refuse entry to or eject groups of four young people gathered together. In addition there are a host of prohibitions upon the wearing of "suspicious" clothes such as bandanas, baseball caps and hoodies. It barely needs to be stated that these centres have no objection to hosting outlets that make millions of pounds selling precisely these items to the very same young people.

This constant low level harassment can actually transform otherwise law abiding youth into understandably resentful young people with criminal convictions. All too often a simmering resentment at the persistent grind and requirement to account for one's actions eventually boils over. The response may be relatively trivial, a few choice words, a refusal to cooperate and a bit of shoving, but it is enough to result in a charge of "Resist", "Obstruct" or "Assault PC". Moreover, the outcome is almost inevitable. Any defence lawyer can attest to the difficulty of persuading a magistrate's court to believe the word of a black or working class youth over that of a police officer.

The overwhelming majority of young people are not involved in gangs, have no interest in them whatsoever and would probably not know where to find them, how to identify them and what, if anything, they do. A much smaller number are loosely affiliated with a vast number of people, especially given the phenomenal growth of social networking sites such as Facebook. By chance therefore they may be remotely associated with some people who are involved in gangs.

A tiny minority of young people are actively caught up in gangs. One of the most detailed and regularly updated websites calculated that in 2011 there were 250 active gangs in London involving at an "upper confidence level" around 12,360 people and at a "lower confidence level" 5,750. The site suggested that there were 3,000 "hardcore" gang members which it characterised as frequent or prolific offenders. This equated to 0.4 percent of all young people in London aged ten to 19.[48]

The Metropolitan Police accepted this figure but justified the establishment of a 1,000-strong task force under the control of Operation Trident by claiming that these gangs were responsible for 22 percent of serious violence, 17 percent of robberies, 50 percent of shootings and 14 percent of rapes in London.[49]

In their desperation to combat gangs the police are prepared to go to extremes even if this means that they end up criminalising other young people. The concept of "joint enterprise" is used to prosecute two or more people who are said to have committed a crime. It is a complex and highly controversial law with each party being "liable for the acts done in pursuance of that joint enterprise", including "liability for unusual consequences if they arise from the execution of the agreed joint enterprise".[50]

In recent years the police have adopted what lawyers have described as a "dragnet approach", in the use of joint enterprise to sweep up young people who they allege are involved in violent or supposed gang related crimes. Individuals who happen to be on the periphery of an outbreak of violence have been rounded up and charged with serious crimes on the flimsiest of evidence. The law assumes that if they are "voluntarily present" among a group engaged in threatening behaviour, there must be a case for them to answer.[51] As this book was being written, the Metropolitan Police was regularly touring schools with a YouTube video entitled "Who killed Deon?" It is a frightening and blood curdling film which ends with the chilling caption: "If your presence, knowledge, or actions lead to a murder you'll be charged with murder under Joint Enterprise".[52]

The real challenge is not simply to acknowledge the figures about gang involvement, but to critically analyse the underlying factors. Of course young people experiment, push boundaries and take risks; that is what growing up and learning are all about. It is ludicrous to suggest that those who are involved in gangs peddle drugs or imperil their own lives by wielding knives and guns just for the sake of it. Those who are involved take the risk because they think it is worth it.

As we emphasise throughout this book, black people are disproportionately poor, unemployed or located in the lowest paid jobs. Those who are excluded from school or have already attracted criminal convictions have little hope or expectation of a lucrative career in the mainstream economy. In such circumstances therefore, warehousing and selling drugs, stealing from others and trading in stolen goods may offer an alternative. It is an alternative that the overwhelming majority reject and do not participate in. Most people eventually find work, though for many it is at the bottom end of the labour market, some of it is in the informal economy and their working lives may be punctuated by frequent bouts of unemployment.

For a minority of the minority there is serious money to be made from crime, particularly drugs. These are the people who, allegedly, cruise round in fancy cars, designer clothes and expensive jewellery. For the majority of that minority, there is instead the daily challenge of evading the police as they hawk and hustle in a bid to survive and prosper. The misery of modern life means that there is usually a fairly steady supply of customers for their wares. A National Health Service report suggested that as many as 20 percent of young adults in England had used one or more illicit drugs in 2009/10.[53]

The precariousness of their predicament can lead to one gang straying onto another's patch in an effort to protect or improve their position. Those that peddle drugs or stolen goods compete just as others do in a market economy. Clearly, however, these rivals cannot rely on the courts or regulatory authorities to resolve disputes. Instead they have to take matters into their own hands and protect their turf by whatever means are at hand. The very nature of their activity means that gangs have to be tight. Their members need to be able to trust each other and thus codes of behaviour and fraternity become established. Gang members habitually refer to each other in familial terms. Disloyalty may be dealt with in the most summary and brutal fashion.

To describe such activities is not to condone them. For example, no decent person can simply dismiss or excuse the circulation of young women among some male gang members for sexual gratification. The fundamental point about the phenomenon of gangs is that they are a product of the oppression and exclusion that blights so many lives. It is a measure of the alienation they experience that a tiny cohort of young people are left to define themselves by, restrict themselves to and fight over small pieces of territory.

### Deaths in custody

It is not possible to predict with any certainty what the catalyst for any revolt will be. Nevertheless it came as no surprise that in 2011 the spark turned out to be a death at the hands of the police. Such fatalities are nothing new, as the preceding chapters have shown.

As we have noted, the abandonment of any effective controls on stop and search led to an exponential increase in the use of such powers to harass and bully people on the streets. Most of the time those who are harassed depart with just their pride bruised. Far too often, however, the outcome has been much worse, and indeed fatal. According to the government's own research, 5,998 people died in state custody between 2000 and 2010—an average of 54 every year.[54]

The injustice suffered by those who have been killed and the lack of accountability of the police and authorities are heart wrenching and infuriating. For example, Christopher Alder, a former paratrooper, was left to die on the floor of a Hull police station in April 1998. In 2012 it emerged that the body his family had buried in 2000 was in fact that of a 77 year old woman. Christopher's body remained undiscovered in a mortuary until November 2011.

The sheer callousness and inhumanity of the state have been well documented by Inquest, an outstanding organisation which has spent 30 years supporting victims and campaigning for change. In addition, those who have suffered have not done so in silence. Instead they have formed a network, the United Families and Friends Campaign, which has struggled gallantly to demand that those responsible are held to account in coroners and criminal courts.[55]

## The death of Smiley Culture

Less than five months before the August riots one such fatality captured national headlines and the reaction served as a warning of what was to come. In the 1980s David Emmanuel had been a successful musician, reaching the charts using the moniker Smiley Culture with hits such as "Cockney Translator" and "Police Officer". On the surface, these appeared to be catchy but lightweight songs which always raised a loud cheer at parties. Beneath the jaunty beat and jokey delivery, however, are words with genuine meaning which captured something of the reality of young life in Britain during that period. "Police Officer" recalls the predictable experience of a black man, Smiley himself, being stopped and having his car searched. Fortunately the officers recognise him as a popular artist and send him happily on his way when he agrees to sign autographs for their children.

Sadly in real life in 2011 things were not to end so happily. Police arrived at Emmanuel's house with a warrant to arrest him for possession with intent to supply Class A drugs. Under UK law, police officers are entitled to use "reasonable force" in the execution of their duties, but nevertheless, they have a duty of care towards those they detain. We will never know what really happened behind those doors nor will the truth about the criminal allegations be discovered because Emmanuel was dead before he emerged from the building.

In the wake of Smiley's death a number of angry meetings were held in towns and cities around the country and a protest march descended on New Scotland Yard, the headquarters of the Metropolitan Police, to demand justice. The IPCC's response was characteristically spineless. It raised concerns about "several aspects of the operation" including "operational planning and risk management". As in so many cases, however, it concluded that "there were no individual failings which, for the purposes of the Regulations, amounted to misconduct".[56]

## Burning and looting

Mark Duggan's death in August 2011 was therefore a tipping point. In the months immediately preceding that terrible event many activists around the country could sense a growing feeling of resentment and there was widespread speculation that things would explode. For example it was raised and discussed during a packed Sunday morning session led by Professor Paul Gilroy at the SWP's annual Marxism festival in London in July 2011 and at various public meetings organised by Black Activists Rising against the Cuts (BARAC) in the wake of Smiley Culture's death.

Clearly deaths in custody, though far too frequent, are not everyday occurrences. Low level and regular harassment at the hands of the police is, however, quite simply a fact of life for black youth, particularly in the inner cities. When Mark Duggan was gunned down on a north London street in broad daylight enough was enough. Those young people who witnessed the encounter knew that there had been no gunfight with police officers in which Duggan had fired first as the police and IPCC were quick to claim. Duggan's family demanded answers but were ignored as senior officers carried on with the holidays. When the family led a march to the police station they discovered that officers had prioritised the stewarding of a pre-season football match. When officers moved in to arrest a young woman the anger erupted.

For many of those who took to the streets this was payback time. It was Mark Duggan who was killed, but they felt that it could have been any one of them. The rage was a manifestation of the fury that they felt about police brutality and oppression. Direct confrontation with the constabulary was not limited to that first evening on the streets of Tottenham. Rather a number of the episodes that occurred in nearby Hackney and elsewhere were pitched battles between young people and the police. In this respect they were an expression of the same bitterness, anger and alienation that that had burst out on a number of student demonstrations in 2010 and 2011.

Mark Duggan's death and the anger it unleashed were swiftly glossed over by the pundits and politicians who focused instead on the looting that followed in its wake. They sought to dismiss any suggestion that there was a link between the riots, police brutality and wider factors such as welfare cuts. Government ministers were scathing in their denunciation of those who sought to draw a link between the abolition of the Education Maintenance Allowance, a small weekly grant intended to support young people who decided to stay on in education, and the anger expressed by the youth on the streets. The dismissal of such behaviour as "pure criminality" allowed them to ignore, at least temporarily, a few inconvenient truths.

The British ruling class's imperial adventures are a lesson in looting against which the activities of a few thousand young people over a few days one summer hardly bear comparison. What happened in August 2011 lays bare the cynical attitude those with power and wealth have towards black and working class youth.

Eventually, one of the causative factors behind the looting that was belatedly recognised was the aggressive marketing deployed by multinational companies. Huge corporations such as Nike, Apple and Sony deliberately target their advertising at young people. Their marketing preys on the notion that respect and status are achieved by the possession of the latest trainers, the newest mobile phones and games consoles and the sharpest threads.

Black youth are invariably regarded as the trendsetters where these matters are concerned. This was something that the Canadian writer Naomi Klein observed at the turn of the millennium in her bestselling book *No Logo*. She identified a phenomenon called "Bro-ing" that was used by Nike. This essentially involved the company's designers swooping into inner city neighbourhoods, armed with a load of the latest "sneakers" and asking "Hey, bro, check out the shoes." One of these designers boasted proudly:

> We go to the playground, and we dump the shoes out. It's unbeliev-able. The kids go nuts. That's when you realize the importance of Nike. Having kids tell you Nike is the number one thing in their life—number two is their girlfriend.[57]

The expectation is that other youngsters would notice and hot foot it to their nearest store, in order to catch up with these fash-ion leaders.

## Black culture?

This apparent pre-eminence of black youth is not restricted to their role as models for sportswear but is also manifested in music and language and many of the leading and most charismatic sports stars are black. It was his undisguised horror at this apparent transformation of the British landscape which lay behind David Starkey's disparaging remarks when commenting on the riots that the "chavs", as he sneeringly described white working class people, had "turned black".

Sport in general and football in particular are not, of course, part of an exclusively black culture. Rather they are pastimes pursued and watched by millions of people of all backgrounds. It is certainly true, however, that the situation today is in stark contrast with the period that existed prior to the 1980s. It was not until 1978 that the first black footballer was picked to play for England.[58] Today it is not uncommon for more than half the team to be black. A decade after Viv Anderson's breakthrough racist stereotypes remained, such as Crystal Palace Chairman Ron Noades' assertion that "the black players at this club lend the side a lot of skill and flair, but you also need white players in there to balance things up and give the team some brains and common sense."

Today it is not uncommon for black players to captain the side. Similarly, black people are increasingly prominent in other sports including athletics, boxing and even motor racing.

It should also be noted that despite the successes, racist attitudes persisted well into the new millennium. In one particularly notorious episode former manager Ron Atkinson was captured on air describing Chelsea defender and World Cup winner Marcel Desailly as a "fucking lazy thick nigger".[59] Seven years later no less a figure than the England captain John Terry was prosecuted for calling a fellow player a "fucking black cunt".[60]

As with sport, music is not a specifically black cultural phenomenon, but it is arguable that "music of black origin" dominates the popular music charts. Similarly, much of the language, codes of behaviour and styles that dominate the streets and clubs is derived from black dominated "urban" music.

On one level, rather than being indicative of a distinct and developing "culture" this increasing visibility is simply a manifestation of demographic changes, though the successes are to be welcomed. On another level the focus on sport and music is indicative of the narrow strata into which young people are pushed.

## Role models and black self-esteem
The pre-eminence of what is therefore rather loosely characterised as "black culture" creates something of a problem for detractors such as Starkey but also for those who are supposedly concerned about the plight of black youth. For many years there was a consensus that black kids struggled because they had low self-esteem as a result of the absence of successful role models for them to look up to.

This argument is barely credible if black culture is now as omnipresent as some would claim. The theory has therefore been adapted to suggest that these youth have a high, indeed an inflated, sense of self-esteem which is not warranted by anything they have actually achieved. More problematically for these observers, it is derived from the "wrong" sort of role models, from uncouth and greedy rappers or sports stars rather than entrepreneurs and civic minded figures of authority. In turn it leads these youngsters to demand "respect" and gratification regardless of whether it is actually earned and deserved. It is the concern about this and a belief that urban youth should learn to accept their place that leads to the sneering denunciations of "black culture".

A widespread consensus around the importance of role models eventually emerged to the extent that one of the key planks of education policy was a drive to encourage respectable professionals to act as mentors to supposedly disaffected or belligerent youth. The aim of such schemes, some of which included boot camps and military style drills, was to teach these youngsters to have a proper sense of respect and perspective. Few of them have proved successful.

## Hip hop hypocrisy
It is within this broad context about role models and self-esteem that we should consider the lazy, predictable and, frankly, hysterical denunciations of hip hop music and Music Television (MTV) that accompanied the commentary about the riots. At its centre is

an argument that the cultural references and moral compass of too many young people are drawn directly from rap music and MTV Base. Starkey spoke out of pure ignorance, but David Lammy too railed against the "toxic" influence of rap and he is certainly not alone in arguing that:

> parts of popular culture have served to perpetuate and entrench...
> problems rather than ameliorate them... Aside from the get rich or
> die trying culture propagated by mainstream rap acts, there exists a
> more sinister strand of rap music that reproduces a narrative of dis-
> possession and nihilism.[61]

It is undoubtedly the case that much of the material broadcast on channels such as MTV Base is deeply offensive, particularly in its portrayal of women. A depressingly large proportion of songs and videos are obsessed with the three "Gs", guns, gangs and scantily clad "girls". Sexism in pop music, videos and the industry generally is by no means limited to hip hop, however. Rather it has been a constant feature of the whole genre throughout its history. Many of the most successful women artists from Madonna through to Rihanna and Lady Gaga have been almost obliged to appear semi-nude on stage, screen, record covers or in promotional articles. Meanwhile male per-formers have habitually boasted about their sexual conquests and used their fame to exploit, often very young, women. In the UK MTV made its name in 1981 on the back of a breathtakingly sexist video for the white, Birmingham-based band Duran Duran's single "Girls on Film".

For years after its establishment meanwhile, the broadcasting policy of MTV was openly racist. Quite simply "black" music did not appear on its playlist. It was forced to change this policy only because of the phenomenal crossover success of Michael Jackson. All of a sudden MTV executives realised that there was a large black audi-ence out there with money to spend. Their hostility to black people notwithstanding, this was too good an opportunity to miss. The time had come to cash in.

Hip hop is neither more nor less intrinsically progressive than any other popular musical genre. Where it sits on the spectrum is dependent upon a number of factors, only one of which is the personal perspective of the artist who writes and records the material.

An example of this can be seen in the short, tragic life of Tupac Shakur, one of the most iconic figures in hip hop. He was born in 1971 to a single mother who was a member of the Black Panther Party and he was named after a group of Peruvian guerrillas. As a teenager Tupac had been a talented poet and actor, but he was unable to achieve success as a rapper with his early more socially conscious material. This all changed dramatically when he abandoned the political rhymes and began recording lyrics that bragged about the "thug life". Most of this output amounted to crude misogyny, materialistic boasts and macho feuds with other artists. Even here though there was an underlying message to those that controlled society. The acronym "THUG LIFE" actually stood for "The Hate U Give Little Infants Fucks Everything". Like the riots therefore it was a rage against a racist society, but with little sense of how to move things forward.

At its outset hip hop did represent an energetic and innovative new form of black culture. Its origins lay in the huge block parties that black youth organised among themselves in New York to relieve the exclusion and boredom they experienced in the 1970s. There DJs such as Kool Herc and Afrika Baambaata rediscovered and scratched classic old tracks and mixed them in with other tunes. In turn, quick witted youngsters took to the microphone to add words to the music. There was something both liberating and democratic about early hip hop. It was not necessary to have years of classical training or expensive instruments to make music, just a few old records, access to a sound system, a microphone and a sharp turn of phrase.

Today hip hop is huge and lucrative, but most of the cash ends up in the coffers of the corporations who own and control the record companies and TV stations that once derided it. The executives of these companies could not care less about the content of the material they broadcast as long as they continue to profit. Indeed, in many respects it serves their interests if the artists they promote encourage the most rampant, individualistic and acquisitive materialism.

A small but not insignificant number of artists have made vast fortunes. It is little wonder that a minority of youngsters, excluded from other occupations, aspire to emulate Jay Z, Kanye West or Missy Elliott. Moreover the advent of modern technology makes it even easier to make music than before and networking sites such as YouTube ensure its availability to a potentially sizeable audience.

The same is true in the UK of both hip hop and its peculiarly British offshoot, grime. Much of it, like most popular music, is simply throwaway nonsense. Some of it is materialistic, sexist, homophobic and offensive. The most gifted artists are, however, able to capture something of the reality of life for young people living in urban society. Anyone genuinely wishing to understand some of the anger and alienation that occasionally explodes in riots could do worse than listen very carefully to a song such as Tupac's "Nothing to Lose".

There is a final point to be made. Manning Marable, one of the most thoughtful and progressive students of black American history, characterised those people who came of age in and around the new millennium as the "hip hop generation". By this he meant more than that they were simply fans of the music. Rather he observed among them the same creativity, restless energy and drive, that one can hear in the songs, but also the incoherence, competitiveness and acquisitiveness. The music reflected and symbolised the anger, desperation and alienation experienced by modern youth.

In conclusion, young people in the 21st century have watched their life chances diminish catastrophically as the rich have got ever richer. David Lammy himself cited research which revealed that 10,000 people in Haringey, the borough in which his Tottenham constituency is situated, were competing for 367 job vacancies at the time of the 2011 riots. In Hackney there were 11,000 unemployed and 500 available jobs. Further north in Wolverhampton a third of 16 to 24 year olds were unemployed and in Birmingham 4,000 young people had been unemployed for more than six months.[62] Indeed, the Office for National Statistics estimated that between 2008 and the end of 2011, unemployment among young black men doubled from 28.8 percent to 55.9 percent.[63] Meanwhile over the same period, the provision of services for young people was decimated. These youth were not as stupid as their detractors might think. They were able to see through the favoured mantra of the coalition government that we were "all in it together".

Yet when young people refuse to obey society's rules, or protest or step out of line they invariably find themselves harassed, intimidated and incarcerated. The suffocating reality of such oppression was brilliantly portrayed in HBOs *The Wire*, arguably the outstanding television series of the early 21st century, or in the UK in mini-series such as Channel 4's *Top Boy*.[64]

Not surprisingly the hip hop generation has little faith in the strategies that have been used to promote black people from the 1970s onwards. Indeed, it is often people from their own ethnic background—and frequently the very same people who benefitted from black struggles in the 20th century—who are immediately responsible for the misery these young people experience.

Here in Britain, David Lammy can identify many of the real problems but his proposals for change are woefully inadequate. Thus he accepts that:

a market economy today feels much like the weather—not something anyone has chosen, just part of the background to life in Britain. The big question in politics is how we civilise capitalism, not whether or not to abolish it.[65]

His party, New Labour, was in office for much of the period during which the market was allowed to let rip, when inequality accelerated and finally the edifice collapsed. He himself held ministerial office for a significant chunk of that time. Indeed, he was a higher education minister impotent in the face of the elitism and exclusion that we described earlier in this chapter.

The transformative potential of music should not be exaggerated, but for many young people there is something wonderfully defiant and exhilarating about the best hip hop just as there was about jazz and pop in the 1960s and punk and reggae in the 1970s. Some of that spirit was present on the streets of England in August 2011. Many of those who participated in those riots expressed no regrets whatsoever, describing their involvement as the best days of their young lives. Their presence though was invariably as individuals lashing out rather than as part of a collective with a clear focus and coherent agenda. It was for precisely this reason that the riots captured our attention for a few days, weeks even, but were swiftly dealt with by a wave of reaction.

There can be little doubt that there will be further explosions of anger in a society of such glaring inequality, exploitation and oppression. Our aim must be to ensure that these eruptions do not simply end in the participants being isolated and incarcerated followed by a return to the status quo. Instead we must consider what it will take to draw people together, channel our energies, create a better world and, in so doing, enable future generations to finally "touch the sky".

## Black women and the impact of racism

It has also been suggested that the tale of woe that we have described in these pages is really a story about the failure of African-Caribbean males. Supposedly they are the ones failing at school, joining gangs and going to prison. In sharp contrast, for much of the 1990s and 2000s it was argued that their female counterparts were doing well, knuckling down, gaining qualifications and moving into fulfilling careers. One slightly bizarre concern that emerged from this consensus was a fear that these successful women would use their higher "social capital" to abandon their male brethren and increasingly form bonds and have families with white men.[66] The consequence of this would be that the "pure" African or African-Caribbean family would become a thing of the past and the children of such associations would emerge with a confused sense of identity.

Clearly there is some truth in the claims about black women and the education system and labour market and it is a positive thing if some are making progress. Contrary to popular wisdom however, the grim reality is that the lives of most black women in Britain in the new millennium are not so far removed from those of black men. The truth of this is not concealed from those in power and authority. The Home Office's own Equalities Office published a comprehensive survey in 2010 entitled *Ethnic Minority Women's Poverty and Economic Well-Being*. Among its findings was the following acknowledgement:

Women of all ethnic groups have lower individual incomes than men in the same ethnic groups. Pakistani and Bangladeshi women have the largest gap and Chinese and Black Caribbean women the lowest.

It continued:

Poverty rates are higher for women in all ethnic groups compared to White British men, Pakistani and Bangladeshi women having the highest poverty rates at around 50 percent.[67]

By that time Britain was already in the grip of a deep and profound economic recession caused by the banking crisis at the end of the previous decade. To address this decline the coalition government elected in 2010 introduced a savage programme of cuts in public sector pay, pensions and employment. A detailed TUC toolkit entitled *Women and the Cuts* considered the likely impact of this austerity drive. It noted for example that "women are more likely to lose their jobs as the majority (65 percent) of public sector workers are women". Moreover, "£6 billion of the projected £8 billion to be raised in net revenue by 2014-15 will be from women".[68] The toolkit went on to observe that nearly half of all black Caribbean women and 37 percent of Pakistani and Bangladeshi women were employed in the public sector. This concentration of women in particular occupations is, in itself, a measure of the discrimination that they—and black women in particular—experience in the labour market. Indeed, the Fawcett Society has calculated that:

Black and minority ethnic women are...four times more likely to be working in jobs for which they are overqualified and disproportionately represented in routine or semi routine and insecure temporary jobs.[69]

There can be little doubt that the predicament worsened as the impact of the recession took effect. More broadly, it was anticipated that the isolation and exclusion of black women would be increased by cuts in funding for English language classes, mental health provision, support for lone parents and services for those fleeing violence.

Despite this it would be wrong to suggest that women are weak, helpless and simply waiting for the welfare cheque or for their men-folk to ride to the rescue. Millions of black women remain in work. Moreover, at an estimated 34.5 percent, "Black women have a greater propensity to join unions than any other group".[70] Far from being totally excluded and powerless therefore black women are deeply integrated into the UK workforce and have the potential to play a leading role in the struggle for a better world.

## CHAPTER 5

# The rise of Islamophobia

**Talat Ahmed**

> This mass terrorism is the new evil in our world today. It is per-
> petrated by fanatics who are utterly indifferent to the sanctity of
> human life and we, the democracies of this world, are going to have
> to come together to fight it together and eradicate this evil com-
> pletely from our world.[1]

Those were the words with which Britain's Prime Minister Tony
Blair responded to news of a series of terror attacks on the US on 11
September 2001.

On that bright clear morning two aeroplanes smashed into and
destroyed the iconic twin towers of the World Trade Centre in
New York City. A third jet crashed into the Pentagon building in
Washington while a fourth, reportedly headed for the White House,
came down in a field in Pennsylvania following a revolt by passengers. Almost 3,000 people were killed by acts which within days were
being characterised as "epoch making" and as having changed "the
landscape of geopolitics as indelibly as they have defaced the skyline
of Manhattan".[2]

That assessment is not wrong. The enormity of those events is
such that it is rarely necessary to recount in detail what happened.
All that is required is a mention of the date 9/11.

### The world since 9/11

Tony Blair's supposedly measured and "statesmanlike" response that
day seemed in marked contrast with that of his United States counterpart George W Bush. The president was sat in a reading class with
a group of schoolchildren when the news was conveyed to him. His
body language was that of a man paralysed by shock and indecision

as he struggled to comprehend the news. He subsequently vanished from sight for several hours as White House officials feared that he might be the target of a further attack.

Briefly therefore it was Blair who, having abandoned his prepared speech to the Trades Union Congress in Brighton appeared to have assumed the mantle of leader of the free world—the man who could provide wise and soothing words at a time of trauma and confusion.

By the following day the US administration had recovered its step. Donald Rumsfeld, the defense secretary, who had been inside the Pentagon when it was attacked, made it clear that diplomatic niceties would not get in the way of a military response when he belligerently declared, "I don't care what the international lawyer says." Bush himself was even more forthright: "We are going to kick some ass".[3]

It soon became crystal clear whose asses would be kicked. "Islamic terrorists" sponsored by the Saudi dissident Osama Bin Laden and his Al Qaeda network were quickly identified as the perpetrators of the attacks. US officials talked of terrorist cells operating globally and in the decade after 9/11 they were to become the focus of a new "war on terror". This so called "Islamic terrorism" was regarded as an irrational and unpredictable enemy, its very statelessness underlining its global reach.

News coverage of 9/11 combined horrific images of the burning twin towers with headlines such as "Day that changed the world" and "Suicide hijackers blitz America".[4] Fox News set the terms of debate when its anchorman stipulated, "This is an attack in the very soul and heart of our nation." It was seen as "the ultimate crime of terrorism", ushering in a new age of fear.

The demand for retaliation was enormous. The pro-war lobby went into overdrive demanding action and Bush insisted, "You are either with us or against us". Tony Blair stood "shoulder to shoulder" with Bush and was to become his most loyal ally offering a metaphorical blood pledge and unconditional support for military action. Meanwhile the leaders of Russia, China, Europe and the Middle East all lined up to demand retaliation.

On 7 October 2001 Operation "Enduring Freedom" was launched

as US forces pounded Afghanistan, the state that was said to be harbouring Bin Laden. This was followed by an attack upon Saddam Hussein's Iraq in March 2003. In the name of defending democracy and civilisation, death was rained down on Afghanistan and Iraq, killing millions of ordinary people in the process.

Rumsfeld's words in the immediate aftermath of 9/11 had been a chilling warning of what was to come. Human rights, supposedly enshrined in international law, were systematically abandoned or ignored. The most notorious example occurred at Guantanamo Bay, the US base in Cuba where prisoners of war were reclassified as "enemy combatants" and subjected to torture.

## Britain experiences blowback

Suicide bombing is regarded as the preferred method of war of these supposed "Muslim extremists". Four years after 9/11 Britain experienced this itself when a series of bombs detonated by suicide attackers rocked the London transport network in July 2005.

On this occasion Blair responded by promising the "most intense" police and security operation to bring those responsible to justice. He added, "It is through terrorism that the people who have committed this terrible act express their values and it is right at this moment that we demonstrate ours." In characteristically opportunist fashion he also declared, "It is particularly barbaric this has happened on a day when people are meeting to try to help the problems of poverty in Africa".[5]

Within a month Blair was announcing a series of new measures aimed at "rooting out extremism" with the spine chilling declaration:

> Let no one be in doubt. The rules of the game have changed. If you come to this country from abroad, don't meddle with extremism, because if you do, or get engaged with it, you are going to go back out again.[6]

In the name of defending freedom at home, Blair's administration enacted a series of draconian laws. Immediately following the 9/11 attacks the government had introduced legislation which enabled them to detain foreign terrorism suspects without trial. In short, this amounted to indefinite detention but, unhappily for Blair, it was declared unlawful by the UK courts. The government responded by introducing control orders, a form of curfew, that allowed the authorities to place almost total restrictions upon the movement and freedom of association of those under suspicion. In order to ensure that these measures would not be struck down by the courts, control orders could be used against both "foreign" suspects and British citizens.

In addition, "extremist" clerics were to be deported without appeal and oppositionist Islamist groups proscribed. Meanwhile a database of individuals regarded as posing a threat to British society was to be drawn up with anyone on it potentially barred from the UK.

This then is the global context within which we must consider the exponential growth of a particularly virulent form of racism. Islam is viewed as the main threat confronting liberal Western democracies in the 21st century. Fear of "Islamic terror" has been used to whip up a frenzy of anti-Muslim racism. The demonisation of Muslims as the "enemy within" has reached frightening proportions. Thus, for example, in the US, Fox News host Brian Kilmeade could pronounce with impunity in 2010, "Not all Muslims are terrorists but all terrorists are Muslims".[7]

Throughout this period fascist organisations have been quick to jump on the anti-Muslim bandwagon and have stoked up fears of Islam representing values inimical to Western ones. The revival in activity by the racist English Defence League (EDL) following the murder of off-duty soldier Lee Rigby in the spring of 2013 is an ominous example of this, as we shall read in the next chapter.

### Islamophobia across Europe

Such scaremongering has fed into fears of a "population time bomb"; of Europe becoming "Eurabia". This "concern" has been most consistently articulated in France and resulted in Marine Le Pen's fascist Front National achieving almost 18 percent of the vote in the first round of the 2012 French presidential elections. This was the highest vote for a fascist party recorded in post-war French history and was built directly on the scapegoating of France's North African Muslim community. Her job was made easier by the craven manner in which the then president Nicholas Sarkozy pandered to racism by claiming the French were being force-fed halal meat and calling for the labelling of halal and kosher meat.

The fallout from the war on terror has normalised anti-Muslim bigotry to such an extent that in January 2011 the then co-chair of the Tory party, Baroness Sayeeda Warsi, herself a Muslim from West Yorkshire, noted how prejudice against Muslims has "passed the dinner-table test".[8] State racism at the top of society has filtered downwards and directly fuelled the growth of far-right fascist groups such as the EDL and its Scottish and Welsh counterparts, who have tried to mobilise on the streets against Muslims, feeding off this "acceptable" racism.

Given this poisonous atmosphere it was no surprise that on 22 July 2011 Anders Breivik went on a murderous spree in Norway resulting in the killing of 69 people in Utoya at a Labour Party youth camp and eight people in a bomb blast outside government buildings. In a belligerent defence in which he boasted of links with the EDL, he claimed this was an act of "self-preservation" to protect the "indigenous" population of Norway against the threat of "Islamification". He targeted young members of the Norwegian Labour Party because to him they represented the "multicultural elites" and "cultural Marxists" who are "soft" on immigration and unwilling to defend "the Christendom of Europe" from an "infestation" of Muslim hoards.

Breivik's 1,000-page manifesto is a document of neo-Nazi hate that specifically aims his diatribe at Islam as incompatible with Western values. Alas, these are not the rantings of a lone lunatic but represent a pernicious development that has become part of the mainstream. Breivik, Le Pen, the Nazi defence leagues and Sarkozy all claim that these views are not racist but simply to do with the irreconcilability of Islamic values with Western norms.

Sadly the pathetic attempt to dress Islamophobic racism up as cultural incompatibility is not the sole preserve of the right. Many in the liberal intelligentsia and even some on the left have bought into this and in some instances acted as the main protagonists in perpetuating hostility towards Muslims. So Christopher Hitchens, one time critic of US imperialism, could pronounce:

> If you ask specifically what is wrong with Islam, it makes the same mistakes as the preceding religions, but it makes another mistake, which is that it's unalterable. You notice how liberals keep saying, "If only Islam would have a Reformation"—it can't have one. It says it can't. It's extremely dangerous in that way.[9]

Hitchens also became the most articulate spokesperson for equating some Islamic movements with fascism and for defending the term "Islamofascism". Sharing this analysis his sidekick, the novelist Martin Amis, provides us with this illumination: "So Islam, in the end, proved responsive to European influence: the influence of Hitler and Stalin…" because like them Islam is "anti-Semitic, anti-liberal, anti-individualist, anti-democratic, and, most crucially, anti-rational".[10]

Hitchens and Amis clearly abandoned any pretence at being critics of capitalism, but many others who remained on the anti-capitalist left were not immune to crude and simplistic formulations. In 2001 Susan George, anti-globalisation campaigner, talked of "fascist fundamentalists" led by a "megalomaniac who wants to take power over the world".[11] The megalomaniac she was referring to was Bin Laden, not George Bush, because on this view "fundamentalism" and "terrorism" are the worst things afflicting the modern world and consequently Islamists are as dangerous as, if not more than, international capitalism.

What unites these apparently disparate perspectives is the belief that Islamist ideas—religious or political—are totally incapable of being reasoned with because the ideology itself is static and monolithic. As Chris Harman argues, they see Islamism as "reaction incarnate, as a form of fascism".[12]

Faced with this onslaught, many Muslims have concluded that Islamophobia is a specific form of racism that is unique, completely unrelated to and independent of wider racism. Rooted in religion as opposed to skin colour, they claim that it requires a specific response. Religion here is synonymous with culture and Muslims feel they are targeted because of this.

Many commentators have traced this anti-Muslim racism to the war on terror, to be understood purely through the lens of imperialism. As we have already demonstrated, US imperialism's recent escapades have clearly fuelled hatred towards Muslims and Arabs to quite unprecedented levels. Nevertheless, it would be wrong to assume that the roots of Islamophobia begin here. Anindya Bhattacharyya has rightly pointed out that Islamophobia should be seen as the cutting edge of racism, as it carves out a space for all the other forms of racism to persist, and so cannot ultimately be separated from them.[13]

This chapter will proceed to show that contemporary Islamophobia is not simply a recent phenomenon but rather one that can be traced to events over 30 years ago, decades in which the process of racialising the category "Muslim" took root and crystallised. Providing a historical context will demonstrate how anti-Muslim racism is inextricably linked to wider racism and will also show how it can be challenged.

## Popular images of Islam and reality

Notions of contemporary Muslim societies in the Middle East frame public perceptions of Islam. This is not surprising, given that the region was colonised by British and French imperialism and deeply shaped by that experience. In the post-war era the US has replaced European powers as the central player in this region. The critical importance of oil as the key raw material has shaped Western policy in the latter half of the 20th century and continues to do so today.

Consequently, wider imperial politics has determined relations with Middle Eastern governments and framed attitudes towards Islamic states.[14] Constructions of the "Muslim" as the enemy have been used to advance Western interests but Western powers have been extremely selective as to which Islamic states are friends and foes. Two examples below illuminate the realpolitik behind this.

### 1 The Iranian Revolution

The Iranian Revolution of 1979 resulted in the overthrow of the US-backed Peacock Throne with the Shah and his entourage fleeing Tehran for their lives. A hated despot who presided over a tyrannical regime was brought to his knees by popular revolt from below. This is not the place to discuss the history of the Iranian Revolution but it is important to note that just as in the 21st century with the Arab

Spring and Mubarak's removal as president from Egypt, the revolution in Iran re-drew the Middle East map and was vital to weakening US interests in the region.

The events in Iran were disturbing but also perplexing for the West. Initially Western press outlets and mainstream politicians tended to regard the activities as part of a "democratising" process and were not overtly hostile. Thus, for example, the *Sun* ran the headline "Hail the Messiah"[15] as Ayatollah Khomeini made his trip from exile in Paris to Tehran in February 1979. By the end of the year however, fears of "Islamic mobs" and "Muslim rioters" were writ large.

On 4 November 1979 students stormed the US embassy in Tehran and took over 100 hostages. Some people were released, including all the black Americans, leaving behind 52 people held by students loyal to Khomeini. The siege was to last 14 and half months. Newspapers roared "The Flames of Hate" as 2,000 Libyan students protested outside the US embassy in Tripoli.[16] A protest by Iranian students against US imperialism in London that month was labelled "That hate filled demonstration" and to underline the irrationality of "Muslim hoards" the papers noted a banner stating "I am ready for martyrdom" carried by a seven year old boy.[17] The newspapers' message was unmistakable—Islam as a creed is bloodthirsty and inhumane. Daily pictures of women clad in black from head to toe and men with beards wielding clubs and guns dominated TV screens.

In the US anti-Iranian and anti-Muslim sentiment reached fever pitch with routine burnings of the Iranian flag becoming as common as saluting the Stars and Stripes. "Nuke Iran" and "Ayatollah: Assaholla" stickers were as commonplace on college campuses as in suburban America. These were the real flames of hate but they were directed towards Muslims who had the temerity to oppose Western interests.

When the hostage crisis ended in January 1981 a *Daily Mail* editorial concluded with the hope that the incoming presidential administration of Ronald Reagan would do something "to limit the ominous forces of instability now convulsing the Middle East".[18]

Though the revolution was unmistakably anti-imperialist, some on the left did not share this assessment, choosing instead to line up with Western regimes as "progressive" compared to the clerical barbarism of Islam. Hitchens and Amis were therefore not the first to characterise Islamist movements as crypto-fascist. In 1979 the *New Statesman* carried a piece by Fred Halliday, former member of the editorial committee of *New Left Review*, referring to the Iranian regime as "Islam with a fascist face".[19] Though he attempted to qualify the assertion, his views came to exemplify the mass of ideological confusion that blighted and continues to blight the left-liberal intelligentsia. The conflation of Islam as a religion, which is as heterogeneous, multi-faceted and contradictory as Christianity, with a variety of political groupings calling themselves Islamist had led to lazy assumptions, crude stereotyping and racist triumphalism about the "inherent" benefits of Western civilisation.

## 2  Saudi Arabia—death of a princess

The reaction to revolutionary Iran was in sharp contrast to events in another Islamic state. On 9 April 1980 the British TV channel ATV broadcast a drama documentary entitled *Death of a Princess*. This purported to document the execution of a Saudi princess for adultery. It was based on the life of Princess Masha'al bint Fahd al Saud, the 19 year old grandniece of the then monarch of Saudi Arabia, King Khaled, who was publicly executed in front of her lover on 15 July 1977. The broadcast caused a diplomatic brouhaha as the Saudi government did everything possible to prevent the programme airing, including a reported £5 million bribe by King Khaled to the ATV network for suppressing the film.[20] The channel refused but was forced to run the following introductory credits:

> The programme you are about to see is a dramatised reconstruction of certain events which took place in the Arab world between 1976 and 1978. We have been asked to point out that equality for all before the law is regarded as paramount in the Moslem world...[21]

This did nothing to quell the enormous rift between the Thatcher government and a loyal Middle East ally.

Sensitive to British interests in Saudi Arabia, the Foreign Secretary Lord Carrington issued a statement "profoundly regretting any offence" caused. Despite this a displeased Saudi government expelled the British ambassador and cancelled contracts worth millions of pounds.[22] Carrington's deputy Sir Ian Gilmour stated that "the whole [dramatised documentary] genre was something to which the Independent Broadcasting Authority and BBC should be giving very careful attention".[23]

Tory wrath went much deeper. Nicholas Winterton, MP from Macclesfield, called on the government to "apologise to the Saudi government and Royal Family for the film". Alleging that the film maker, Antony Thomas, "had a history of producing inaccurate and biased films", Winterton wanted the government to ensure that "these left wingers do not have the power to undermine the best interests of the UK".[24] By July the British ambassador was back in Jeddah, and within a few months it was business as usual as normal privileges were restored to British businesses operating there.

Was this just a minor tiff between Britain and the highly autocratic and theocratic regime? It may seem like a storm in a teacup but the episode was a catalyst in firmly implanting the idea that Islam and Islamic practices were, at best, antiquated and, at worst, barbaric and inhumane; ideas of medieval rulers keeping women in a state of virtual slavery, meting out unspeakable penalties for the slightest infringement, loomed large in public perceptions.

There was and is nothing new in Western notions of Asiatic societies as inherently backward and monolithic. With several qualifications, Edward Said's concept of orientalism as a prism through which colonial fantasies of Africa and Asia were constructed is apt. At the time no one with a Muslim background could escape interrogation as to the specific and peculiar nature of Islam. "Why do Muslim women have to cover their head/face? Why do they walk three paces behind their men? Why do you have arranged marriages? Why are Muslim men so dominant? Why is Islam so intolerant?" Islamic culture was defined not only as qualitatively different but, crucially, inferior and in need of "civilising".

Such issues seem synonymous with present-day depictions of Islam but like all nasty prejudices, the demonisation of contemporary Muslims utilises imagery from previous periods and reinvents it to fit current needs. In the process older forms of racism can be accommodated and given space to spew their bile relatively unhindered. The fact that the above attributes are not unique to Muslim-dominated societies, much less an accurate historical account of how Islam emerged and expanded, is of course irrelevant to such racial stereotyping. At the time of these controversies socialists condemned the racist bigotry and pointed to the hypocrisy of Western politicians claiming the high moral ground as "defenders of women's rights" in Iran, yet oblivious to the plight of Saudi women.

These two events highlight the double standards that enshrine Western ruling class attitudes towards Islam. A despotic feudal relic may cause the occasional diplomatic spat but as long as Saudi oil continued to pump and profit Western industries all could be forgiven. By contrast, revolutionary Iran posed a direct assault upon Western strategic, political, economic and military interests. Consequently its brand of Islam had to be condemned.

At this time the "problem" of Islam was largely confined to the Middle East and Asia and was therefore external to Western society. This perception was to change dramatically over the next decade.

## The new racism: Islamophobia under Thatcher
In the 1980s the language over race in Britain shifted to "culture" with the debate over immigration and racism coded in terms of social cohesion and integration into "British culture". This turn shifted attention from race as defined in biological terms to one emphasising language, custom and religion.

This did not mean the disappearance of crude biological notions of race. The "new" racism made use of older imagery but redefined it to fit the period of post-war migration and permanent settlement of Asians and African-Caribbean people in the UK.

Chapter 2 has already highlighted the significance and impact of Thatcher's notorious "swamping" speech. Later she declared, "So, if you want good race relations, you have got to allay people's fears on numbers".[25] Thatcher was not only making a direct correlation between immigration, numbers and racial harmony but more perniciously using "culture" as a euphemism for race:

We are a British nation with British characteristics. Every country can take some small minorities and in many ways they add to the richness and variety of this country. The moment the minority threatens to become a big one, people get frightened.[26]

The impact was unmistakeable. Tabloid newspapers were full of racist hysteria about hoards of immigrants settling in Britain whose customs, language, religion and values were different. The image of hoards was particularly directed at Asians arriving in the UK following their expulsion from East Africa. Socialists and anti-racist activists challenged this scapegoating; the front page of *Socialist Worker* asked "Whose Culture?"[27] and went on to expose the Tory racism. In response to attacks on Malawi Asian immigrants from Africa socialists fought back with the declaration, "They're Welcome Here".[28]

Thatcher's use of the race card gave legitimacy to racists who could now confidently talk in terms of "cultural" differences and "British values". This shift helped set the terrain for debates about assimilation, integration and the "problem" with accommodating "outsiders" into mainstream British society. Outsiders were defined by skin colour but the question of Muslims in Britain and their "failure" to integrate and absorb British values would be played out against the background of debates over multiculturalism throughout Thatcher's three terms.

### Ray Honeyford and the attack on multiculturalism, 1982-85

Vengeful and hypocritical attacks upon the failures of multiculturalism have become common currency among political leaders in the 21st century. A particularly spiteful example is the lecture that British Prime Minister David Cameron delivered at a NATO security conference in Munich in February 2011.[29] There is nothing new in this. As long ago as 1984 an article appeared in the *Salisbury Review* arguing that "cultural enrichment" entailed "the determined efforts of misguided radical teachers to place such as the following alongside the works of Shakespeare and Wordsworth":

Wi mek a lickle date
fi nineteen seventy eight

An wi fite and wi fite
An defeat di state[30]

The author of the article was Ray Honeyford, a Bradford comprehensive school headmaster. Over 80 percent of the pupils at his school were Asian and largely Muslim, with eleven languages spoken. Honeyford claimed the education of white children would suffer if they were in a minority. He criticised Asian parents for taking their children to the subcontinent for long periods of time and described a parents' meeting in his school as representing the "hysterical political temperament of the Indian subcontinent" where a "half-educated and volatile Sikh usurped the privileges of the chair by deciding who was to speak".[31]

Community outrage was such that the local education authority rightly suspended him in April 1985. Honeyford won a High Court hearing and was back in post in September that year, only to accept £160,000 from the council to retire early.

In the mid-1980s his words provided succour to every racist and reactionary who suddenly felt emboldened. The press howled with rage at how Honeyford was forced out of his job and hounded for his beliefs. The reality was that he was not some poor innocent. His diatribe against Asian Muslim pupils called for an end to mother-tongue teaching an emphasis on Christian instruction, and he queried the dress code of Muslim girls. Like Thatcher he claimed that his views were not racist but rather an expression of the problems of cultural difference that Muslim values posed. He did not call for integration or assimilation, but expressed open hostility to the very existence of non-white migrant communities in the UK.

Honeyford's legacy is all too obvious when over 20 years later the *Sunday Telegraph* republished the entire article, saluting his "courage and intellectual integrity, which has been so clearly vindicated by recent events". The paper declared him a "martyr to multiculturalism".[32]

The *Salisbury Review* is not some objective publication, however. It is a "journal of conservative thought" representing the new right. Throughout the 1980s the social forces behind it had been baying

*Say it Loud*

for blood over every progressive policy they termed "loony" left. Previously its views had not been part of mainstream Conservative ideology but in Honeyford the new right found their hero.

Roger Scruton, its editor, boasted, "This episode was our first great success, and led to the 600 subscriptions that we needed".[33] Its target remained the left but, as the Honeyford episode demonstrates, education became the battleground over racism where Muslim communities would bear the brunt. The site of the next battle would be Yorkshire.

### Race schools row

In September 1987 a row broke out in the small West Yorkshire town of Dewsbury which would crystallise fears over "Muslim" influence and anxieties over multicultural education, and result in a racist backlash. Twenty six white parents refused to send their children to Headfield Middle School where 500 out of 590 pupils were of Asian origin. Instead they took their children to Overthorpe Junior and Middle School where 90 percent of the pupil intake was white.

From the beginning the parents denied that their actions were motivated by racism, simply stating that they wished to exercise choice over their children's education.[34] However, this choice entailed concerns over "language" and a lack of emphasis on "Christian" teaching. The accusations levied against Headfield were that it did not celebrate Christmas and that the children made chapattis instead of pancakes on Shrove Tuesday. These claims were completely untrue but nevertheless the case was a beacon for the new right.

The campaign went on for a year and eventually the white parents got their way following a carefully orchestrated campaign which had condemned multicultural education as "political correctness gone mad" and maligned the local Asian Muslim community for refusing to integrate into British societal norms. On a more fundamental level it had achieved relative success in helping to cement the notion of cultural difference as a legitimate form of discourse to guide public opinion and policy.

The parents' campaign had powerful backers. The legal adviser was John Whitfield, a former Conservative MP. Honeyford was also involved, stating that he would be happy to advise the parents, insisting that "you really have to emphasise that a school is English instead of having the nonsense of a multi-racial school".[35] A retired headmaster from Harrogate, Kenneth Dransfield, turned up fully equipped with stationery, books and paper to take classes, stating that he could not possibly stand by when these children were in need.[36] Meanwhile the Parental Alliance for Choice in Education (PACE) provided media advice. This was not some benevolent civic pressure group; its founder Fred Naylor was a determined opponent of comprehensive education.

The campaign also received active support from the Freedom Association, a nasty right wing organisation founded in 1975 by Norris and Ross McWhirter. Better known to some readers as editors of the *Guinness Book of Records*, these brothers had a shady history. The Freedom Association was established with the explicit aim of challenging trade union power and the Campaign for Nuclear Disarmament (CND), and it campaigned against sanctions and the sporting boycott of apartheid South Africa.[37]

The McWhirters' intervention in the schools race dispute determined the ideological parameters of the row. It framed arguments about "choice" and "freedom" in education with reference to "cultural" specificities of heritage, language and religion. This is how a veneer of intellectual respectability was provided to nasty racist stereotypes about Asians in general and Muslims in particular.

The headteacher of Headfield School, Gordon Hibbert, countered the spurious allegations stating:

> If we talk about Christian traditions we also talk about Islam. If we talk about Christmas we also talk about Eid. We talk about Buddhism as well as Christianity and Islam. We hope that by living together they will learn tolerance. They live better together if they are aware of one another.[38]

This was irrelevant to the school's opponents. Deliberate falsehoods and misconceptions drove some parents into the campaign but other claims were simply racist. So Avril Cater could say, "There are a few Asians living on our street but they keep themselves to themselves. They go their way and we go ours".[39]

The schools issue became a lightning rod for dormant fascism in West Yorkshire as the BNP and remnants of the National Front were galvanised from their moribund state to enter the fray. Anti-Asian graffiti was daubed on the buildings of local schools, housing estates and taxi ranks.

The local area was and still is predominantly Asian, made up of Gujarati Indians and Pakistanis who migrated in the 1950s and early 1960s to work in the town's textile mills. By the 1980s the textile industry had been decimated, resulting in high levels of unemployment, which though high for all groups was racially structured. So unemployment for whites stood at 11 percent between 1985 and 1987 compared to 21 percent among those of Caribbean origin, 16 percent for those of Indian origin and 29 percent for those of Pakistani and Bangladeshi origin.[40] This material reality lay at the heart of the schools dispute and shaped feelings of disadvantage and oppression.

The Tory government's education policy encouraged the Dewsbury row. Kenneth Baker's 1988 Education Act enshrined the principle of so-called "parental choice", permitting schools to opt out of local education authority (LEA) control if a majority of parents supported such a move. The notion of choice was a misnomer as most parents did not have a choice, but what mattered was the symbolic challenge to comprehensive education. This legislation would lead to more Dewsburys.

Avtar Jouhl of the Indian Workers Association predicted at the time that the opt-out clause would also be utilised by socially conservative elements within the Asian community to demand separate faith schools and further increase segregation.[41] He was right. Ibrahim Hewitt, general secretary of the Islamic Circle, called for "Hindu, Muslim and other religious groups to open their own voluntary-aided schools".[42] Riaz Shahid, secretary of the Muslim Parents Association, went further and attacked inter-faith education as a "fraud".[43]

This was the material and political context in which the demand for separate Muslim schools was raised in Dewsbury. Asian parents called for Zakaria Girls School to be turned into a Muslim school.

These parents were pilloried as "reverse racists". The fact that a boycott by white parents of a predominantly Asian school had ignited the schools row was conveniently forgotten.

Socialists campaigned against the racist lies of the media and the backers of the 26 parents from Dewsbury and understood that the demand for separate Muslim schools was a reaction to the racist stereotyping fuelled by the Dewsbury parents' actions. The demand for separate Muslim schools was understandable but wrong and socialists argued against it, campaigning instead for a robust defence of co-educational comprehensive education. But many on the left missed this nuanced approach, instead maintaining the view that Muslims were "fundamentalists" and "medieval" in their attitudes towards women's education, and failing to differentiate between the racism fuelling the Dewsbury parents' campaign and the oppression that was the background to calls for Muslim schools.

The battle over education and the Honeyford affair demonstrate the manner in which Muslims began to be perceived as a serious problem within British society. Muslim parents were blamed for seeking separate education for their children, thereby refusing to integrate into mainstream British norms. The language of culture was used to highlight notions of difference based on religion, language and custom. Thatcher's emphasis on "Britishness" was reinforced by right wing commentators seeking to provide some intellectual cover to the scapegoating of Muslims. This creation of the "Muslim" as the "other" would find a fuller expression at the end of the 1980s as anti-Muslim ideas were cemented over a work of fiction.

### The Rushdie Affair, 1989

In February 1989 daytime TV presenter and former Labour MP Robert Kilroy-Silk announced, "If Britain's resident ayatollahs cannot accept British values and laws then there is no reason at all why the British should feel any need, still less compulsion, to accommodate theirs".[44]

The reference was to Muslim protests over Salman Rushdie's novel *The Satanic Verses*. The book had been published in 1988 and was immediately banned in India in October of that year. No

Western government took such steps but there were large-scale protests by Muslims demanding its ban.

In Britain the first protest took place in Bolton on 2 December 1988, where the book was torched at a rally of 7,000. The media largely ignored this but they would not do so again. On 14 January 1989 a large demonstration in Bradford ended with the book being set alight. The front page of the *Daily Telegraph* had a picture of over 1,000 Muslims cheering a public burning.[45] Fearing reprisals two branches of WH Smith in the city withdrew copies from their shelves.

Passions were further inflamed on 14 February 1989 when Ayatollah Khomeini issued a fatwa (death sentence) on Rushdie. A media storm ensued. The *Daily Mirror* referred to Khomeini as "that Mad Mullah"[46] while the front page of the *Daily Telegraph* announced that "1,000 fanatics might answer call".[47]

These protests were compared to 1930s Nazi-style book burnings and to the witch hunts and inquisitions of earlier times: "It would be the first burning of a heretic in Europe in two centuries".[48] Peregrine Worsthorne, former editor of the Tory *Sunday Telegraph,* feared that with Europe's growing Muslim population:

Islamic fundamentalism is rapidly growing into a much bigger threat of violence and intolerance than anything emanating from, say, the fascist National Front; and a threat, moreover, infinitely more difficult to contain since it is virtually impossible to monitor, let alone stamp out.[49]

The liberal intelligentsia was not much better. Bill Buford of literary magazine *Granta* declared, "To give into pressure to stop the distribution of a book on the day the book is banned invokes images of censorship and, in WH Smith's case, spinelessness".[50] Fay Weldon, the novelist and feminist, waded in by denouncing the Muslim community: "That a minority group should be able to terrorise the literary community in this way seems bizarre".[51] She later added that the Bible provides "food for thought" out of which "you can build a decent society". The Qur'an offers "food for no thought. It is not a poem on which a society can be safely or sensibly based. It forbids change, interpretation, self-knowledge, even art, for fear of treading on Allah's creative toes".[52]

The issue was too good for an unpopular Thatcher government to pass up. So on 1 February 1989 Home Secretary Douglas Hurd ruled out any changes to the blasphemy law and cajoled British Muslims to "join the mainstream". Such a patronising attitude continued with his successor, John Patten, who in July 1989 sent a condescending letter to a number of British Muslim organisations which included homilies on the need to gain fluency in the English language and lessons on how democracies worked, particularly what it means to be a British Muslim.[53]

Nazis also seized upon the Rushdie affair to scapegoat Muslims. On 24 June 1989, 1,700 police defended the right of the BNP to hold a rally in Dewsbury, where they sieg heiled and chanted "Rushdie, Rushdie". Incidents such as these led some Muslims to conclude that the police, fascists and Rushdie were the same ilk.

In fact Rushdie lamented the fact that that the controversy fed Western stereotypes of "the backward, cruel, rigid Muslim, burning books and threatening to kill the blasphemer".[54] A day after the fatwa was issued Rahul Patel and Gareth Jenkins interviewed him for *Socialist Worker* and as precarious as his life was Rushdie still understood the scapegoating and vilification taking root:

> It's no pleasure to me to be supported by the *Sun* when it's referring to Asians as rats. I'm not on the *Sun*'s side in that. I'd sooner be with the rats.[55]

This is what made the protests against him so regrettable. Far from abusing Islam *The Satanic Verses* probed issues of police racism, immigration controls and the lives of British Asians. Instead of embracing this debate, self-appointed community leaders, who had presumably never read the book, simply called for laws on blasphemy to be extended to Islam.

While some on the left defended Rushdie by attacking Muslims as intolerant thugs *Socialist Worker* defended him against censorship but also fought tooth and nail with other anti-racists to defend Muslims against the barrage of abuse directed at them. In an editorial the paper argued, "Rushdie is not a racist nor is he a friend of those who defend the entrenched racism of British society. He is one of the sharpest critics of it".[56]

The Rushdie affair represented another decisive shift in the characterisation of Islam as an internal problem for the West. Islamic fundamentalism was no longer confined to the Middle East; Muslims were a now "problem within". Book burning was evidence of Muslim fanaticism, comparable to the fascist regimes of the 1930s. It also marked a key moment whereby the liberal intelligentsia labelled Islam monolithic, repressive and irrational, distinct from Christianity, which at least had experienced the Reformation and the Enlightenment.

The row over education and multiculturalism fused with the Rushdie affair to emphasise the Tory notion of "Britishness". The terrain of debate shifted to talk of "non-British" cultural practices and culture became a euphemism for race. This would be a toxic mix as the decade concluded with the end of the Cold War and the emergence of a new world order.

### The New World Order

In 1993 Harvard professor and sometime US government adviser Samuel Huntington published a highly influential essay, "The Clash of Civilisations?" Later expanded into a full length book it argued that the world was entering a new historic phase where the primary struggle would be between the "Christian West" and the "Islamic East".[57] For Huntington, Islam represented a "different civilisation whose people are convinced of the superiority of their culture and are obsessed with the inferiority of their power". For good measure he added that Muslims have a "high propensity to resort to violence".[58]

Two years later NATO secretary-general Willy Claes warned that:

> Muslim Fundamentalism is at least as dangerous as communism was. Please do not underestimate the risk…because it represents terrorism, religious fanaticism and exploitation of social and economic justice…[59]

This speech heralded a reconfiguration of the world as the Cold War ended with the fall of the Berlin Wall in November 1989 and the subsequent collapse of the Soviet Union in 1991. Western powers crowed at the demise of the Soviet Union and as they congratulated themselves talked in terms of a new world order, where publicly at least, peace and prosperity were the order of the day. However, as Claes's statement demonstrates, a new bogeyman loomed on the horizon; Muslim terrorism signified the new threat and the rise of Islam replaced Soviet tyranny as public enemy number one.

In the same speech Claes defined NATO not simply as a military alliance but as one "defending basic principles of civilisation that bind North America and Western Europe". These ideas helped normalise racism against Muslims as well as justifying imperial attacks on Muslim countries under the banner of civilisational conflict.

### The First Gulf War

On 2 August 1990 Saddam Hussain's Iraq invaded neighbouring Kuwait over disputed oil refineries and contested territory. A week earlier the US ambassador in Baghdad, April Glaspie, was reported to have told Saddam, "We take no position on these Arab affairs." For the Iraqi dictator this signalled American acquiescence and seemed a just reward for Iraq's role in helping to contain revolutionary Iran during the 1980s. Iraqi troops had invaded Iran in September 1980. Two years later the Iranians began a counter offensive that proved successful. At this point US power tilted in favour of Saddam Hussein. Ronald Reagan removed Iraq from the US's list of "state sponsors of terrorism", declaring that the US "could not afford to allow Iraq to lose the war to Iran" and that the United States "would do whatever was necessary" to ensure that.

The US was true to its word. Western allies in the Gulf States provided the bulk of funding for Iraq but the US was heavily implicated over what came to be known as "Iraqgate", a scandal that saw over $5 billion of US taxpayers' money channelled into Saddam's coffers from the presidential administration of George Bush Sr. And under Bush Sr's watch US technology was exported to help Baghdad build a massive arsenal of chemical and biological weapons.

What ensued was a horrific eight-year war dominated by trench warfare and the use of chemical weapons against Iranian troops. The death toll was estimated at 1 million but Iraq emerged strengthened and able to launch its attack on Kuwait in August 1990. Saddam had miscalculated, however. Two days later the US policy of neutrality switched and Saddam was now characterised as a dictator who had to be overthrown. A build-up of American forces began in the Gulf with 150,000 US troops dispatched to Saudi Arabia. This would increase to 400,000 with further reinforcements from Britain, Australia and other Gulf states.

The Gulf War was framed in terms of democracies fighting to safeguard liberty against an irrational, zealous ideology. Bush and Thatcher argued that "democracy" and "the rule of law" had to be upheld. They claimed that Iraq represented a usurping power that had to be neutered and Kuwait's sovereignty returned.

The reality was that Kuwait was neither a democracy nor an innocent small country. It was, and remains, a vicious dictatorship, ruled by the Al-Sabah family. In a kingdom of over 2 million people only 60,000 had the vote. The Al-Sabah clan owned fabulous wealth amounting to £60 billion on the world stock markets; the family kept servants in virtual bonded slavery with maids and cleaners locked up for months and beaten with electrical flex for the slightest disobedience. This was the reality of the society that Bush and Thatcher wanted to defend.

In a calculated attempt to popularise the US led invasion, Second World War analogies were deployed with Western forces described as "Allies", Saddam as the new Hitler and poor little Kuwait as Belgium. The build-up to war demonstrated the degree to which US imperial interests once again coalesced with a form of cultural racism that demonised Islam with innate anti-democratic tendencies. If Saddam was a modern Führer, Islam was characterised as representing a quasi-fascist ideology with values inimical to Western virtues of tolerance and liberty.

Torrid stories of Iraqi atrocities appeared in the tabloids. A particularly notorious example involved a woman claiming to be a nurse in Kuwait City hospital. She appeared before the US Congress and presented an account of Iraqi soldiers pulling babies out of incubators, throwing them to the ground and leaving them to die. This was used as the final justification for a strike on Baghdad in the name of humanitarian intervention. Even Amnesty International accepted these charges as valid. Not only was the story a lie but the woman was revealed to be a member of the Kuwaiti royal family who did not even live in the Emirate.

In the middle of the night of 17 January 1991 the US led coalition began an aerial bombardment of Iraq. Operation Desert Storm had begun. This was the most hi-tech combat the world had hitherto seen. US cable networks described it as "the 4th of July" as bombs rained death on Iraqi cities. The war was to last just over five weeks and was the first to see "embedded" journalists reporting from the "front line". TV journalists and newspaper correspondents dutifully reported US military briefings as fact.

This war introduced the world to "smart" bombs and "surgical strikes" which created an impression of a "clean" war where only bad guys got killed. Western forces were described as patriotic and highly professional while Iraqi troops were rapists and mutilators. The term "collateral damage" was repeatedly used to sanitise the human carnage resulting from American bombs and the language of Arab Muslims as bloodthirsty fanatics was normalised in an attempt to dehumanise their suffering.

The collateral damage was in fact hundreds of thousands of slaughtered Iraqi civilians. In an act of sheer military arrogance US forces bombed retreating Iraqi soldiers on the Basra Road. This venal, cowardly act was matched by callous CNN reports that gleefully described the massacre as a "turkey shoot". Over 200, 000 people were incinerated that day. And in a final act of complete barbarism Western forces came across a large underground trench system where thousands of Iraqi soldiers tried to surrender as they approached. Instead the defenders of democracy and freedom overran the trenches with bulldozers, burying many of the Iraqis alive.

In Britain the Tory government's job of backing Bush was made easier by the craven support shown by Neil Kinnock, then leader of the Labour Party. A former member of CND and supposed "peacenik", Kinnock accepted the need to deploy whatever measures and force were considered necessary to remove Iraq from Kuwait.

*Say it Loud*

Liberal academics provided intellectual gloss for the war. Canadian broadcaster Michael Ignatieff wrote that the US Secretary of State should show Saddam "a video demonstration of the shortest way to turn Baghdad into a car park. The dictator is a military man: the West must speak his language".[60] Fred Halliday declared, "The military action against Iraq was legitimate, just as in the 1930s and 1940s it was justified to support the war against fascism".[61] He was the key public intellectual to back the drive to war and in case there was any doubt he insisted, "If I have to make a choice between imperialism and fascism, I choose imperialism".[62]

The perception of Islam as irrational, anti-modern and oppressive was a necessary component of cementing the "clash of civilisations" notion. Demonising Muslims and the Arab world was central to fusing US imperial interests with this cultural racism. Some still on the left echoed these views. So LGBT activist Peter Tatchell referred to Islamic revivalism as the "new dark ages" as it "revived religious obscurantism and intolerance".[63] This was all the more tragic as the Tories and media ratcheted up racism and the scapegoating of anyone looking Arab/Muslim. So in January 1991 more than 170 Arabs were rounded up in midnight raids and over 80 were deported because they posed a "threat to national security". Many of them were students who had opposed Saddam's regime.

Socialists argued that this was a war for oil and fought tooth and nail against the drive to conflict. On 1 September 1990 the SWP organised a demonstration in London against intervention and war and campaigned throughout the offensive with others under the slogan of "No blood for oil" and "US and UK out of Iraq". The demonstration was only a few thousand strong but was imperative to challenging the widespread acceptance of Western intervention as just and necessary. But we also challenged the lazy and inaccurate associations made between Islam and fascism. This was not straightforward. Some on the left wanted the slogan to be "US and UK out of Iraq" and "Iraq out of Kuwait". Others demanded sanctions as the "humanitarian" alternative to war and there were those who had illusions in the United Nations. Even Tony Benn, the veteran left wing MP, believed that with the end of the Cold War the United

Nations now had the possibility of operating some form of just global governance.

The equation of US aggression with Iraq's invasion as if they were the same led some on the left to abstain on the question of war. Theoretical confusion resulted in some people accepting the lie about Islamic societies being inherently aggressive and tyrannical.

This weakened the position of some socialists who had no truck with Saddam. He was a brutal dictator who tortured and murdered thousands of opponents and used chemical weapons to attack the Kurdish town of Halabja in 1988, killing thousands. But he was able to do this precisely because of the aid provided by the US, UK and other governments for over ten years while he attacked Iran. These administrations had turned a blind eye to human rights violations throughout his reign and supplied the weapons and gas which he used to commit those atrocities. The same powers that denounced him as the new Hitler in 1990 had refused to even criticise him in 1988.

The cynicism of our rulers was exposed when Lawrence Korab, former US assistant defence secretary, admitted, "If Kuwait grew carrots we wouldn't give a damn." Therein lay the true motive—to protect oil supplies, and if that meant waging a bloody war to re-install an absolute monarch, then so be it.

Eventually millions of people across the world saw through the lies and joined the anti-war movement; 100,000 marched against the war in London on 12 January 1991.

The New World Order was a historic moment in the political and cultural shift that would shape the last decade of the 20th century and was to have major implications for the new millennium. Politically the first Gulf War was a decisive victory for Western powers and particularly for the US, which could confidently declare the end of the "Vietnam syndrome", its reluctance to engage in direct military interventions following its humiliation in Vietnam.

With the demise of the Soviet Union the American ruling class saw an opportunity to make clear that it was the only superpower with the ability to wage war to defend its interests in the oil-rich Middle East. As with the post 9/11 conflicts therefore, the case for war was built on a tissue of lies. Talk of humanitarian intervention was used to provide a cloak of respectability for naked imperialist aggression.

If Saddam was the new Hitler then Islam was the creed and the conflation of Islam with fascism was popularised to stoke up racist hysteria for a domestic audience. Older stereotypes of zealous and intolerant Muslims were reinforced with notions of Islamic terrorists hell bent on destroying civilisation.

Following his expulsion from Kuwait, Saddam remained in power in Iraq but the doctrine of Western intervention to pursue so-called aggressors had been established. Far from the New World Order heralding peace and prosperity the 20th century ended with a world dominated by instability and war where the vilification of Islam had crystallised into a full blown global menace fit for the new millennium.

## The myth of self-segregation

The summer before 9/11 a series of riots had broken out in the north of England. These would be used to stigmatise Muslim communities as violent and intolerant but also, just as insidious, as isolated and apart from mainstream society. The riots were instigated by racist provocation and fascist activity as the BNP organised demonstrations in Bolton, Burnley and Bradford. Yet the focus of mainstream commentary was not on racist scapegoating but rather on Asian Muslims who were blamed for supposedly mindless criminality.

A 2001 report commissioned by the Home Office and written by Professor Ted Cantle of Coventry University's Institute of Community Cohesion concluded that people in Britain were leading "parallel" and "polarised" lives where those from different backgrounds did not mix. It called for a meaningful concept of citizenship, which could include an oath of allegiance setting out "a clear primary loyalty to this nation".

A review of the Oldham riots blamed deep-rooted segregation, which authorities had failed to address for generations. It warned, "Segregation, albeit self-segregation, is an unacceptable basis for a harmonious community and it will lead to more serious problems if it is not tackled."

A third report, on the Burnley riots, called for local and government action to tackle the deprivation and "disillusionment" of young people, which has led to "violence and prejudice". A previous report into Bradford's troubles by former Commission for Racial Equality (CRE) chair Lord Ouseley also painted a grim picture of a fractured city with mistrust between different communities.

The response of the Labour government was not to denounce the BNP for whipping up racist violence, or to criticise the police handling of these riots. Instead the then Home Office minister John Denham insisted that it was crucial to identify "shared values and common citizenship" to help bind Britain's diverse ethnic communities. The implication of this was that Muslims did not share these common values. Four years later Trevor Phillips, successor but one to Ouseley at the CRE, would cause a sensation when he argued that Britain was "sleepwalking to segregation". This was not the result of racism or deprivation. Rather it was the fault of certain communities who had "self-segregated". So he announced:

> Residential isolation is increasing for many minority groups, especially South Asians. Some minorities are moving into middle class, less ethnically concentrated areas, but what is left behind is hardening in its separateness. The number of people of Pakistani heritage in what are technically called "ghetto" communities trebled during 1991-2001; 13 percent in Leicester live in such communities (the figure was 10.8 percent in 1991); 13.3 percent in Bradford (it was 4.3 percent in 1991). But too many communities, especially those of Pakistani and Bangladeshi heritage in some cities, are up around the 60s and the 70s, even in London.[64]

However, these claims and the figures they are based on have been challenged by academics who specialise in demography. Nissa Finney and Ludi Simpson argue that there is no evidence to support Phillips's claim that Britain is becoming increasingly ghettoised and no statistical evidence of "white flight" from inner-city areas with high numbers of minority ethnic residents.[65] They note that only six out of 408 districts in Britain contain any ward with more than three quarters minority ethnic residents.

Finney argues that the only areas that could be claimed to resemble ethnic ghettos were those with almost exclusively white populations. She notes, "The average white person lives in an elected ward which has more than 90 percent white people in it".[66] Just as the language of cultural difference has been employed to normalise racism, so the language of ghettos and self-segregated communities has become the coded way of blaming Muslims for not integrating.

Similarly, Danny Dorling questions Phillips's ability to interpret statistics. He argues that for all ethnic minority groups identified by the census, the indices of segregation fell between 1991 and 2001. These are the very indices which Phillips referred to in his speech. They fell fastest for people identified as being of black and "other Asian" origin.[67]

Dorling makes a distinction between a segregation index and an isolation index. The former is a measure of the proportion of people who would have to move home for a group to be evenly spread across the country. This he explains is falling for all minorities. By contrast, the isolation index is a measure of how often individuals from a particular group are likely to meet other individuals from their group. Communities suffer high levels of isolation if most of them live together with few other ethnic groups. Low levels of isolation come in communities where ethnic minority groups are more spread out and where other groups live in relatively high numbers. The two are related but do not measure the same thing.

The index of isolation is thus not necessarily a good measure to use, but Dorling argues that if one does, it is highest in Britain for Christians, followed by people with no religion. The most segregated religious groups in England and Wales are people of the Jewish and Sikh faiths, not Muslims as is often supposed; while the levels of geographical isolation of people of Catholic faith in Scotland exceed those of any minority religious or ethnic group in England.

Statistics can of course be manipulated but as Dorling makes clear the empirical evidence simply does not support Phillips's thesis about self-segregation. Therefore the riots were unjustifiably used as another stick with which to berate Muslims.

## 9/11 and the War on Terror

As we acknowledged at the beginning of this chapter, 9/11 has been the defining event of the new millennium. The response to the events of that day marks the point at which the Islamophobia which had accelerated at varying speeds in the final decades of the 20th century went into overdrive.

The perpetrators of the 9/11 attacks were Arabs: 15 from Saudi Arabia, two from the United Arab Emirates, one Egyptian and one Lebanese. Yet these men were not illiterate and medieval zealots, hell bent on taking us back to 7th century Arabia. They were highly educated, worked in professional occupations and were thoroughly "modern".

What fuelled these men's anger was resentment at US imperialism. In particular, the hijackers' motives were the demand to remove US troops stationed in Saudi Arabia, close to the sacred cities of Mecca and Medina; anger at US imposed sanctions on Iraq following the first Gulf War, sanctions that had left a million Iraqis, mostly children, dead; and opposition to US foreign policy particularly its continued support for Israel. The sense of injustice for Palestinians has raged within the Arab world for six decades and US funding for Israel reinforces Western interference in the region.

The hijackers' rage was also directed at dictatorships in Islamic countries which the US backed to the hilt. They had been brought up to respect their religion but then saw powerful people in Saudi Arabia and the Gulf States openly flouting religious convention. In turn they came to associate hypocritical Muslims with alcohol, sex and extravagance.

Though the official enemies in the "war on terror" were Bin Laden and the Al Qaeda network, the 9/11 attacks provided Western powers with the justification to pursue a far wider agenda. The US ruling class was still smarting at the loss of Iran and therefore saw this as its opportunity to re-draw the map of the Middle East in its interests.

Spearheaded by a cohort of neo-conservative thinkers, a section of that class calculated that the US could offset its relative economic decline by utilising its overwhelming military superiority and might as the world's one remaining superpower to ensure that control of critical resources such as oil did not fall into the hands of competitors such as China.

The neo-conservatives' strategy was dubbed the "Project for the New American Century" and with their front man George W Bush Junior in the White House in 2000 they were itching for an opportunity to implement it. 9/11, such a spectacular assault upon American pride and power, provided them with the justification to try and turn this blatantly imperialist dream of "full spectrum military dominance" into reality.

Once the Bush regime responded to the attacks not by launching legal action to bring Al Qaeda to justice but by launching war on Muslim countries, the racist backlash against Muslims at home received official state legitimation and became inevitable. Similarly in Britain we witnessed an intensification of hostility towards Muslims. Mosques were attacked, women had their scarves/veils ripped off, and many people were spat at or verbally abused and denounced as fanatics and terrorists.

The New Labour government's craven support for the "war on terror" led to the propagation of lies not simply in order to try and justify such a policy—most notoriously over Iraq's mythical "Weapons of Mass Destruction" but also to try and silence any criticism of the increasingly unpopular wars at home, particularly from Muslims.

The depths to which New Labour would sink were revealed in November 2001 when an article was published in the *Observer* newspaper under the name of backbench MP Khalid Mahmood. Headlined "The Five Myths Muslims Must Deny",[68] this claimed to be an authentic "Muslim" voice in support of the war. A few days later it was revealed that the article had not been written by Mahmood, but by Denis MacShane, Minister of State at the Foreign and Commonwealth Office. A further disclosure showed that Mahmood agreed to put his name to the article after the Labour peer Lord Ahmed refused. Inayat Bunglawala, then of the Muslim Council of Britain, quite rightly condemned Mahmood's actions, saying, "MacShane then found Mahmood—universally regarded as being not exactly the brightest spark in parliament—to be a more willing instrument for his scheme".[69] In November 2003 the same Denis MacShane declared that Muslims more than others must choose between "the British way" and "the terrorist way". His meaning was explicit: if you support the anti-war movement you are a traitor.

Abuse from politicians was matched by vitriolic anti-Muslim hysteria in the tabloids and mainstream TV news outlets. Suddenly anyone wearing a headscarf or turban, with a beard or just looking Muslim was fair game.

Many liberals, some of whom had been previously on the left such as Hitchens and Nick Cohen, rushed to support the "war on terror". Others who remained on the left and who had been leading lights in the anti-capitalist movement had bought into fashionable ideas about globalisation and the resulting declining power of nation states. Therefore they never combined their often powerful critiques of corporate power with an analysis of state power.

This lack of theoretical clarity about imperialism led to political defensiveness in the face of war. So Susan George, interviewed during a conference at the London School of Economics organised by global justice campaign ATTAC in February 2002, was asked about the "war on terror" and replied:

> I think that after the attack and the resulting trauma in America Bush had no political choice other than invasion. I think his decision was determined by the context and by the attacks on the World Trade Centre and Washington. It would have been very difficult to act otherwise.[70]

Others on the left were enmeshed in a theoretical confusion of their own about Islam, adopting the position that "Islamic fundamentalism" was equally as reactionary as American imperialism and so raising the slogan "No to war, no to terrorism" after 9/11. This position disarmed the left in France where the anti-war movement remained weak, and a lack of clarity about the nature of religion, Islamic political movements and imperialism disoriented anti-racists to such a degree that the French left was not able to effectively challenge Islamophobic currents.

Had such arguments been accepted in Britain they would also

have led to a weaker anti-war movement, or worse, two separate anti-war movements—with Muslims demonstrating on one day and other anti-war campaigners marching the next. Fortunately, there existed here a cadre of socialists with a clear Marxist understanding of both Bush's drive to war as an imperialist bid for US supremacy and control of oil and also the contradictions of religious belief. In such circumstances the need to stand shoulder to shoulder with Muslims against racism was absolutely imperative. The outcome was the creation of a mass, united and powerful anti-war movement.

The front page of *Socialist Worker* after 9/11 was headlined "Horror in the United States: Bitter fruit of US policy".[71] It stressed the anger and hatred that exists internationally against US imperialism and highlighted the wider barbaric history of Western state terrorism.

That week the SWP and other socialists played a critical role in forming the Stop the War Coalition and winning the argument that this organisation should be based around just three critical slogans: "Stop the war", "No to the racist backlash", "Defend civil liberties". A mass international anti-war movement was subsequently galvanised after arguments at the European Social Forum in Florence in 2002 around these slogans. It culminated in an international day of action against the impending attack on Iraq on 15 February 2003, which had been called at Florence. Worldwide an estimated 30 million people marched and rallied to the common slogan of "Stop the war". In Britain, where there had been mass anti-war demonstrations even before the attack on Afghanistan, an estimated 2 million people marched. This remains the largest political march in British history. Perhaps the best tribute to this movement came when people watching the London demonstration on Al-Jazeera on the streets of Cairo asked in amazement, "Are all these people marching Muslim?"

## 7/7 bombings

The most positive element about the anti-war movement in Britain was its ability to hold people together and unite them under an umbrella of unconditional opposition to the war. It correctly identified Western powers as the main enemy and refused to countenance on any grounds the scapegoating of Muslims and Islam. This unity was put to its severest test with the London bombings in 2005.

On the morning of 7 July that year four explosions on the city's transport network left 56 people dead, including the four bombers. Almost 800 people were injured, many severely. In the hours that followed it became evident that the men responsible were British Muslims from West Yorkshire. The "war on terror" had come home and "Muslim extremism" was now revealed to be a domestic problem. Denunciations of supposed Islamic extremists were swift with Blair taking the lead, declaring, "This is a religious ideology... Those who kill in its name believe genuinely that in doing it, they do God's work; they go to paradise".[72]

Though Blair was at pains to point out that this was not representative of all Muslims his insistence that this was "a strain within the worldwide religion of Islam" served to crystallise a powerful image of all Muslims as potential terrorists. Not only were Muslim terrorists home grown but there was a specificity to Islamic doctrine that encouraged such atrocities and had to be rooted out.

The message was not lost on racists. The BNP used a photograph of the bombed London bus for an election leaflet with the slogan, "Maybe now it's time to start listening to the BNP." Though Home Secretary Charles Clarke condemned the BNP for its cynical opportunism, it was New Labour ministers who used the attacks to launch an offensive against anyone who opposed the war and dared to suggest that London had been targeted because of Blair's craven support for George Bush's war.

The London bombers left video recordings explaining that their actions were in protest at Britain's support for war in Afghanistan and Iraq, but politicians and media pundits were not interested in probing and addressing this. Instead a whole raft of policies were introduced by New Labour including control orders, curfews and racial profiling, all of which hounded Muslims and helped create moral panics about Islamist terrorists.

The backlash against anyone "looking" Muslim was pronounced. The Institute of Race Relations conducted a survey of newspaper coverage of racial violence following the bombings and their findings are shocking. The *Liverpool Daily Post* (30 August 2005) reported a four-fold increase in religiously and racially motivated crimes in the Merseyside area. The Merseyside Racial Monitoring Unit received 200 calls in the six weeks after the London bombings, compared to 48 in the six weeks prior to the bombings. Police figures show an 87 percent increase in incidents reported, compared to the same time the previous year. The *Kent Messenger* (11 August 2005) carried a report about a 19 year old Muslim man being kicked and punched by a gang of four white men who first asked him if he was Muslim. The *Asian News* (26 August 2005) reported that a Muslim family from Hyde, Manchester, were accused of being bombers by a white family as they entered Alton Towers fun park. Security guards insisted on searching the Muslim family's car for "bombs". The *Bristol Evening Post* (11 August 2005) reported that Sachin Singhal had been targeted by racists who poured acid over his car. The *Edinburgh Evening News* and *BBC News* ran a story about a 20 year old Sikh man who was racially abused by two white men in the city centre. The men repeatedly pushed him from behind. They then punched him to the ground and ripped off his turban and jacket.[73]

These incidents demonstrate how attacks on Muslims rocketed but also how other Asians were targeted. It is tempting to conclude that racists do not know the difference between Muslims, Sikhs and Hindus, much less care. What it clearly reveals is how a heightened racist atmosphere affects all minorities. Indeed, the most tragic and high profile victim of this hysterical climate was a young man who was neither Asian nor Muslim.

### The death of Jean Charles de Menezes

7/7 had been particularly humiliating for the Metropolitan Police. There had been scenes of joy across the capital the previous afternoon as the announcement was made by the International Olympic Committee that London would host the 2012 summer Games. On the morning of 7 July Metropolitan Police Commissioner Sir Ian Blair appeared on Radio 4's flagship *Today* programme and reassured listeners that his organisation was well equipped to handle such an enormous event. He confidently declared that the Met was "the envy of the policing world in relation to counterterrorism". The four bombers were embarking upon their suicide mission at precisely the time when Blair's words were being broadcast.

Exactly two weeks later, on 21 July, London commuters were subjected to further trauma when four more devices were discovered on the Underground network. This time the bombs failed to detonate and the perpetrators were captured on CCTV fleeing the station platforms. The police were determined to act swiftly and set up surveillance the following morning outside a flat in Tulse Hill, south London, after finding the identity card of a man named Hussein Osman in one of the rucksacks they had recovered. They then followed a suspect to Stockwell station and assassinated him in full view of a carriage of stunned commuters on the train that he had boarded. The intelligence had been mistaken and the man killed was in fact a 27 year old Brazilian electrician, Jean Charles de Menezes.

In the immediate aftermath of de Menezes's shooting the police launched a damage limitation exercise which would be repeated in years to come following the deaths of a white newspaper vendor, Ian Tomlinson, as well as Mark Duggan. It was claimed that de Menezes had been wearing unseasonably bulky clothing and was seen to be furiously texting on his mobile phone as he began his fateful journey. He had then added to the suspicion by getting off a bus at Brixton station only to re-enter the same vehicle and head to Stockwell. The most damning allegation was that he had vaulted the ticket barrier at Stockwell station in what must surely have been a clear act of defiance and an indication of his criminal intent. He then reacted "aggressively" when confronted by the pursuing officers who shouted "Armed police". It was this final act which prompted the firing of the fatal shots.

The truth was very different. De Menezes had been using his mobile phone to let his employers know that he was running late for work. He re-boarded the bus he had initially taken because he discovered that Brixton Underground Station was closed. The allegation that de Menezes had leapt over the ticket barrier was a bare faced lie. He had in fact paused to collect a free newspaper before using his travel card to pass through the gates. In addition, fellow passengers gave evidence on oath to say that no warning was given before seven bullets were fired into his head.

De Menezes was never at any point positively identified as the terror suspect. The flat was under surveillance for several hours, with the police's intention being to allow anyone leaving to walk a short distance before being detained and their identity checked. There was no footage of de Menezes departing because the officer responsible for this task had apparently gone to the toilet.

Even if de Menezes had been the wanted man, the police still had plenty of time to apprehend him. Instead he was allowed to catch a bus which travelled for almost two miles on busy roads at the height of the morning. The commanding officer of this operation was Cressida Dick. As de Menezes entered Stockwell station it was she who ordered his detention only to change her mind seconds later. On her command therefore armed officers rushed in. By the time they reached the platform radio contact was lost and de Menezes's fate was sealed.

As with so many other cases, the de Menezes family was subjected to further injustice at the hands of the state following his death. Firstly, the Crown Prosecution Service concluded in July 2006 that there was "insufficient evidence" to take action against any individual officers. Instead, and even here only because there was a high profile family campaign demanding justice, the Met was prosecuted for breaching its duty of care to non-employees under the Health and Safety at Work Act 1974. The police still refused to accept liability and entered a not guilty plea. Jean Charles's family therefore had to endure a five-week trial. The Old Bailey jury did ultimately find the force guilty and a fine of £175,000 and £385,000 costs was imposed. This was, of course, paid out of public funds.

Following the verdict, the judge, Mr Justice Henriques was damning in his criticism of the Met, stating, "Every single failure has been disputed. Some of these failings have been simply beyond explanation. There has been no single admission to any one of the alleged failings".[74]

Ian Blair resisted widespread calls to resign in the wake of this debacle. As with Condon, he received the backing of the Home

Secretary, on this occasion Jacqui Smith, and also that of Prime Minister Gordon Brown. Meanwhile Cressida Dick was subsequently awarded the Queen's Police Medal and promoted to the position of Assistant Commissioner.

Further injustice was meted out to the de Menezes family in 2008 when an inquest jury was instructed by the coroner that it could not conclude that Jean Charles had been unlawfully killed. The family were devastated and walked out of the hearing in disgust. Despite the coroner's ruling, the jury did what it could by announcing an open verdict and its answers to a series of questions clearly demonstrated that its members did not believe the testimony of those officers who had given evidence.

### Muslim baiting in the mainstream media

The media plays a key role in society and has been centrally involved in stirring up hostility to Muslims. Baiting Muslims became so mainstream that in September 2005 a Danish newspaper published a series of 12 cartoons depicting denigrating images of the prophet Mohammed and claimed that this was its contribution to the debate on censorship and criticism of religion. Upon publication there was uproar across the Muslim world at what was perceived as yet another insult to their faith.

The reality was that this was not probing, critical journalism. The cartoons were not intended to extend debate about the nature of humour, much less contribute to an honest discussion about race relations and racism. They were an example of crude and simplistic tabloid journalism designed to whip up anti-Muslim hysteria and fuel an Islamophobic juggernaut.

More broadly, Muslims were told to "clean up" their backyard and root out extremists. Asian and Arab student societies were targeted on university campuses as lecturers were asked to spy on students for "fundamentalist" tendencies. Even parents were asked to "keep an eye" on children and report any sudden change in behaviour. All this was seen as a test of "loyalty" to concepts of "Britishness" and "shared values".

As long ago as 1997 Polly Toynbee, widely regarded as one

of Britain's most liberal commentators, happily declared in the *Independent,* "I am an Islamophobe and proud." A decade later the demonisation was becoming more extreme with *Sunday Times* columnist Rod Liddle describing Muslims as "savages" and boasting, "Islamophobia? Count me in." Not to be outdone, *Sunday Telegraph* columnist Melanie Phillips published an entire book, *Londonistan,* in which she argued that Britain is creating a "terror state within". By 2006 the notion of the "Muslim" as the "enemy within" was firmly etched into the popular imagination and routine public debate.

## Resistance

In spite of this difficult and at times hostile atmosphere there was resistance to the Islamophobic onslaught. Up to 2 million people, black and white, from all religions and none, marched against the war in the biggest demonstration in British history on 15 February 2003. When George Galloway was elected MP for Bethnal Green and Bow in May 2005 it was on an explicitly anti-war ticket. In his victory speech he declared that this was a defeat for Blair over Iraq. This sentiment resonated with millions across the country.

Similarly, when Galloway ran rings around the Senate hearings over profiteering from illicit oil deals, he lambasted US imperialism over the war. After the bombings he and Labour MP Jeremy Corbyn were lonely voices in parliament in their condemnation of the Blair government for bringing the war home.

On a smaller though no less important scale, in 2005, socialists in Leeds took the initiative and worked with community activists, faith communities and trade unionists to establish "Beeston United" under the slogan "Peace and Unity in our Community". Beeston is the area of south Leeds where three of the 7/7 bombers came from. The ideas of the anti-war movement were pivotal to this campaign.

The slogan of "No to war, no to the racist backlash and defend civil liberties" came to full fruition in Leeds as activists fought to defend the Muslim community and raise questions about why London was targeted. If the dominant ideas of the Stop the War Coalition had been to equivocate over questions of imperialism, racism and Islamism or to concede in any way to the notion of

Islamic exceptionalism, the wider resistance to Islamophobia would have been so much weaker. If that had been the case, control orders, curfews and dawn raids might have affected every single Asian household in Leeds in the aftermath of 7/7.

The arguments that underpinned Beeston United were not easy or straightforward to win but they were absolutely indispensable and succeeded in preventing a racist lynch mob atmosphere from gripping the city. The role of the anti-war movement and socialist ideas at the core of it was critical to challenging the prevailing Islamophobic offensive.

## Islam and the veil

The question of the veil is firmly etched into public consciousness as exclusively Islamic. It is taken as one of the most visible representations of everything that is wrong with Islam, particularly its treatment of women. France banned the veil in April 2011 and since then incidents of women having their scarf or veil ripped off have been widely reported.

In Britain the then New Labour Leader of the House of Commons Jack Straw made an issue out of the veil, describing it as a "visible statement of separation and of difference", and he asked women visiting his surgery to consider removing it. He wrote in his column for the *Lancashire Telegraph* that he feared women "wearing the full veil was bound to make better, positive relations between the two communities more difficult". Asking women to consider showing their mouths and noses would lead to true "face to face" conversations with constituents, enabling him to "see what the other person means, and not just hear what they say".[75] He would later ask, "Would those people who do wear the veil think about the implications for community relations?"

Phil Woolas, New Labour MP for nearby Oldham and Minister of State for Borders and Immigration, backed Straw and went further in demanding that teacher Aishah Azmi should be sacked. Azmi was a teaching assistant in a school in Dewsbury, who had been suspended for wearing the veil. Woolas told the *Sunday Mirror* that she had "put herself in a position where she can't do her job".

He continued, "She cannot teach a classroom of children wearing a veil." Astonishingly he attempted to gain the high moral ground: "By insisting she will wear the veil if men are there, she's saying: 'I'll work with women, but not men.' That's sexual discrimination." He went on to warn, "There are limits to liberal democracy. There are boundaries in a democracy and this is one of them. It's a boundary we can't cross".[76] Woolas claimed Muslims did not understand that to non-Muslims veiling and covering the face is "frightening and intimidating".[77] An editorial in the same newspaper argued, "The veil is a cultural symbol, not a religious one, and it is self-evident that wearing it promotes separateness and a sense of them and us".[78]

Woolas was subsequently exposed as a man who had no business lecturing anybody about democracy. In 2010 his victory in that year's general election was overturned and he was barred from office for three years. He had been found guilty of making false statements about his Lib Dem opponent Elwyn Watkins during the campaign. In keeping with the opportunism of so many desperate Labour careerists he had pandered to racism. His election literature had included the bogus suggestions that Watkins was being funded by a rich Arab sheikh and receiving support from Muslim extremists.

The Tories were not far behind New Labour in the chorus of condemnation of Islam. Following the London bombings the then Shadow Home Secretary David Davis wrote that multiculturalism had failed Britain and called for Muslims to unite behind "common cultural values of nationhood". A year later he argued that "multiculturalism had led to a divided society and a splintering of loyalties" and he blamed governments for tiptoeing around the issue, particularly with reference to Muslim communities.[79] Davis went on to question whether a form of "voluntary apartheid" was being inadvertently encouraged. He used a newspaper column to speculate, "Do Muslims really want apartheid here?" and he lectured the Muslim community for being "excessively sensitive to criticism, unwilling to engage in substantive debate". Finally he suggested that they believe they should be "protected from criticism, argument, parody, satire and all other challenges that happen in a society that has free speech as its highest value".[80]

Attacks on the veil have provided a further means of marginalising Muslims and planting the notion that "they" are the problem. Once again responsibility for this has been placed upon Muslims, in this case women, who are told they only have themselves to blame for insisting on being "apart" from the British mainstream.

## Conclusion

Islamophobia is the critical cutting edge of contemporary racism in Britain and internationally. This flows from the wider politics of empire, from the loss of Iran as a loyal ally of the United States, to the end of the Cold War and the need for a new ideological justification for Western military power after the so-called "collapse of Communism". Given this wider continuing context of imperialist war, Islamophobia will not disappear any time soon.

This racist "othering" of Muslims in the West is propagated in a respectable manner by politicians like David Cameron and Angela Merkel with their attacks on the "failure" of multiculturalism. It is given an intellectual gloss by both reactionary and liberal commentators alike in the media, and then seeps down into popular consciousness. It ends with organised neo-Nazi groups attacking mosques and other racist attacks on Asian people in the streets.

Islamophobia is in many ways the last respectable form of racism in British society, for the basic reason that many people agree with *Daily Telegraph* editor Charles Moore, who insisted, "Britain is basically English speaking, Christian and white, and if one starts to think it might become basically Urdu speaking and Muslim and brown one gets frightened".[81]

A survey in the *Guardian* suggested 53 percent of people supported Jack Straw in 2006 in thinking that veils create a barrier between Muslims and other people. Ted Cantle, author of a report on the Oldham riots of 2001, warned that Muslims were being forced into a corner and becoming more embittered by such attitudes.[82]

In the face of this racist offensive, which is often either propagated or legitimised by the state and elite politicians, there have been various responses from Muslims themselves, all of them perfectly understandable. One response has been to turn inwards, identify more with one's religious faith as a way of handling oppression in the outside world, and in general retreating into the Muslim community. In Britain in particular, this "quietism" has possibly been the dominant response particularly since 7/7.

Another response has been to try and counter racism by seeking to identify more with the national identity, stressing one's "Britishness" and loyalty to the nation at every opportunity in order to avoid the accusations of extremism. This has been the response of many so-called "community leaders" and those seeking to make careers for themselves in mainstream political parties.

Finally, a minority of young Muslims have defiantly identified with the Islamists as a way of resisting the prevailing racism. One expression of this has been the formation of online Muslim Defence Leagues in Dewsbury and east London as a counter to Nazi groups. Another outlet has been Muslim youth identifying with global Islam and supporting Islamist/jihadist groups to counter imperial aggression. Though these seem very disparate responses the common strand is the belief in a mythical "Muslim" community that is homogenous.

As a result of these various responses to increasing state repression, the level of participation by Muslims since 7/7 in joint political projects with the left and other radicals in Britain around such campaigns as Stop the War has fallen markedly. Nevertheless many Muslims have courageously rejected such pressures towards "respectability" and worked for example with anti-racists in groups such as Unite Against Fascism to stand up to racist provocations from organised fascist groups.

Despite the prevailing high levels of hostility and racism to Muslims, akin in many ways to the anti-Semitism suffered by Jewish people a century ago, there are reasons to be optimistic about the future. Firstly, Muslim people are much more integrated in British society than popular headlines in the media would lead us to believe. Moreover, and critically, Muslims are more integrated into the wider British working class movement than ever before—joining trade unions for example. There is now a long and rich history of Muslim working class struggles in Britain.[83]

Building anti-racist unity on the base of this class unity, collective organisation and collective struggle is the best hope of a long-term means of resisting and overturning Islamophobia. This can only be done, however, if the left makes the wider labour movement a place in which Muslim people feel comfortable and respected.

As this chapter has tried to show, there is a cadre of socialists who have had the theoretical clarity about race, religion and imperialism to enable them to lead the fight against Islamophobia over the past 30 years in Britain. That socialist tradition has been so clear because it is rooted in the classical Marxist tradition that had to face similar arguments about anti-Semitism a century and more ago. This is a proud tradition that can enable us to fight Islamophobia effectively today.

## CHAPTER 6

# Beating back the fascist threat

**Weyman Bennett**

THE GREEK prime minister, Antonis Samaras, warned Europe that his country was on the edge of a Weimar Germany-style social collapse. What I have seen on the streets of Athens convinces me this is not rhetoric. There is a violent far-right party, its MPs committing and inciting violence with impunity; a police force that cannot or will not prevent Golden Dawn from projecting uniformed force on the streets. And a middle class that feels increasingly powerless to turn the situation round.[1]

Those dire words of warning were made by BBC *Newsnight* reporter Paul Mason and were broadcast in October 2012. The rise of Golden Dawn, a fascist party, is as rapid as it is shocking. The general election in Greece held in August 2012 saw Golden Dawn poll 6.9 percent of the vote, gaining 18 MPs. This was an astonishing vote given that only a year before it was unable to register even a half percent of support in national opinion polls.

The rise of Golden Dawn was primarily caused by the deep and profound economic crisis that swept Greece. By 2013 unemployment reached 27 percent and among young people aged between 15 and 24 the level was 59.3 percent. Reductions in wages, unemployment and huge public sector cuts had created enormous levels of bitterness and instability. This proved to be fertile ground from which Golden Dawn could grow.

The rise of fascism was by no means limited to Greece. From Brussels to the Black Sea, from Malmö to the Mediterranean, fascist and extreme far-right organisations have grown at an alarming rate. Their representatives have been elected to the national parliaments in Austria, Belgium, France, Hungary, Netherlands, Sweden and Ukraine. We would have to go back to the 1930s to witness a time when fascism and the far-right have garnered such support.

The rise of fascism has not been limited to the ballot box. Since the collapse of the Stalinist regimes in Eastern Europe we have also seen the growth of fascist and racist gangs. They have been involved in violent attacks on ethnic minorities and democratic institutions. In Britain we have seen the rise of the racist street movement the English Defence League (EDL) and there have been the murderous attacks carried out by Anders Breivik in Norway, Wade Michael Page in the US and David Copeland in Britain. Their bombings and shootings show that a small number of Nazis are out of desperation prepared to turn to terrorism in order to try to spark a "race war".

Fascist and far-right movements have not grown in a vacuum. Mainstream political parties from both the right and the left have adopted many of the policies of the far-right. From the Second World War until the early 1990s most of Europe's leaders placed a "cordon sanitaire" around extreme right parties; they refused to work with them and shunned their policies. This is clearly no longer the case. Just as in the 1930s, governments have played the race card in order to divert minds from the real causes of the crisis. More and more mainstream parties, the state and the media have vilified minority communities.

Since the 1990s European governments of all political persuasions have implemented laws that have criminalised and persecuted asylum seekers. As we have indicated in earlier chapters, this process intensified after 9/11. Chapter 5 described how Muslims became the new enemy within and Islamophobia became the anti-Semitism of the 21st century. European leaders from Angela Merkel to Nicholas Sarkozy to David Cameron have lined up to denounce multiculturalism and preach a form of mono-culturalism.

The problem is not just the electoral success of far-right/fascist parties; their success has led mainstream parties to adopt even more severe xenophobic and anti-Muslim policies.

Some sections of the left have gone along with the idea that Islam is more backward than other religions and have supported anti-Islamic legislation like the banning of wearing the hijab in public. Once structures of exclusion are erected for one group in society, they can easily be adapted for others.

Far from marginalising the extreme right and fascist parties, the adoption of some of their policies and the language of the racists by the mainstream parties has enabled many of these groups to move out from the political fringe. Ruling coalitions in Italy and Austria have even invited fascists into their governments.

## Political trends of fascism and the far-right

The growth of the extreme right and fascist parties has taken the form of four general political trends. The first is racist far-right populism. Parties such as the Swiss People's Party and the Party for Freedom (PVV) in the Netherlands are not fascist parties, but they pursue their racist and nationalist agendas through the democratic system. It is within this trend that the UK Independence Party (UKIP) emerged as a serious force on the British political scene. We will return to the question of UKIP later in this chapter.

The second political trend is the rise of Euro-fascist parties. The Front National in France, the Swedish Democrats and the British National Party (BNP) give the impression they are just right wing populist parties but behind this facade they retain their core fascist ideology.

Third, there are openly fascist parties. These include the likes of Golden Dawn in Greece and Jobbik in Hungary. These organisations do not attempt to hide their fascist ideas and pursue a strategy to win parliamentary support and also create paramilitary and street movements, which terrorise ethnic minorities and democratic forces.

Finally there are street movements. In many Eastern European states we are witnessing the rise of violent ultra-nationalist racist gangs who carry out violent attacks on the Roma, Jews and other minorities. In Britain we have seen the rise of the English, Scottish and Welsh Defence Leagues.

Worryingly for anti-fascists and anti-racists, these different political strands of fascism and far-right organisations have begun to work more closely together, adopting ideas and strategies from each other.

Golden Dawn in Greece and Jobbik in Hungary have both developed along classic fascist lines. They created both an electoral machine and street fighting groups prepared to attack migrants and democratic institutions and workers' organisations.

Because the objective factors generally aid the growth of racist/fascist type parties we witnessed the rise of several of these movements at the same time. In Britain for example the BNP reached a new level of electoral popularity in 2009, winning over 940,000 votes and two seats in the European Parliament. At the same time the EDL was launched. It was as both of their fortunes waned in the face of determined anti-fascist opposition that we witnessed the rise of UKIP. Across Europe vile and rabid racism is the political dynamo of these organisations. The victims vary from country to country; in northern and Western Europe Islamophobia is the dominant form of racism. In Eastern, central and southern Europe both Roma and Muslims are the key targets. In addition as we have witnessed the rise of Islamophobia across most of Europe, we have also seen the revival of older forms of racism such as anti-Semitism.

Of course there are regional and national differences between the different racist and fascist organisations. But there are Europe-wide issues, whether real or perceived, which have promoted their growth. They include the "protection" of national identities against the perceived fear of immigration, the power of the European Union, the impact of the economic crisis and perceptions about crime.

But the picture is not all doom and gloom. It is by no means inevitable that the horrors of the 1930s will be repeated. In particular two phenomena can drive the fascists backwards. The first is the existence of a determined anti-fascist movement that confronts them at every turn. The second is wider workers' resistance to the economic crises that fascists seek to exploit.

In the wake of Golden Dawn's dramatic rise, anti-fascists set about the urgent task of building a movement in opposition to them but crucially also, there have been mass workers' struggles and general strikes in Greece against the cuts. Across Europe we have seen resistance to austerity take place on many levels. We are witnessing the emergence of movements determined to beat back the fascists.

Since its establishment in 2003 Unite Against Fascism (UAF) in Britain has played a central role in challenging and confronting the BNP and EDL. It is here in Britain that the fascists have suffered the most serious decline in their fortunes and struggled to make a significant breakthrough. This has led some commentators to speculate that Britain is different from other European countries and that its political culture means it is not susceptible to the rise of fascism and the far-right. This chapter will consider whether that assessment is correct.

### British exceptionalism?

Under the headline "Le Pen stands for President, Griffin can't get elected" the French newspaper *Le Monde Diplomatique* argued in August 2011 that the BNP were unable to grow in Britain.[2] Ultimately the author of the piece argued that its failure is more to do with style over substance. Without a hint of irony the *Daily Express* put it the most succinctly when it argued, "The British character means that foreign ideologies like fascism and Nazism will never take a hold on these shores...it is just not in our character".[3]

Go back to 2010, and it was a completely different picture. The BNP had two MEPs, a member on the Greater London Assembly and close to 60 councillors. In addition, the racist EDL has at times been able to put thousands of its supporters on the streets protesting against the so called "Islamification of Britain".

The suggestion that Britain is somehow immune to fascism is dangerously complacent. The objective conditions for the growth of fascist parties in Britain are similar to other European countries.

Tables 1, 2 and 3 were produced by Eurostat and were commissioned for the European Parliament.[4] They show the "official" levels of unemployment, youth unemployment and migrant populations across European. The first thing to note is just how sharply unemployment levels increased across Europe in the aftermath of the 2008 banking crisis. Secondly, while unemployment levels in the UK were lower than in Greece, Spain, Portugal and Ireland, they were similar to France and Hungary and higher than Sweden, Netherlands and Denmark where far-right and fascist parties have polled well in elections.

## Table 1: Unemployment levels in Europe from 2001-2012

| | Foreigners | | | | | | Foreign-borns | | | | | |
|---|---|---|---|---|---|---|---|---|---|---|---|---|
| | Total | | Citizens of other EU countries | | Citizens of non-EU countries | | Total | | Born in other EU countries | | Born in non-EU countries | |
| | 1000s | % | 1000s | % | 1000s | % | 1000s | % | 1000s | % | 1000s | % |
| EU-27 (1) | 20709.9 | 4.1 | - | - | - | - | 32967.0 | 6.5 | - | - | - | - |
| Belgium | 1224.9 | 11.0 | 778.6 | 7.0 | 446.3 | 4.0 | 1699.2 | 15.3 | 797.1 | 7.2 | 902.1 | 8.1 |
| Bulgaria | 42.4 | 0.6 | 11.3 | 0.2 | 31.1 | 0.4 | 88.1 | 1.2 | 32.9 | 0.4 | 55.1 | 0.8 |
| Czech Rep | 423.0 | 4.0 | 151.3 | 1.4 | 271.7 | 2.6 | 390.8 | 3.7 | 138.2 | 1.3 | 252.7 | 2.4 |
| Denmark | 358.7 | 6.4 | 134.9 | 2.4 | 223.8 | 4.0 | 531.5 | 9.5 | 169.2 | 3.0 | 362.3 | 6.5 |
| Germany | 7409.8 | 9.1 | 2744.8 | 3.4 | 4665.0 | 5.7 | 9931.9 | 12.1 | 3453.4 | 4.2 | 6478.5 | 7.9 |
| Estonia | 206.6 | 15.7 | 14.4 | 1.1 | 192.2 | 14.6 | 210.8 | 16.0 | 19.8 | 1.5 | 191.0 | 14.5 |
| Ireland | 487.9 | 10.6 | 388.8 | 8.5 | 99.1 | 2.2 | 685.5 | 15.0 | 504.7 | 11.0 | 180.8 | 3.9 |
| Greece | 975.4 | 8.6 | 151.2 | 1.3 | 824.2 | 7.3 | 1259.9 | 11.2 | 320.7 | 2.8 | 939.2 | 8.3 |
| Spain | 5562.1 | 12.0 | 2354.5 | 5.1 | 3207.6 | 6.9 | 6555.0 | 14.2 | 2353.4 | 5.1 | 4201.6 | 9.1 |
| France | 3858.3 | 5.9 | 1353.1 | 2.1 | 2505.2 | 3.8 | 7358.2 | 11.3 | 2131.4 | 3.3 | 5226.9 | 8.0 |
| Italy | 4825.6 | 7.9 | 1450.1 | 2.4 | 3375.4 | 5.5 | 5457.8 | 9.0 | 1747.7 | 2.9 | 3710.1 | 6.1 |
| Cyprus | 172.4 | 20.0 | 108.3 | 12.6 | 64.1 | 7.4 | 200.3 | 23.2 | 108.5 | 12.6 | 91.8 | 10.6 |
| Latvia | 332.9 | 16.3 | 6.7 | 0.3 | 326.2 | 16.0 | 298.0 | 14.6 | 30.4 | 1.5 | 267.6 | 13.1 |
| Lithuania | 20.6 | 0.7 | 3.0 | 0.1 | 17.6 | 0.6 | 147.8 | 4.9 | 18.1 | 0.6 | 129.7 | 4.3 |
| Luxembourg | 229.9 | 43.8 | 198.7 | 37.9 | 31.2 | 5.9 | 216.2 | 41.2 | 164.7 | 31.4 | 51.5 | 9.8 |
| Hungary | 207.6 | 2.1 | 127.9 | 1.3 | 79.7 | 0.8 | 465.6 | 4.7 | 316.2 | 3.2 | 149.4 | 1.5 |
| Malta | 20.5 | 4.9 | - | - | - | - | - | - | - | - | - | - |
| Netherlands | 697.7 | 4.2 | 360.8 | 2.2 | 336.9 | 2.0 | 1906.3 | 11.4 | 473.1 | 2.8 | 1433.2 | 8.6 |
| Austria | 941.7 | 11.2 | 382.7 | 4.5 | 565.0 | 6.7 | 1332.8 | 15.8 | 550.5 | 6.5 | 782.3 | 9.3 |
| *Poland* | *57.5* | *0.1* | *18.4* | *0.0* | *39.0* | *0.1* | *674.9* | *1.8* | *265.2* | *0.7* | *409.7* | *1.1* |
| *Portugal* | *439.1* | *4.2* | *108.0* | *1.0* | *331.1* | *3.1* | *853.8* | *8.1* | *212.1* | *2.0* | *641.7* | *6.1* |
| *Romania* | *36.5* | *0.2* | *7.0* | *0.0* | *29.5* | *0.1* | *193.5* | *0.9* | *87.1* | *0.4* | *106.4* | *0.5* |
| Slovenia | 85.6 | 4.2 | 6.1 | 0.3 | 79.5 | 3.9 | 230.1 | 11.2 | 21.4 | 1.0 | 208.7 | 10.2 |
| Slovakia | 70.7 | 1.3 | 54.0 | 1.0 | 16.7 | 0.3 | 156.9 | 2.9 | 131.8 | 2.4 | 25.1 | 0.5 |
| Finland | 181.7 | 3.4 | 68.3 | 1.3 | 113.4 | 2.1 | 260.9 | 4.8 | 93.3 | 1.7 | 167.5 | 3.1 |
| Sweden | 646.1 | 6.8 | 276.0 | 2.9 | 370.1 | 3.9 | 1426.4 | 15.0 | 489.5 | 5.2 | 936.9 | 9.9 |
| UK | 4802.3 | 7.6 | 2344.1 | 3.7 | 2458.2 | 3.9 | 7625.8 | 12.1 | 2575.7 | 4.1 | 5050.1 | 8.0 |
| Iceland | 21.0 | 6.6 | 16.5 | 5.2 | 4.5 | 1.4 | 34.6 | 10.8 | 22.4 | 7.0 | 12.1 | 3.8 |
| Liechtenstein | 12.1 | 33.3 | 6.0 | 16.6 | 6.1 | 16.7 | 22.8 | 62.5 | 7.7 | 21.1 | 15.1 | 41.4 |
| Norway | 409.2 | 8.2 | 247.2 | 5.0 | 161.9 | 3.3 | 614.7 | 12.3 | 266.1 | 5.3 | 348.6 | 7.0 |
| Switzerland | 1815.1 | 22.8 | 1141.1 | 14.3 | 673.9 | 8.5 | 2033.7 | 25.6 | 1218.3 | 15.3 | 815.4 | 10.3 |
| Croatia (2) | 23.3 | 0.5 | 7.7 | 0.2 | 15.6 | 0.4 | - | - | - | - | - | - |

(1) Estimated
(2) Population data for HR comes from 2011 Census as on 31 March 2011

Table 3 shows that levels of migrants living in the UK are as high as, if not higher than, in most European countries. Therefore lack of presence cannot be used as a mitigating factor in the failure of the BNP and the EDL to grow. Nor can it be maintained that the political climate has been unfavourable. Only the most dyed in the wool reactionary could claim that mainstream political parties have been soft on Muslims and migrants. David Cameron has spearheaded the attack on multiculturalism. Far from marginalising the fascists, such a toxic atmosphere can help to legitimise them by giving credence to their ideas.

**Table 2: Youth unemployment (15-24 years of age)**

| | 2001 | 2002 | 2003 | 2004 | 2005 | 2006 | 2007 | 2008 | 2009 | 2010 | 2011 | 2012 |
|---|---|---|---|---|---|---|---|---|---|---|---|---|
| EU-27 | 8.6 | 8.9 | 9.1 | 9.3 | 9.0 | 8.3 | 7.2 | 7.1 | 9.0 | 9.7 | 9.7 | 10.5 |
| Euro area | 8.1 | 8.5 | 9.0 | 9.3 | 9.2 | 8.5 | 7.6 | 7.6 | 9.6 | 10.1 | 10.2 | 11.4 |
| Belgium | 6.6 | 7.5 | 8.2 | 8.4 | 8.5 | 8.3 | 7.5 | 7.0 | 7.9 | 8.3 | 7.2 | 7.6 |
| Bulgaria | 19.5 | 18.2 | 13.7 | 12.1 | 10.1 | 9.0 | 6.9 | 5.6 | 6.8 | 10.3 | 11.3 | 12.3 |
| Czech Republic | 8.1 | 7.3 | 7.8 | 8.3 | 7.9 | 7.1 | 5.3 | 4.4 | 6.7 | 7.3 | 6.7 | 7.0 |
| Denmark | 4.5 | 4.6 | 5.4 | 5.5 | 4.8 | 3.9 | 3.8 | 3.4 | 6.0 | 7.5 | 7.6 | 7.5 |
| Germany | 7.9 | 8.7 | 9.8 | 10.5 | 11.3 | 10.3 | 8.7 | 7.5 | 7.8 | 7.1 | 5.9 | 5.5 |
| Estonia | 12.6 | 10.3 | 10.1 | 9.7 | 7.9 | 5.9 | 4.6 | 5.5 | 13.8 | 16.9 | 12.5 | 10.2 |
| Ireland | 3.9 | 4.5 | 4.6 | 4.5 | 4.4 | 4.5 | 4.7 | 6.4 | 12.0 | 13.9 | 14.7 | 14.7 |
| Greece | 10.7 | 10.3 | 9.7 | 10.5 | 9.9 | 8.9 | 8.3 | 7.7 | 9.5 | 12.6 | 17.7 | 24.3 |
| Spain | 10.5 | 11.4 | 11.4 | 10.9 | 9.2 | 8.5 | 8.3 | 11.3 | 18.0 | 20.1 | 21.7 | 25.0 |
| France | 8.2 | 8.3 | 8.9 | 9.3 | 9.3 | 9.2 | 8.4 | 7.8 | 9.5 | 9.7 | 9.6 | 10.2 |
| Italy | 9.0 | 8.5 | 8.4 | 8.0 | 7.7 | 6.8 | 6.1 | 6.7 | 7.8 | 8.4 | 8.4 | 10.7 |
| Cyprus | 3.9 | 3.5 | 4.1 | 4.6 | 5.3 | 4.6 | 3.9 | 3.7 | 5.4 | 6.3 | 7.9 | 11.9 |
| Latvia | 12.9 | 12.8 | 11.3 | 11.2 | 9.6 | 7.3 | 6.5 | 8.0 | 18.2 | 19.8 | 16.2 | 14.9 |
| Lithuania | 17.4 | 13.8 | 12.4 | 11.3 | 8.0 | 5.2 | 3.8 | 5.3 | 13.6 | 18.0 | 15.3 | 13.3 |
| Luxembourg | 1.9 | 2.6 | 3.8 | 5.0 | 4.6 | 4.6 | 4.2 | 4.9 | 5.1 | 4.6 | 4.8 | 5.1 |
| Hungary | 5.6 | 5.6 | 5.8 | 6.1 | 7.2 | 7.5 | 7.4 | 7.8 | 10.0 | 11.2 | 10.9 | 10.9 |
| Malta | 7.6 | 7.4 | 7.7 | 7.2 | 7.3 | 6.9 | 6.5 | 6.0 | 6.9 | 6.9 | 6.5 | 6.4 |
| Netherlands | 2.5 | 3.1 | 4.2 | 5.1 | 5.3 | 4.4 | 3.6 | 3.1 | 3.7 | 4.5 | 4.4 | 5.3 |
| Austria | 3.6 | 4.2 | 4.3 | 4.9 | 5.2 | 4.8 | 4.4 | 3.8 | 4.8 | 4.4 | 4.2 | 4.3 |
| Poland | 18.3 | 20.0 | 19.8 | 19.1 | 17.9 | 13.9 | 9.6 | 7.1 | 8.1 | 9.7 | 9.7 | 10.1 |
| Portugal | 4.6 | 5.7 | 7.1 | 7.5 | 8.6 | 8.6 | 8.9 | 8.5 | 10.6 | 12.0 | 12.9 | 15.9 |
| Romania | 6.6 | 7.5 | 6.8 | 8.0 | 7.2 | 7.3 | 6.4 | 5.8 | 6.9 | 7.3 | 7.4 | 7.0 |
| Slovenia | 6.2 | 6.3 | 6.7 | 6.3 | 6.5 | 6.0 | 4.9 | 4.4 | 5.9 | 7.3 | 8.2 | 8.9 |
| Slovakia | 19.5 | 18.8 | 17.7 | 18.4 | 16.4 | 13.5 | 11.2 | 9.6 | 12.1 | 14.5 | 13.6 | 14.0 |
| Finland | 9.1 | 9.1 | 9.0 | 8.8 | 8.4 | 7.7 | 6.9 | 6.4 | 8.2 | 8.4 | 7.8 | 7.7 |
| Sweden | 5.8 | 6.0 | 6.6 | 7.4 | 7.7 | 7.1 | 6.1 | 6.2 | 8.3 | 8.6 | 7.8 | 8.0 |
| United Kingdom | 5.0 | 5.1 | 5.0 | 4.7 | 4.8 | 5.4 | 5.3 | 5.6 | 7.6 | 7.8 | 8.0 | 7.9 |
| Croatia | - | 14.8 | 14.2 | 13.7 | 12.7 | 11.2 | 9.0 | 8.4 | 9.1 | 11.8 | 13.5 | 15.9 |
| Turkey | - | - | - | - | 9.2 | 8.7 | 8.8 | 9.7 | 12.5 | 10.7 | 8.8 | 8.1 |
| Norway | 3.4 | 3.7 | 4.2 | 4.3 | 4.5 | 3.4 | 2.5 | 2.5 | 3.2 | 3.6 | 3.3 | 3.2 |
| Japan | 5.0 | 5.4 | 5.3 | 4.7 | 4.4 | 4.1 | 3.9 | 4.0 | 5.1 | 5.1 | 4.6 | 4.3 |
| United States | 4.8 | 5.8 | 6.0 | 5.5 | 5.1 | 4.6 | 4.6 | 5.8 | 9.3 | 9.6 | 8.9 | 8.1 |

There is another factor that has aided the growth of fascist and far-right parties. Across most of Europe we have seen the decline in influence, membership and support of the mainstream parties of the centre-left and centre-right. This has opened up a space for parties of the far-left and far-right to exploit. It is also an interesting fact that fascist parties have often grown when social democratic parties are in office and have betrayed a section of their core support. This was true in France, Britain and more recently in Greece.

Objectively the political and economic conditions in Britain are similar to other European countries, and do not explain the failure of fascist type parties to make a sustained political breakthrough. There is, however, one subjective factor. Every time fascism has raised

*Table 3: Foreign and foreign-born population by group of citizenship and country of birth, 1 January 2012*

|  | Youth unemployment rate | | | | Youth unemployment ratio | | |
|---|---|---|---|---|---|---|---|
|  | 2010 | 2011 | 2012 | 2012Q4* | 2010 | 2011 | 2012 |
| EU-27 | 21.1 | 21.4 | 22.8 | 23.2 | 9.0 | 9.1 | 9.7 |
| Euro area | 20.9 | 20.8 | 23.0 | 23.7 | 8.7 | 8.7 | 9.6 |
| Belgium | 22.4 | 18.7 | 19.8 | 22.0 | 7.3 | 6.0 | 6.2 |
| Bulgaria | 21.8 | 25.0 | 28.1 | 28.4 | 6.7 | 7.4 | 8.5 |
| Czech Republic | 18.3 | 18.1 | 19.5 | 19.3 | 5.7 | 5.4 | 6.1 |
| Denmark | 14.0 | 14.2 | 14.1 | 14.2 | 9.4 | 9.6 | 9.1 |
| Germany | 9.9 | 8.6 | 8.1 | 7.9 | 5.1 | 4.5 | 4.1 |
| Estonia | 32.9 | 22.3 | 20.9 | 19.3 | 12.6 | 9.1 | 8.7 |
| Ireland | 27.6 | 29.1 | 30.4 | 29.4 | 12.0 | 12.1 | 12.3 |
| Greece | 32.9 | 44.4 | 55.3 | 57.9 | 10.0 | 13.0 | 16.1 |
| Spain | 41.6 | 46.4 | 53.2 | 55.2 | 17.8 | 19.0 | 20.6 |
| France | 23.6 | 22.8 | 24.3 | 25.4 | 8.9 | 8.4 | 9.0 |
| Italy | 27.8 | 29.1 | 35.3 | 36.9 | 7.9 | 8.0 | 10.1 |
| Cyprus | 16.6 | 22.4 | 27.8 | 31.8 | 6.7 | 8.7 | 10.8 |
| Latvia | 37.2 | 31.0 | 28.4 | 24.7 | 13.9 | 11.6 | 11.4 |
| Lithuania | 35.3 | 32.2 | 26.4 | 24.2 | 10.4 | 9.0 | 7.7 |
| Luxembourg | 15.8 | 16.4 | 18.1 | 18.5 | 3.5 | 4.2 | 5.0 |
| Hungary | 26.6 | 26.1 | 28.1 | 28.8 | 6.6 | 6.4 | 7.3 |
| Malta | 13.1 | 13.8 | 14.2 | 14.5 | 6.7 | 7.1 | 7.2 |
| Netherlands | 8.7 | 7.6 | 9.5 | 9.8 | 6.0 | 5.3 | 6.6 |
| Austria | 8.8 | 8.3 | 8.7 | 8.7 | 5.2 | 5.0 | 5.2 |
| Poland | 23.7 | 25.8 | 26.5 | 27.5 | 8.2 | 8.7 | 8.9 |
| Portugal | 27.7e | 30.1 | 37.7 | 38.4 | 8.2 | 11.7 | 14.3 |
| Romania | 22.1 | 23.7 | 22.7 | 22.2 | 6.9 | 7.4 | 7.0 |
| Slovenia | 14.7 | 15.7 | 20.6 | 23.2 | 5.9 | 5.9 | 7.1 |
| Slovakia | 33.9 | 33.5 | 34.0 | 35.1 | 10.4 | 10.0 | 10.4 |
| Finland | 21.4 | 20.1 | 19.0 | 19.3 | 10.6 | 10.1 | 9.8 |
| Sweden | 24.8 | 22.8 | 23.7 | 24.1 | 12.8 | 12.1 | 12.4 |
| United Kingdom | 19.6 | 21.1 | 21.0 | 20.7 | 11.6 | 12.4 | 12.4 |

*The quarterly youth unemployment rate is seasonally adjusted.

e = estimate

its ugly head there have been mass movements created to counter it. It is the rise of these fascist organisations and the movements that opposed them that we will now consider.

Since the end of the Second World War there have been three waves of fascist revival in Britain. The first was the emergence of the National Front between 1968 and 1979 which we examined in chapter 2. The second was the short-lived success of the BNP in the early 1990s. The third is the rise of both the BNP and the EDL that we have battled against in more recent years.

### The BNP's first electoral breakthrough

The BNP was formed in 1982 as a splinter group from the NF. Throughout the 1980s the BNP absorbed a number of NF branches and a myriad of other Nazi grouplets joined it. It claimed a membership of 2,500 and its leader was John Tyndall, who was previously the chair of the NF. In the 1980s it remained on the fringes of British politics. At the 1983 general election it fielded 53 candidates, winning a grand total of 14,621 votes, and it lost every deposit. It also polled very poorly in local council elections.

The situation was to change dramatically in September 1993 when Derek Beackon won a by-election in the Isle of Dogs and was elected onto Tower Hamlets Council. It was the first electoral breakthrough for the Nazis since the 1970s. Suddenly the BNP was in buoyant mood. Its paper, the *British Nationalist*, predicted:

> The party is now poised to take control of up to two local councils in east London. This would give the BNP a taste of real power, with control of multimillion-pound housing budgets. More importantly, winning control of a local council would give the BNP electoral credibility... Whatever happens on 5 May, the BNP is set to dominate British politics during the 1990s.[5]

Two questions are of importance to us: what were the causes of the BNP's electoral breakthrough and how where they thwarted?

There are a number of reasons for the BNP's initial electoral success. First there were significant economic developments taking place across parts of Tower Hamlets at that time. Canary Wharf on the Isle of Dogs was chosen as a new hub for banking and finance. Skyscrapers and huge office blocks sprang up all over the south of the borough. This created jobs and wealth for some but for most local people the reverse happened. The building projects blighted their neighbourhoods and very few people were employed in the new industries. Fabulous wealth sat side by side with high levels of poverty.

The *London Evening Standard* ran a story reporting, "Many working class people live in conditions of poverty and distress more associated with the 19th century." Unemployment remained twice as high as the national average, with health and housing being some of the worst in Britain. The failure of the three main parties to address these issues exacerbated the situation and pushed some people towards drawing racist conclusions.[6]

The Labour Party and Liberal Democrats vied for control of the council but neither tackled the poverty found in the area. In fact, the Liberal Democrats, who controlled the council in 1993, made the BNP's racism respectable. Housing was and remains a key issue for working class people and a potential source of racial tension. The Liberal Democrats introduced a "sons and daughters" housing scheme that prioritised housing through a points scheme based on the length of residency of people's parents. This scheme favoured white residents and pushed migrant workers further down the housing priority list. One local paper reported that a Liberal Democrat councillor was travelling to Bangladesh to argue that Tower Hamlets had "no room for immigrants". In the run up to the 23 September 1993 council elections they produced leaflets suggesting that they favoured white residents.

Instead of taking a firm stand against all this the local Labour Party caved in and implied that they supported the "sons and daughters" policy. Worse, in order to weaken the Liberal Democrat challenge Labour published false canvassing returns suggesting that the BNP could win. The idea behind this crazy plan was to win Labour voters back, but all it did was legitimise the BNP.

Fascist groups have a long tradition of organising in east London, stretching right back to Oswald Mosley's British Union of Fascists in the 1930s. As the magnificent Battle of Cable Street in 1936 demonstrated, they have frequently been beaten back by fierce anti-fascist resistance, but by the early 1990s the BNP was able to tap into the bitterness that ordinary people felt. The fascists had a thriving branch in Tower Hamlets including many members who had been activists in the NF back in the 1970s.[7]

The BNP was buoyed up by the success of its European counterparts, most notably Jean-Marie Le Pen's National Front (FN). This French fascist party's claim to have around 100,000 members was probably exaggerated but its influence was undeniable. It sold around 200,000 copies of its weekly paper and boasted 1,700 municipal councillors and 11 MEPs.[8]

Le Pen was the architect of what is now called Euro-fascism. He understood that if the FN simply lived out its Nazi fantasies it would remain on the political fringes of French society. He argued that in order to build up the FN's strength its members could no longer openly proclaim their dedication to Hitler and genocidal racism. Instead they would present themselves as nationalists who were concerned about immigration, identity and multiculturalism. Le Pen famously described his politics as "neither left nor right, but French".

Inspired by the FN's success and change in political presentation, the BNP attempted, in a very crude fashion, to adopt some of Le Pen's strategies and tactics. The local BNP branch found new ways to tap into the frustration and discontent in the borough. It organised a "Rights for Whites" campaign and demonstration in 1990 after a local white boy was injured in a fight with a gang of Asian youths. This was not your usual Nazi protest. The Nazi regalia and flags were absent and the skinheads were told to stay away. This was a demonstration coordinated by Nazis in their Sunday best joined by 300 to 400 local people waving St George's flags and singing "chirpy" cockney songs.

The BNP boasted that it was able to speak to "literally thousands of local people, selling them papers and creating the image they wanted to create of the BNP, as opposed to the negative media stereotype". It tried to project its members as local activists and pillars of the community but the brutal reality was never far from the surface. In 1992 BNP thugs organised several attacks on Anti Nazi League stalls in Tower Hamlets and just a week before the election a gang of 30 to 40 BNP members went on the rampage on Brick Lane, a predominantly Asian area of Tower Hamlets, attacking shops and breaking windows.

Nevertheless the new strategy began to make headway. In 1992 the BNP stood Barry Osborne in a council election in the Millwall ward on the Isle of Dogs. He captured 20 percent of the vote. A Labour candidate resigned in the ward shortly afterwards, sparking another by-election on 16 September 1993. Derek Beackon was chosen as the candidate and he ran a campaign emphasising "Rights for Whites". The BNP flooded the area with canvassers and won the election gaining 1,480 votes (33.9 percent).

## Defeat and decline

The reaction by the left to the BNP victory was instant. An SWP member and Unison union steward led a section of Tower Hamlets council workers out on strike. This was inspiring but it was clear to local anti-racists that a more long-term strategy would be required to defeat the BNP.

As we have already established, the ANL had been re-launched in 1992 in response to the resurgence of fascist activity. It adopted a strategy that involved bringing together MPs, MEPs, trade unions, celebrities and thousands of black and white anti-racists. It built a broad based campaign that confronted the Nazis wherever they tried to mobilise but also went door to door arguing with those who were considering voting Nazi. It was this mass activity that ensured that the BNP was not able to consolidate Beackon's success.

Within three days of his election BNP members were driven off their only regular sale in Brick Lane by 1,000 ANL members and local people. Instead of celebrating Beackon's victory they were seen on national television running away, and have not dared to sell openly on the streets of Tower Hamlets since. Within a month 60,000 marched against presence of the BNP headquarters in Welling, south east London. This march forced the TUC to call its own demonstration against racism some months later through the heart of London's East End, where 50,000 gathered and the BNP was made to look insignificant.

The ANL was not just active in east London. Across the country it was central to organising a high publicity campaign against the BNP. In cities like Leeds, Cardiff and Manchester where the BNP were trying to organise, the ANL held demonstrations and protests.

The next round of council elections took place in May 1994. Not only was Beackon's seat up for re-election, but also a whole swathe of seats were being contested in east London. Seeking to capitalise on their recent success the BNP stood candidates in most wards in Tower Hamlets and neighbouring borough Newham. ANL members leafleted every house in these wards, anti-BNP meetings were held across the country and local gigs opposing fascism were held.

Not only did the mass campaigning ensure that Beackon was defeated; no other BNP candidate was elected.

The main beneficiary of the "Don't vote Nazi" campaign was the Labour Party which saw its share of the vote increase significantly across the country. The success of the campaign was celebrated at an ANL carnival in May 1994, which attracted around 150,000 people.

There can be no doubt that the election of Derek Beackon put the anti-racist movement to the test. Anti Fascist Action (AFA) drew the conclusion from the rise of the BNP that white workers are racist and have no role to play in the struggle against the Nazis. Rather than attempt to build a mass movement to smash the Nazis therefore, AFA and a handful of other similar organisations have relied on a small group of street fighters to confront the fascists. In the end this always leads to secretive organisation that by definition excludes the vast majority of people. Small groups of people attacking groups of Nazis have never smashed them, as the lessons of the 1930s and 1970s demonstrate. It is only mass action coupled with serious door to door and union campaigning around the issues that breed fascism that has broken Nazi movements.

Following Beackon's defeat the BNP attempted to regroup. There were four further council by-elections in the East End of London in 1994/95. The Nazis stood candidates and in each one they saw their vote decline. The Poplar by-election in December 1994 was a major setback for them. The BNP felt they had a chance of winning as whites made up nearly 90 percent of the ward. They stood Beackon again with the slogan on a leaflet, "Only fools and horses vote BNP". The prediction proved correct. The BNP came third with less than 20 percent of the vote. Anywhere else in the country 19 percent would be a good vote for the fascists, but they had secured 44 percent two years previously and 28 percent in the neighbouring ward in the May 1994. When set against these figures therefore it was a serious decline. Reporters observed that BNP supporters at the count were visibly shaken. In subsequent elections the BNP saw its vote diminish even more.

The defeats sent the BNP into a decline which saw it return to the political fringes for nearly a decade. It suffered a major haemorrhaging of its membership with branches reporting a 50 percent decline. Even more serious for the Nazis, the failure at the ballot box saw some of their members turn towards individual attacks and harassment. For those suffering at the hands of Nazi terror, it is a truly harrowing experience, but it was a sign of their frustration and weakness. Violence gives the members a quick fix, but ultimately it will lead nowhere. It isolates them from the vast majority of people and on its own will not build a mass Nazi movement.

## The Nazi revival

In 1999 Tyndall was displaced as the BNP's leader by Nick Griffin—also a longstanding neo-Nazi and Holocaust denier, but one with a marginally more "respectable" background than Tyndall. Griffin sought to emulate the electoral success of Jean-Marie Le Pen's Front National and embarked on a course of transforming the BNP's public image.

Griffin signalled this change of direction in an article for the BNP's *Patriot* magazine. He wrote, "Politics is always the art of the possible, so we must judge every policy by one simple criterion: is it realistically possible that a decisive proportion of the British people will support it?"[9]

He called for the BNP to "scale down our short-term ambitions" and focus on tactics that would bring the party a "step closer to our eventual goal". In particular he urged BNP members to drop—in public at least—the culture of hooliganism and Hitler worship that had become the party's stock in trade.[10]

It is important to note that the changes proposed by Griffin were cosmetic only. The turn away from overt racism, Nazism and Holocaust denial, and the adoption of a more populist style of campaigning were designed to win support at the ballot box, not to fundamentally alter the fascist nature of the party. Griffin spelt this out explicitly in his *Patriot* article: "Of course we must teach the truth to the hardcore. But when it comes to influencing the public, forget about racial differences, genetics, Zionism, historical revisionism and so on".[11]

By 2002 this new Le Pen-style Euro-fascist strategy was beginning to bear fruit. The BNP won three council seats in the northern town of Burnley that year and took a further 13 seats the next year. Its total number of councillors had risen to 49 by the May 2006 local elections. In electoral terms at least, it had become the most successful fascist organisation in British history.

This change in tactics by the BNP necessitated a change in tactics by anti-fascists in Britain. The collapse of the BNP in the early 1990s meant that the ANL had atrophied. What was needed was a broader, inclusive anti-fascist organisation.

## Unite Against Fascism

In late 2003 several campaigning groups and trade unions came together to form Unite Against Fascism (UAF), with the explicit aim of countering the rise of the BNP. Its component parts included Labour Party members, the revolutionary left, anti-racists rooted in black community struggles, religious groups and trade union activists.

UAF was consciously modelled on previously successful anti-fascist coalitions, notably the Anti Nazi League. Another key influence was the "united front" tactic advocated by Leon Trotsky in the late 1920s and early 1930s. Trotsky had called for Germany's social democrats and communists to join forces against their common enemy, Hitler's Nazi Party.

While UAF's roots were in previous anti-fascist struggles, it adapted its approach to fit the contemporary climate. Fascist organisations are characterised by the dual nature of their tactics: seeking respectability through the ballot box, but also organising violence against the left and black people on the ground. In turn therefore, anti-fascists had to combine anti-BNP electoral work—primarily exposing and campaigning against the BNP on the doorstep—with a willingness to build mass demonstrations against the fascists when necessary. But in the mid-2000s it was the electoral side that was reaping benefits for the fascists, and therefore this was the arena that UAF initially focused upon.

In many European countries there exist anti-fascist organisations that have official endorsement and mass support but restrict themselves to passive and legalistic campaigning. These are typically complemented by more radical groups that advocate more militant tactics, but are unable to win the wide-scale support that would make these tactics effective precisely because of their hostile and sectarian approach to mass campaigns. The aim of UAF was to counteract this tendency and ensure that both wings of the movement would work together, whatever stresses and strains this would involve.

In terms of propaganda during elections, UAF focused primarily—though by no means exclusively—on ripping off the mask of respectability that the BNP was seeking to wear. UAF's reasoning was that the BNP's electoral gains had been predicated on the party ditching its previous overt racism and adopting a softer language of populist opposition to immigration, multiculturalism and Muslims. Anti-fascists, therefore, needed to demonstrate that behind this "respectable" bigotry lay an organisation led and run by hardened fascists. This intuition was buttressed by research, which made it clear that labelling the BNP as Nazis was the single most effective message when it came to dissuading its potential voters.

While exposing the BNP as Nazis was important, it was not the only message UAF put out. The BNP's populist turn could only happen because of the rise of a "new racism" that repackaged old racial prejudices in "cultural" clothing. Consequently, any effective anti-fascist strategy would have to take a principled stance against this disguised "cultural" racism. In particular, UAF took a strong stand against Islamophobia, arguing that the emerging anti-Muslim racism, which was popular even in liberal circles, was acting as a breeding ground for fascism.

This insistence on opposing Islamophobia was controversial among some sections of the left that had categorised "Islamic extremism" as a variant of fascism. The other controversial aspect of UAF's approach was rejecting the dogma popular among liberals that blamed the BNP's rise on "white working class alienation". According to this argument, the rise in BNP votes was driven not so much by racism but by economic factors such as unemployment and housing shortages. It followed that those opposed to the BNP should refrain from campaigning against or even mentioning racism, and stick instead to economic issues.

It is undeniable that lack of jobs and houses had severely damaged the social fabric in many of the areas in which the BNP had made electoral gains. It is also true that the BNP exploited these issues for its own propaganda purposes—typically blaming the shortage in jobs or services on immigrants. But all the empirical studies showed that BNP voters were not, in the main, particularly poverty stricken or badly affected by the running down of public services. On the contrary, they typically tended to come from the better off sections of the working class or the lower middle class. This again was in keeping with the traditional pattern for fascist organisations, which root themselves in the middle class (petty bourgeoisie) and attempt to build a mass base from there. In particular, it was a grave mistake to assume that white working class people were inherently susceptible to racist arguments. Such assumptions only served to undermine anti-BNP campaigning by misunderstanding the nature of the BNP's growth.

One further aspect of UAF's armoury involved a "cultural front". The Love Music Hate Racism (LMHR) campaign was launched in 2002 specifically to spread anti-fascist and anti-racist messages through the music scene. LMHR helped to organise hundreds of gigs, DJ nights and festivals involving a wide range of artists, black and white, spanning a variety of musical styles. Over 150,000 attended the LMHR carnival in east London in 2008, 24,000 in Stoke in 2009 and 10,000 in Barnsley in 2010. Just as important was the fact that LMHR encouraged young people to set up their own gigs and events against the Nazis. In 2008 over 300 events were arranged by local groups.

### 2009: A turning point

The year 2009 was a turning point for fascists in Britain in two respects. First, the BNP achieved a breakthrough at national level, winning two seats in the European Parliament on top of around 50 council seats that it had picked up and held over the years. Second, that year saw fascists return to Britain's streets for the first time in over a decade, with the EDL emerging as the leading force behind a series of anti-Muslim rallies and racist rampages. In 2010 the EDL was organising on average a demonstration every two weeks and was able to put up to 5,000 people on the streets.

The EDL was an organisation that attracted large numbers of football hooligans, who were prepared to unite together in order to oppose Islam. As it grew it broadened its opposition and its supporters attacked trade union meetings, picket lines and protests. Its leadership threatened to smash up the Occupy camps and student demonstrations. What began life as an anti-Islam group morphed into a fascist street movement. While the majority of EDL supporters were not fascists, the vast majority of its leadership had links to previous or existing fascist groups.

UAF's work over the previous years had put it in a position where it could respond swiftly to both these developments. A mass demonstration was organised outside the BNP's "Red, White and Blue" annual rally in the Derbyshire countryside that year (a rally that Griffin had explicitly modelled upon Le Pen's "Bleu-Blanc-Rouge" fete). Thousands of anti-fascist protesters blockaded the routes into the BNP event, effectively shutting it down for a day. The publicity this action gained sent a message out that mass resistance to the BNP was both necessary and possible.

At the same time UAF started organising counter-demonstrations to oppose EDL attempts to target mosques and Muslim communities up and down the country. At the heart of this strategy was an insistence that it was vital to mobilise against the fascists and a belief that the streets should not be ceded to racist gangs without any visible or active opposition.

The initial results of these counter-demonstrations were mixed. In some cases, such as Harrow and Birmingham, united demonstrations consisting of Muslim youths, the left and the wider community successfully chased the EDL off the streets. In others, such as Stoke-on-Trent, the counter-demonstrations were much smaller, and the EDL were allowed to run rampant through the streets attacking Asians and anyone else who stood in their way.

Again these tactical shifts proved controversial among some sections of the left. Hope not Hate, an anti-fascist organisation with strong connections to right wing sections of the Labour Party in particular, argued strongly against demonstrations and rallies against the fascists. It focused instead on mostly futile appeals to the authorities to act against the EDL threat.

The media's response to the BNP's electoral breakthrough was similarly mixed. On the one hand, sections of the media offered the BNP a cloak of legitimacy. The BBC in particular invited Nick Griffin onto its flagship *Question Time* programme. On the other hand, UAF's key message—that despite appearances the BNP was still a Nazi and racist organisation—began to seep through into the mainstream. UAF responded to Griffin's *Question Time* appearance by announcing a demonstration outside the BBC studios. This received huge publicity on newspaper front pages and reinforced the growing sense that the BNP was under siege.

At the same time UAF continued its electoral work, building a strong anti-fascist coalition in the London borough of Barking and Dagenham, where the BNP had a dozen councillors. This coalition brought together socialist activists, local church groups, black community organisations and the local Labour Party. Campaigners went door to door in Barking in the local and general elections in May 2010, where Griffin was standing for parliament. In consequence Griffin crashed to third place and the BNP lost all 12 of its councillors. In 2011 UAF along with a local anti-BNP group organised a similar campaign in Stoke-on-Trent, which again wiped out a long-standing BNP presence on the local council.

These electoral defeats for the BNP at the hands of a mass, visible physical opposition to it threw the organisation into crisis. It was torn apart by faction fighting, purges and mass resignations and many of its members defected to the EDL.

### The EDL: fascists return to the streets

As the fascists' electoral fortunes collapsed, many of its activists responded by turning to the streets. The EDL started life as a motley crew of racists and football hooligans, with a network of fascists at its centre acting as its ideological and political organising force. Despite its claims to the contrary, many of the EDL's leading figures had a history of involvement with fascist organisations. Its leader Tommy

Robinson—real name Stephen Yaxley-Lennon—was a small businessman and former BNP activist from Luton.

UAF built up a consistent record of organising mass opposition to the EDL even in the face of bitter police harassment, as happened in Bolton in 2010. It also exposed the organisation's Nazi links, despite its frequent attempts to pose as a "peaceful" and legitimate protest movement concerned merely with "Islamic extremism".

Two counter-demonstrations organised by UAF and local community groups appeared to break the back of the EDL. The first was in Tower Hamlets and took place on 3 September 2011. UAF worked with local trade unionists and mosques in the borough to help build a 5,000-strong march against a proposed EDL assembly. Faced with this mass opposition the EDL abandoned its plans, with Robinson admitting to the media that it would have been a "suicide mission". Instead it marched to the edge of the borough and were turned away. The failure of the protest left the EDL demoralised and defeated.

The following year the EDL announced that it was going to march through the multiracial east London neighbourhood of Walthamstow on 1 September. Once again UAF played a key role in bringing together a coalition of anti-racists, trade unionists and mosques to oppose it. On the day the EDL only managed to put 200 supporters on the street. Meanwhile the anti-fascist protest numbered well over 4,000. They blocked the route of the EDL march, forcing the police to take the EDL down local side streets where they were attacked by local youth and anti-fascists. Under massive pressure the police forced the EDL to call off its demonstration. It was a rout and a vindication of the hard work anti-fascists had put in over years to build a united front that could respond quickly when put to the test.

In the immediate aftermath of the Walthamstow demonstration and in a moment of madness the EDL announced that it was going to return to the borough less than two months later on 27 October. Once again anti-fascists mobilised. Fearing a full-scale riot the police refused to let the EDL take to the streets. Instead a handful of EDL members were allowed to protest miles away outside parliament, while over 1,000 UAF supporters celebrated the defiant unity that had been achieved in Walthamstow.

*Say it Loud*

The EDL's failures in Tower Hamlets and Walthamstow appeared to mark its demise. The organisation turned in on itself. There were splits and mass defections and although it continued to announce marches, the numbers attending dwindled.

The situation changed dramatically after the murder of a British solider outside an army barracks in Woolwich, south London, on 22 May 2013. The EDL had previously announced plans for a demonstration in Newcastle on 25 May but anti-fascists had been confident that the turnout would not be big. Indeed it was rumoured that Robinson himself was so demoralised that he would not bother attending. In the event, the murder of Drummer Lee Rigby gave both the EDL and BNP a fillip. They latched on to the fact that the two black men arrested at the scene with knives and blood on their hands were purporting to act in the name of Islam.

That evening Robinson turned up with dozens of supporters in Woolwich to rampage through the streets. Three days later the Newcastle demonstration attracted up to 1,500, outnumbering the 1,000-strong anti-fascist mobilisation. Two days later, despite the efforts of anti-fascists, up to 1,000 EDL supporters were able to march down Whitehall in central London to the Cenotaph. Meanwhile Griffin arrived in Woolwich to lay flowers at the makeshift shrine to Lee Rigby. He claimed that this was not a political intervention and that he was simply paying his respects as the MEP for the constituency in which Lee Rigby's family lived, but within days the BNP had announced that it would march in Woolwich on 1 June. UAF immediately responded by announcing that it would organise a counter-demonstration.

The police refused to allow the Nazis to march and instead directed that they should assemble in Westminster where they would be allowed to lay a wreath at the Cenotaph. Again anti-fascists announced a counter-demo. The BNP was able to muster less than 100 supporters who remained cowered behind police lines as 1,000 anti-fascists blockaded their path. Elsewhere on the same day, in over 30 towns and cities, EDL protests were comprehensively outnumbered by anti-fascists.

The Help for Heroes military charity, whose T-shirt Lee Rigby was photographed wearing, announced that it would refuse to accept money raised by the EDL. A more alarming development was the dramatic increase in Islamophobic attacks. In the week after Lee Rigby's death the group Tell Mama: Measuring Anti Muslim Attacks announced a 15-fold increase in such incidents compared to the previous year. There were reports of Muslim women having their veils ripped off and being punched, and an Islamic centre in Muswell Hill, north London, was burned to the ground. The words EDL were daubed on the wreckage and its supporters blogged in celebration and suggested that mosques should be similarly targeted during Friday prayers. Lee Rigby's family issued a heartfelt plea that his "friends' different cultures and religions made no difference to Lee". They proceeded to state that "Lee would not want people to use his name as an excuse to carry out attacks against others".[12]

The events of May 2013 serve as a warning that anti-fascists can never rest on our laurels. There have frequently been times when fascist groups have been down but it does not follow that they are out for the count. As long as the threat remains it is vital that we mobilise and cement our unity in the most effective way.

### What about UKIP?

Like other right wing populist parties, UKIP is not a fascist party which seeks to smash working class organisation or democratic institutions. Nor does it seek to build a street army. It began life in the early 1990s as a right wing split from the Tory party representing those British capitalists whose interests lay outside the European Union. Nigel Farage, its long-term leader, was educated at public school and made a fortune in the City, while treasurer Stuart Wheeler was educated at Eton and Oxford and worked for the derivatives trading firm IG Group.

Arguably therefore, these were men who should be held to account for the economic crisis that gripped the country after 2008. Instead of admitting any culpability however, at the 2010 general election these men proposed a flat rate of income tax and a reduction in public spending to 1997 levels with the loss of 2 million public sector jobs. In short, their solution was misery for ordinary working people.

*Say it Loud*

Thus their public focus is on nationalism and xenophobia. At a parliamentary by-election in the Sussex constituency of Eastleigh in March 2013 UKIP ran a viciously racist campaign scapegoating Bulgarians and Romanians. It was claimed that millions of people from these countries were preparing to flood into the country taking jobs, claiming benefits and putting a squeeze on public services once EU border controls were lifted in 2014. Its candidate won 23.9 percent of the vote, taking second place behind the Liberal Democrats who were defending what had previously been a fairly safe seat. It is widely believed that had Farage, by far UKIP's dominant personality, stood, he would have claimed the party's first Westminster seat. Two months later UKIP consolidated its vote in county council elections, increasing its number of councillors from just eight in 2009 to 147.

More important than the votes and number of seats gained was the effect that UKIP's rise had upon the wider political climate. In essence, the centre of debate was dragged to the right as all the mainstream parties rushed to ramp up their anti-immigrant rhetoric. This in turn provides a boost to those even further to the right who argue that they are the most consistent opponents of immigration and that they can provide a more thoroughgoing solution.

## Why fascism is different

Ever since Benito Mussolini and his fascists took over the Italian state in 1922 and Adolf Hitler's Nazi Party was handed control of the German state in 1933 socialists have attempted to understand the political phenomenon of fascism and Nazism. What distinguishes fascism from other forms of dictatorship is the methods it deploys, its ultimate political goal and the social base of the movement.

Of course racism and anti-Semitism are profoundly important to fascists. They use racism to hold their supporters together and create a scapegoat for discontent. But the main aim of fascism is not restricted to the annihilation of one racial group within society. For example, Mussolini's Blackshirts did not use anti-Semitism to build their organisation. Since Mussolini, however, fascist parties have increasingly used racism as a way of gaining support. The victims vary from country to country. In Hitler's Germany the main target was the Jews; in Hungary today it is the Roma.

However, there is much more to fascism than racist ideology. Its primary aim is to destroy working class organisations and democracy, and to install a dictatorship. The Russian revolutionary Leon Trotsky argues:

> Fascism is not merely a system of reprisals, of brutal force and of police terror. Fascism is a particular governmental system based on the uprooting of all elements of proletarian democracy within bourgeois society... To this end the physical annihilation of the most revolutionary section of the workers does not suffice. It is also necessary to smash all independent and voluntary organisations, to demolish all the defensive bulwarks of the proletariat, and to uproot whatever has been achieved during three quarters of a century by the Social Democracy and the trade unions.[13]

Fascism is different from other counter-revolutionary movements. It is a mass movement of the petty bourgeoisie—shopkeepers, doctors, low-level officials, foremen and the self-employed. This class occupies a contradictory position in society. When capitalism is relatively stable the petty bourgeoisie tends to tail either the main capitalist parties or the parties of the working class. But during extreme economic crises the petty bourgeoisie can look to create its own movement—a movement of despair.

In the 1920s and 1930s fascist parties built mass movements based on the middle class. Fascist movements use a dual strategy of an army of thugs to smash democratic and left forces using and creating a "respectable" political facade.

Fascists could not take power without the political and financial support of the ruling class. Hitler's NSDAP Nazi Party was bankrolled by business leader Fritz Thyssen and other sections of German capitalism. Mussolini's fascists were backed by the Pirelli brothers and other industrialists. The fascist parties offered the ruling class a solution in the form of a mass movement of counter-revolution.

Across Europe each anti-fascist group has had to develop tactics and methods to suit its own individual situation and circumstances.

But if there is one thing we can learn from the ANL and UAF campaigns that is the centrality of the united front.

## The importance of the united front

The united front tactic was first consciously developed by the Communist International in the years following the Russian Revolution. The Communist International was a worldwide revolutionary organisation whose conferences discussed political issues, strategy and tactics. The "Thesis on Comintern Tactics" of 1922 stated:

> The united front tactic is simply an initiative whereby Communists propose to join with all workers belonging to other political parties and groups, and unaligned workers, in a common struggle to defend the immediate, basic interests of the working class against the bourgeoisie. Every action, for even the most trivial everyday demand, can lead to revolutionary awareness and revolutionary education; it is the experience of struggle that will convince workers of the inevitability of revolution and the historic importance of communism.[14]

Later Trotsky further developed the theory of the united front tactic, which he saw as the central weapon in the fight against fascism in the 1930s. To see why, we have to look at what happened in the case of Germany in this period.

Hitler and his Nazi Party polled just 2.6 percent of the vote in the German general election of 1928. The two main parties of the left were far stronger. In the same election the combined vote of the social democratic SPD (the equivalent of Britain's Labour Party) and the Communist Party (KPD) was over 40 percent. Votes alone underestimate the strength of the left—the SPD had a million members and the KPD up to 60,000.[15]

Two years later the German economy was in ruins as the worldwide slump hit. It was the equivalent of Greece today. Industrial output fell by half, public sector jobs were decimated and the official unemployment figure reached over 3 million, though some historians estimate that the true total was closer to 6 million, 40 percent of the workforce.

From nowhere Hitler's Nazis became a major political force. They gained 18.3 percent of the vote in 1930 and 37.4 percent in the July 1932 elections. This was the highest vote they achieved and by the November 1932 elections it had fallen to 33.1 percent. But just like Golden Dawn and Jobbik, Hitler's Nazis were not primarily an electoral machine. The Nazis built a terrifying organisation that attacked democratic organisations and Jews. They had over 1 million members and a private army of 400,000 stormtroopers. They also had the support of some major sections of German capitalism.

The combined vote of the SPD and KPD was greater than that of the Nazis in every free election except July 1932. But, as Trotsky wrote in 1931, you cannot judge the balance of forces by votes alone:

> The main strength of the fascists is their strength in numbers. Yes, they have received many votes. But in the social struggle, votes are not decisive. The main army of fascism still consists of the petty bourgeoisie and the new middle classes... On the scale of electoral statistics, 1,000 fascist votes weigh as much as 1,000 Communist votes. But on the scales of revolutionary struggle 1,000 workers in one big car factory represent a force 100 times greater than 1,000 petty officials, clerks, their wives and their mothers in law. The great bulk of fascists consist of human dust.[16]

But there was one massive problem—the two main left parties failed on a national and local level to unite against the Nazis in the workplaces and on the streets. They did not come together to campaign against the Nazis during the elections.

The SPD leadership refused point blank to work with the KPD. One leading member argued, "We have our methods of combating the NSDAP, the KPD have theirs...we do not need them".[17] The fact was the SPD leadership was totally committed to working through parliament and the state institutions. At the start of 1933 the SPD leaders even accepted Hitler's appointment as chancellor on the grounds that it was carried out in a constitutional manner. While the leadership of the SPD did not want to confront Hitler other than through the ballot box, that was not the case with very large sections of the SPD members.

The problem with the KPD was not its failure to confront the

Nazis. Its members regularly fought them on the streets. The problem was that it adopted an approach that made it impossible to unite in struggle with the SPD. In line with the "third period" policy imposed on Communists everywhere by Joseph Stalin the KPD branded the SPD and not the Nazis as the main enemy. It even called the SPD "social fascists". This disastrous policy cut the KPD off from the SPD.

There were massive differences between the politics of the reformist SPD and the revolutionary spirit of the KPD. No one should underestimate the difficulties of working together to beat a common enemy; after all some in the SPD leadership authorised the murder of two of Germany's most brilliant Marxists and founders of the KPD, Rosa Luxemburg and Karl Liebknecht, in 1919. Yet despite those ideological differences and personal hatreds, it was imperative that those forces came together. After all, when Hitler sent the left to the concentration camps he did not distinguish between KPD and SPD members.

The failure to unite the two wings of the left in a common struggle against the Nazis enabled Hitler to drive through the middle. In a series of articles about the events in Germany, Trotsky argued, "Worker communists, if fascism comes to power it will ride like a terrific tank over your skulls and spines. Your salvation lies in merciless struggle. Only a fighting unity with Social Democratic workers can bring victory."

Unity, Trotsky urged, should include all those prepared to back a struggle: "The policy of the united front has as its task to separate those who want to fight from those who do not." That did not mean burying the differences between those who wanted to reform the system and those who wanted to topple it. It meant agreeing to fight round one issue while continuing to argue their positions. Trotsky summed it up: "March separately but strike together! Agree only on how to strike, who to strike and when to strike".[18]

Tragically that never happened. The result was undoubtedly the greatest defeat of the working class in history, one that saw six million Jews and a further 6 million Russians, Poles, Gypsies and trade unionists exterminated by the Nazis.

Events are fast moving, the situation is not yet as serious as

Germany in the early 1930s, but as the Greek prime minister warned, "a whiff of Weimar Germany style social collapse" is taking place in Greece. That means it is vital we argue for unity in the fight against the threat of the far-right in Europe. While it does not mean dropping our political principles it does require everyone to bring together different political forces—trade unions, faith and community groups—to build the widest possible campaigns against the rise of fascist organisations.

But that is not enough. We have to be clear that fascism is not an aberration of capitalism. It is a product of the system, a system that in times of crisis has been prepared to unleash the monster of fascism against working class people. The fight against fascism is an intrinsic part of the wider fight for a society which has no place for exploitation and oppression.

## CHAPTER 7

# Lessons from America

**Yuri Prasad**

MORE THAN any other country in the world, the US has seen the various strategies for defeating racism tested on a mass scale. Mass movements against racism have developed ever since the establishment of racist Jim Crow laws at the turn of 19th century, each characterised by differing approaches to the problem. This short sweep of a number of key battles shows the strengths and shortcomings of the approaches, while offering some valuable insights for all those engaged in the fight today.

### The radical roots of civil rights: How the Communist Party fought segregation during the depression

Communist Party activists in the US waged a war against racial segregation during the 1930s Great Depression. In the teeth of brutal opposition they helped build a multi-racial workers' movement that aimed to smash the divide and rule policies of the bosses—and in the process break the prejudices of white workers. Nowhere was the battle fiercer than in the Deep South—the states that had formed the slave-owning Confederacy during the US Civil War of 1861-65. The vast majority of black people were forced into the lowest paid jobs or to scratch a living as tenant farmers.

As chapter 1 has shown, the Southern ruling class were terrified by the political radicalism and unity that developed between black and white after the Civil War. They knew that the only way a rich minority of landlords and merchants could maintain their rule over a poor majority was to divide them. In the 1890s the Populist Party led a movement of poor farmers of all races in a challenge to the privileged few. Its electoral success scared the rich and they responded in the only way they knew how—with vicious racism. They first disenfranchised most black farmers, along with many poor whites, and from 1900 onwards they instituted Jim Crow, a system of legal segregation that rigidly divided every aspect of life. Legal racism was backed up by the paramilitary terror of the Ku Klux Klan.

All whites were encouraged to think of themselves as superior, despite the fact that the racial divisions among workers and farmers helped to keep poor whites in poverty. The result was pitifully weak union organisation and low wages for the poor—while the rich enjoyed big profits and unchallenged power.

Southern rulers presented their society as unchanging but from the First World War onwards big changes began to sweep the land. The war massively increased the demand for coal, iron and steel—and all sorts of finished goods. Cities desperate for labour sucked in workers from the countryside, while the military demanded that millions of young men of all races join the fight in Europe. The first stirrings of a revolt at home began soon after black soldiers began to return from the bloody battlefields of Europe where they had been told they were fighting for democracy. Now back at home they were greeted with hostility, scarcity and brutal racism. But their return also coincided with an event that was to transfix newly radicalising black workers and farmers—the Russian Revolution of 1917.

Radicals from all over the world were encouraged to travel to Russia and see the new society at first hand. Among the hundreds of Americans who made the trip in the early 1920s were a handful of black activists. What they experienced there was to change their lives forever.

Lovett Fort-Whiteman, who became the first US-born black member of the Communist Party, was astounded by what he believed was "the first state in the history of the world which had actually solved the problem of racial discrimination".[1] For Black Americans used to strict segregation—particularly where friendship and romance were concerned—Russia was a revelation. Homer Smith recalled: "If a Negro was standing in line at a shop, some Russian was sure to tug him by the arm and lead him to the front of the line. If it was a matter of a dance with a Russian girl, a Russian man would always give way".[2]

And the respect for African-American comrades was carried into the organisation back in the US. Black Communist Angelo Herndon wrote, "We were called comrades without condescension or patronage. Better yet, we were treated like equals and brothers".[3] Another recruit, Hosea Hudson, was impressed because Communists spoke to people at the bottom of the heap. He said, "This low class of people was the ones the police was killing what nobody saying nothing about. Outcasts! When the Party come out, these people were somebody. You took these people and made leaders of them".[4]

The Russian revolutionaries believed that African-Americans would form the vanguard of the coming American revolution and the newly founded US Communist Party prioritised recruiting black workers. Communists established themselves in major Northern cities. They made inroads in the Harlem district of New York, the capital of Black America. But most black people lived in the South at the time, and the Communists knew they would have to recruit there. Unfortunately, the new party had few roots in the South and little understanding of its traditions of resistance—or of the terror that would be unleashed against them there.

Their first major test came in 1929 in Gastonia, North Carolina, when the Communist-run National Textile Workers Union called a strike of around 2,000 workers. The town was famed for its mills and terrible working conditions. Communists organised integrated meetings with black strikers speaking—at a time when mainstream unions barely allowed black workers to join. As picket line battles raged, bosses forced thousands of strikers from company-owned homes into "tent cities". Soon more party organisers, black and white, were sent from New York to help the struggle. Bosses understood the threat. Not only were the Communists out for better wages, but also they wanted to break the segregation that served the rich so well.

Company police broke up protests and meetings with clubs, while organisers were targeted with bullets. Striking Communist Ella Mae Wiggins was killed when a group of men jumped out of a car and began shooting. Wiggins was white but chose to live in a black area. The crime was committed in daylight with more than 50 witnesses. Yet five people charged with her murder were acquitted after less than 30 minutes of deliberation. Although the strike was eventually defeated, the knowledge that black and white workers could strike together, even in the South, spread like wildfire. The story of black Communist Otto Hall, who was helping to organise the dispute, was retold countless times. White strikers drove Otto away from a police-inspired mob in the boot of their car. Everyone knew that if the car had been stopped the whites would have been killed too.

The lesson that white workers could be broken from racism—providing no concessions were made to it—was repeated at meetings across the US. Excitement at the revival of an inter-racial workers' movement acted as a recruiting sergeant for the newly-formed party and attracted many into its ranks. Soon the handful of Northern black Communists who had started work in the late 1920s was supplemented by dozens of native Southerners, black and white. They were well schooled in how to answer what were then difficult questions. William Dunne recalls that the first question many would ask a white Communist was, "Would you want your daughter to marry a nigger?" Dunne would reply, "That will be her affair, not mine. But one thing you can rest assured of—I would rather that she jump into a lake than to marry such a yellow-bellied Negro-hater like you".[5]

The Gastonia strike had tested the party but it was the campaign for the Scottsboro Boys that would be the making of it. Nine young black men, aged 13 to 21, were falsely accused and convicted of rape of two white women on a freight train in Alabama in 1931. As soon as news of the arrests spread large groups of white men assembled to "defend their women's honour"—code for lynching any black man who has stepped out of line. The authorities rushed a trial before an all-white jury, knowing a guilty verdict was little more than a formality. Legal lynching of this kind was common and few escaped Southern justice.

In this atmosphere the mainstream anti-racist organisation, the moderate National Association for the Advancement of Colored People (NAACP), initially refused to provide the Scottsboro Boys with lawyers for their appeal. They did not want to be associated with a case that could bring their respectable name into disrepute. But from the very beginning the Communists saw things differently.

This case was a chance to expose Southern racism to the world and build a multiracial defence campaign. A Communist newspaper in the South declared, "There can be no such thing as a 'fair trial' of a Negro boy accused of rape in an Alabama court. Anyone who thinks otherwise is a fool".[6]

Lawyers from the Communist-backed International Labour Defence (ILD) quickly came to their aid and helped spark an international campaign for their release. The ILD's strategy was "to give the Boys the best available legal defence in the capitalist courts, but at the same time to emphasise that the Boys can only be saved by the pressure of millions of workers, coloured and white, behind the defence in the courts".[7]

Communists organised protests across the country but the campaign centred on the cities of the North, where they had started to build a presence in black communities and where it was possible to organise without the constant threat of the KKK. In Harlem the party toured the Scottsboro Boys' families around the black churches and to meetings dominated by NAACP activists that latterly adopted the campaign. When they took to the streets the police battered them. The sight of bloodied, largely white socialists helped seal the Communists' reputation as genuine allies of black workers. After many years of campaigning charges for four of the nine were dropped, and none faced the death penalty. The campaign had been vital to keeping them alive.

Communists took their hard-won reputation as anti-racists into the continuing battles to unionise workers and into the fight against poverty and segregation everywhere, but nowhere more than Harlem. For almost everyone there the Great Depression was a catastrophic experience. The economic crisis took a more concentrated form than in the rest of the country as a huge rise in joblessness and evictions led to destitution. The unemployment rate for blacks throughout the depression was up to three times the rate for whites in New York. But workers and the poor were not the only ones affected—the black middle class also lost much of its limited toehold. The result was a growing radicalisation that had a strong black nationalist flavour, and which included the rapid growth of Marcus Garvey's United

Negro Improvement Association (UNIA). UNIA encouraged a brand of race loyalty that cut against the Communists' strategy of inter-racial class struggle. For example, they organised pickets outside white-owned shops in Harlem to demand that white workers be sacked and replaced by black workers. Garvey and his followers believed that the only solution to racism in America was to leave and found a new black-only colony in Africa.

Though theirs was still a largely white organisation the Communists threw themselves into campaigns dominated by black separatist groups and by force of political argument, audacity, and sometimes sheer bravery they steadily recruited more black members until they were an undeniable force within the black community. Many of those who joined had been members of, or were greatly influenced by, nationalist organisations. They became convinced of the Communist approach when they saw the party's theory applied in practice.

For example, when Communists were faced with the "Don't buy where you can't work" campaign they decided to intervene, despite its demands. Instead of insisting that white workers be sacked, Communists would demand that black workers be hired in addition. When the Communist strategy won results, both workers and anti-racism campaigners scored a victory. When, after the rise of fascism in Italy, black nationalists attacked Italian-American traders, Communists formed a massive march against fascism with a hundreds-strong delegation of Italian workers at its head. Harlem's black nationalists were stunned to hear Italian Communists' chants of "Death to Mussolini", but crowds on the side of the march did nothing but cheer. The black newspaper, the *Amsterdam News*, recorded, "When white workers march in such numbers in such cordiality through a Negro neighbourhood it is something for Negroes to think very deeply about".[8]

The huge potential of the party was shown in the mid-1930s, as fascism grew in Europe and many in the US drew comparisons between the Nazis and the racist South. Communists were only too happy to make the link as the growth of fascism also posed a threat to Stalin's recently entrenched regime in Russia.

*Say it Loud*

But the control of the party by Russia was to prove its undoing. The Communist international bureau, the Comintern, first pushed for a global popular front strategy, which watered down criticism of capitalist governments in Europe and America in the search for new allies against Nazi Germany. In the US the strategy often blunted the party's militant edge, though it did offer limited protection from the constant threat of imprisonment that party organisers faced, particularly in the South.

But in 1939 Russia's leaders decided that their security would be best served by a treaty with Germany. They instructed Communist parties around the world to conduct an about turn. Now the main danger was deemed to be imperialist war with Germany, not fascism at home or abroad. The popular front against racism was suddenly dropped, and almost overnight much of the respect that the party had carefully nurtured over almost two decades was lost. Nevertheless, the victories that Communists had helped win in America did usher in a new era—a fact that would only become clear after the end of the Second World War in 1945.

### The birth of the civil rights struggle

The civil rights movement that emerged in the mid-1950s marked the return of anti-racism in the US after the dormant years of the Second World War. Once again war had seen millions of black Americans fight for democratic freedoms abroad that most were denied at home, including in armed forces that maintained segregation until long after the war's end.

Conditions were worst in the Deep South. In the rural communities it was difficult for poverty stricken sharecroppers to resist the combined pressure of the landlords, the law and the Ku Klux Klan. But the changes that began in the wake of the First World War were accelerating. Almost 2.5 million made the move to the cities in the 1940s and 1950s, largely joining the ranks of the urban working class. In 1910 57 percent of all black men and 52 percent of all black women were farmers and only a sixth of the black population worked in manufacturing. By 1960 38 percent of blacks were industrial workers and just 8 percent worked on farms.[9]

But for most, the move to the cities did not mean any lessening of racism. In the mines, the steel plants and the huge cotton mills of the South black workers found they were restricted to the most menial, dirty and worst paid jobs. Southern states guarded against democratic protest by restricting voting rights for blacks and ensuring that all-white police handed out the roughest justice to those who seemed not to know their place. Things were little better in the North. Millions had made their way to Chicago, Detroit, New York and Los Angeles, lured by the prospect of well-paid work and escape from the prejudice of the South, only to find themselves in monotonous and back breaking jobs by day and dumped in ghetto housing by night. Here it wasn't the law that prevented a black worker from eating in a good restaurant; it was lack of money. Between 1950 and 1960 the average non-white family income in a Northern city was 63 percent of that of the average white family.[10]

These conditions might have led to a renewal of the struggles of the 1930s but the Communist Party that played such a crucial role then was by now a spent force. The twists and turns of its policy on fascism had disorientated even its core membership but that was now compounded by the onset of a Cold War between Russia and America. Washington politicians, led by Senator Joseph McCarthy and the secret services, ran a witch-hunt against US Communists and the left in general, that led most radicals to hide or even abandon their politics. For more than a decade the era of strikes and street confrontations over segregation seemed like a distant memory.

The gap was filled by a struggle that centred on the courts. The NAACP launched a series of legal battles aimed at banning segregation and winning voting rights in the South. The most famous of these was the 1954 Brown vs Board of Education of Topeka, which outlawed the "separate but equal" schools policy that predominated. But the pace of change was slow and even Supreme Court decisions took years to be enacted, if they were ever enacted at all. In 1955 judges insisted that Southern schools should be integrated "with all deliberate speed". Yet ten years later more than 75 percent of schools districts there remained segregated.

The Southern ruling class responded to the legal challenges with a programme of "Massive Resistance", involving both legal and illegal tactics. Faced with a Supreme Court judgement instructing them to desegregate their schools, they endorsed vicious racist protest pickets, which on occasion forced the federal government to send in troops to uphold the law.

Impatience among black people at a grassroots level meant that the slow pace of change would not be tolerated for much longer. The changing class character of black people fed into a new spirit—one that refused to put up with many of the injustices their parents and grandparents had endured. In June 1953 black people in the city of Baton Rouge, Louisiana, organised a boycott after the local bus company refused to end the practice of forcing blacks to take only what seats were available at the back of the bus. In December 1955 the arrest of Rosa Parks in Montgomery, Alabama, for refusing to give up her seat to a white passenger, sparked a year-long boycott on a much bigger scale. She is often portrayed as someone who acted spontaneously, without thinking, but Parks was a longstanding activist who had even spent time in the company of Communists during the Scottsboro Boys campaign and with the left radicals at the Highlander Folk School. She said of herself, "I had almost a life history of being rebellious about being mistreated because of my colour".[11]

Local reverend 26 year old Martin Luther King shot to prominence as the leader of the 40,000-strong Montgomery boycott. The bus boycott tactic he led was repeated in Tallahassee, Florida, and then in Birmingham, Alabama. King was soon coordinating struggles with his Southern Christian Leadership Conference (SCLC). The new leaders of the civil rights struggle were young and prepared to use tactics that the old, more conservative leaders baulked at. One of the participants in Montgomery wrote, "For the first time police... were confronted by Negroes who acted like men... All the threats which had been used to suppress the Negro had lost their potency".[12] But even the new radicals began by thinking that segregation in the South was an aberration that Washington liberals would soon act against if only it were brought to their attention. King later spoke of the campaign in Montgomery, saying:

Feeling that our demands were moderate, I had assumed that they would be granted with little question: I had believed that the privileged would give up their privileges on request. This experience, however, taught me a lesson. I came to see that no one gives up his privileges without strong resistance. I saw further that the underlying purpose of segregation was to oppress and exploit the segregated, not simply to keep them apart.[13]

The church was to play a central role in the movement over the next decade. It was both a religious and a social centre. Ministers, who were employed by their churches, could act with a degree of independence few other black people could match. The biblical parables that spoke of long suffering people ultimately being rewarded by god chimed with many who knew that the fight against segregation would be fiercely contested. Christian doctrines that praised the righteous act of "turning the other cheek" when struck by an oppressor fed the non-violent strategy that came to dominate the struggle for the next ten years.

According to Chris Harman, non-violence fitted the interests of "the middle class which did not want massive social confrontation... but it also seemed to fit the situation that Southern blacks found themselves in. As a poor and unarmed minority, they did not feel they had much chance if it came to physical warfare".[14] Many in the movement accepted the tactical need not to retaliate against racist violence even if they did not necessarily accept the principle.

King's stress on non-violence also functioned as a means of broadening the movement. When he talked of the movement wearing oppressors down with its capacity to suffer he was trying to reassure liberal whites, especially those of the middle class in the North, that they had nothing to fear from the people he led. They could press Washington to grant reforms without risking massive confrontations. But at a national level the US ruling class was in a quandary as to how to respond to the growing pressure for civil rights. On the world stage, it could see that the question of racism badly tarnished its image with the many countries that were throwing off the yoke of colonialism, leaving them open to advances from communist Russia

*Say it Loud*

and China. And at home discontent among black people threatened to spill over into rebellion if nothing was done. But with racism such a cornerstone of American capitalism—and with the Democratic Party machine that ran the South absolutely determined to resist any change—any legislative moves against segregation by Washington would be deliberately small. As far as liberals were concerned, splitting the Democrats along North and South lines was to be avoided at all costs.

The Southern elite sensed hesitation, and King began to feel that only when faced with resistance to racism on a mass scale—the kind that could disrupt the normal functioning of the system and did not limit itself to what is acceptable to Washington—were the wealthy elite of the North and the big business owners in the South prepared to move against the more backward sections that ran the Southern states. As he noted:

> The enlightened white Southerners, who for years have preached gradualism, now see that even the slow approach finally has revolutionary implications. This realisation has immobilised the liberals and most of the white church leaders. They have no answer for dealing with or absorbing violence. They end in begging for retreat, lest things get out of hand and lead to violence.[15]

### The mass action phase

Moderates who hoped for a pause in the movement were to have their hopes dashed as instead the struggle suddenly escalated. On 1 February 1960 four black college students sat down at the "whites only" food counter of the local Woolworth store in Greensboro, North Carolina, and ordered lunch. They were refused service, as they knew they would be, but remained seated until the shop closed. They came back the next day, and the day after that, only now they were joined by 50 fellow students, including two whites. By April some 50,000 students joined the sit-in movement and a new phase of the civil rights movement was born.

A year after the sit-ins began came the Freedom Rides in which groups of black and white bus passengers would test the laws banning segregation on inter-state travel and facilities. Predictably the bi-racial group were met by violence as soon as they reached the South. White mobs burned buses and beat up riders while the racist police jailed blacks who dared sit down in whites-only sections of the bus depots. But as news of the attacks filled newspapers and TV screens, still more young people flocked to the movement.

The new wave of activism led to the foundation of the Student Non-violent Coordinating Committee (SNCC) and the revival of the Northern group, the Congress of Racial Equality (CORE), both of which were to play a crucial role as the radical wing of the struggle. Whereas King and the SCLC had once appeared as the left pole in the movement, they now marked the centre ground. But neither the SNCC's radical tactics, nor its revolutionary rhetoric, was matched by its politics. The legacy of the McCarthy period, which saw the Communists hounded out of public life, meant a widespread hostility to the radical left in general and Marxist ideas specifically. Instead their ideology drew upon a moral indignation at racism in the South and a reformist belief that segregation, and racism more generally, was an aberration of bourgeois democracy—and that the battle to win equal rights for all was the way to fulfil the American Dream.

Despite this, a new dynamic took hold whereby the SNCC pressurised King into ever more dramatic actions, and King in turn pressurised President Kennedy in Washington for more protection and legislation. While this strategy appeared to be getting results there was little need for the SNCC to look for different politics. But the year 1963 became a turning point after which many began to question the very ideals that movement had championed.

Between autumn 1961 and spring 1963, some 20,000 men, women and children were arrested. In 1963 alone another 15,000 were imprisoned. Above all else, two significant actions during that year stand out—the desegregation campaign in Birmingham, Alabama, and the March on Washington.

Historian and activist Manning Marable wrote that Birmingham represented "the citadel of white supremacy":

> No black resident was ever secure from the wide sweep of white terrorism—institutional and vigilante. White police officers in the

city casually picked up black women pedestrians and raped them at gun point. Throughout the 1950s, black homes and churches were bombed... Every aspect of cultural, social and economic life in the town was strictly segregated.[16]

King decided upon a campaign in Birmingham in an effort to create a national crisis that would bring the issue of segregation to national and even global prominence. It would be the biggest action of the movement yet and he needed thousands of working class citizens, not just students and activists, to turn out and defy the police. Marable records the effect of his appeal:

King openly castigated the black preachers who had ignored the demonstrations. "I'm tired of preachers riding around in big cars, living in fine homes, but not willing to take their part in the fight. If you can't stand with your people, you are not fit to be a leader!" ... [Ralph] Abernathy rose to his feet, asking the congregation, "Who'll volunteer to go to jail with me and Martin...?" Men, women and children surged forwards, hands upraised, tears in their eyes, singing and praying.[17]

Over the following weeks TV cameras filmed hundreds of protesters being clubbed, water-cannoned and arrested. Then on 2 May, 6,000 children marched and Birmingham let loose their vicious police dogs as they knelt to pray; 959 children were arrested and jailed. "Across the world, humanity was repulsed by the sickening spectacle of American racism, the reality of white democracy," wrote Marable.[18]

Massive reaction to the open display of Southern brutality forced Kennedy to intervene and get prisoners released. Behind the scenes he pressurised the city business leaders and authorities into agreeing a plan to desegregate public facilities, and not long afterwards his administration announced a new civil rights bill that would outlaw segregation throughout the nation. It was a massive victory for King, but in the process of massing the forces necessary he had brought a new actor on to the stage—the urban working class.

As movement historian Jack Bloom notes:

When King appealed to all the members of the black community to participate, they heeded his call, but then would not be controlled. He had brought into motion the most subdued strata of the population. When they began moving, it was difficult to stop them; they had many of their own scores to settle and would not easily be put aside. One of the ironic results of King's Birmingham campaign was that the great victory for his non-violent strategy ended in the first of the urban riots.[19]

The Birmingham campaign had forced the Kennedy administration to come off the fence over civil rights but they were not prepared to be dictated to by King and the movement. Instead they sought to incorporate the struggle and so determine its tactics and goals. Bobby Kennedy, the Attorney General in his brother's administration, went so far as to call a meeting of CORE and SNCC leaders in his office, at which he told them, "Why don't you guys cut all that shit, freedom riding and sitting in shit, and concentrate on voter registration. If you do that, I'll get you tax-free status."

When a march on Washington was announced for August 1963, radicals in the movement hoped that it would be a mass protest that would paralyse the capital. Airports and railway stations would be closed, schools and universities would shut and businesses would put up shutters as hundreds of thousands of protesters showed their impatience with the slow pace of change. But under the direction of King and white liberals around Kennedy, the march became a celebration and endorsement of the pending civil rights bill. More than 250,000 people, black and white, joined the rally in front of the Lincoln Memorial, which was broadcast live on TV. Speaker after speaker talked of their love for their country, and how great reform was now just around the corner. One activist, John Lewis of the SNCC, wanted to strike a different note by denouncing the Democrats' support for civil rights as "too little, too late", but he was warned to tone down his speech or be taken off the list of speakers.

Now, instead of the left pole of the movement pushing King and he in turn pushing Kennedy, the pressure was coming from the other direction—the Democrats were silencing the radical wing of the movement. This became obvious the following year during the SNCC's Freedom Summer. Thousands of student activists risked their lives to go to the South as part of a massive voter registration drive a great many were injured or jailed—four activists and three Mississippi blacks were killed. In opposition to the racist Democrats in the South, they built a multi-racial alternative called the Mississippi Freedom Democratic Party. But when the national party held its convention in August 1964, it was the white racist Democrats who took all the seats. King and others pleaded with the younger activists to accept a poor compromise and not split the party as this would allow the hard right republicans to win the next election. The SNCC activists rejected the compromise and walked away bitterly disillusioned. They began to break with the common tactical position of the rest of the movement in two crucial areas—integration and non-violence. SNCC leaders increasingly blamed the influence of white liberalism, and those who accommodated to it, for blunting their movement. It wasn't long before they began arguing that whites should have no role in the anti-racist struggle. And, in the wake of the violence of Birmingham and the Freedom Summer, and the higher level of white "Massive Resistance" that followed the Civil Rights Act, the idea of armed self-defence gained a mass appeal.

Activists debated the issues for the next 18 months, in which time the fault lines seemed only to grow. The stage was set for a new phase of the struggle to begin. As Bloom notes, "The Birmingham campaign began the transition from a movement based in the black middle class, whose goal was civil rights, to one with a much broader base that fought under the slogan of 'Black Power'."[10]

## Malcolm X

By the mid-1960s many young veterans of the civil rights struggle were in the midst of a search for a new politics. Malcolm X electrified audiences all over the world with speeches that combined great eloquence, sharp wit and hard politics. He characterised "white American society" as an evil into which no black person should want to be assimilated, and he chastised all those who tried. Malcolm's attacks on the strategy of non-violence in the face of racist brutality initially isolated him from the burgeoning civil rights movement. However, as the South more often resorted to violence to resist change, Malcolm found a growing audience among many disillusioned activists and began to define a radical pole of opposition to King within the movement.

Yet the man who was to be the biggest influence on the coming Black Power phase of the movement would shortly be dead. Malcolm was assassinated as he rose to speak to a meeting in New York in February 1965. The son of Garveyite parents, Malcolm rose to prominence as a minister in the black separatist group, the Nation of Islam. He joined the Black Muslims, as they were known, while still a young man serving time in prison for a series of burglaries and possession of a firearm. Having converted he devoted himself to winning new converts by attacking American society for its racism and hypocrisy and easily found a large audience of black people disillusioned with mainstream religion and politics, especially among those pushed to the margins by drugs and poverty. His appeal was primarily to those trapped in the Northern ghettos, where segregation was supposedly outlawed but where most black people found themselves at the bottom of the pile. By the end of the 1950s he was the Nation of Islam's most famous member, preaching to audiences of thousands, and the organisation now had over 100,000 members.

Malcolm chastised all white people as racist "devils" and the Black Muslims rejected much that the civil rights movement stood for. It was against integration into white society, it was against any alliances with white politicians, and it was against the principle of non-violence. Malcolm said, "Be peaceful, be courteous, obey the law, respect everyone—but if someone puts his hand on you, send him to the cemetery".[21] Why should those campaigners who travel to the South to fight racism face the police and vigilantes unarmed, he asked.

But while the Black Muslims were known for their radical rhetoric, many felt their ban on political involvement meant they offered little by way of practical solutions to the problems of the ghettos. It was a criticism that stung Malcolm, who said, "Privately I was convinced that our Nation of Islam could be an even greater force in the American black man's overall struggle—if we engaged in more action," and, "It could be heard increasingly in the Negro communities: 'Those Muslims talk tough, but they never do anything, unless somebody bothers Muslims'."[22]

Malcolm's relationship with the Nation of Islam became strained as he urged greater involvement in the struggle, until in 1963 he was first suspended and then expelled for ignoring the leadership's instruction not to make a speech in which he pointedly refused to join the wave of mourning that greeted the assassination of President Kennedy. After leaving the Black Muslims, he embraced orthodox Sunni Islam and travelled to Mecca and to many of the countries that had recently won their freedom from European colonialism, where he was treated as though he was the leader of black America. His ideas about the world were to undergo a transformation as he found himself praying alongside Muslims with blond hair and blue eyes, and meeting the leaders of anti-colonial revolts who could not understand his contempt for whites. He returned to the US now determined to play a more active role in the fight against racism. Malcolm even said that he was prepared to work alongside whites who were genuinely committed to the fight against racism. But he was still scathing in his criticism of moderate civil rights leaders who talked of non-violence:

> [As] long as the white man sent you to Korea, you bled. He sent you to Germany, you bled. He sent you to the South Pacific to fight the Japanese, you bled. You bleed for white people. But when it comes time to seeing your own churches being bombed and little black girls be murdered, you haven't got no blood.[23]

In the last year of his life Malcolm grew increasingly radical and started to identify racism with capitalism. He remained a nationalist but one who believed in revolution and thought it possible that black people would work with other sections of the oppressed to achieve change. And, as the Harlem riot raged in 1964, he predicted that in the future America would be gripped by such a spirit.

Tragically, he was not to see how the growing rebellion in the ghettos of the North would feed a new wave of revolutionaries, who were no longer prepared to accept the strategy of non-violence or the limitations of alliances with the Democrats. Malcolm was gunned down by agents from the Nation of Islam who feared his popularity would outstrip their own, and in this they were completely correct.

## The ghetto rebellions and Black Power

While the students in the civil rights movement arrived at the idea of a separate black movement through a long process of disillusionment with white liberalism, in the Northern ghettos the process was sharper. Urban uprisings became a feature of the mid to late 1960s and marked a decisive shift of the struggle from the South to the North. In 1964 Harlem exploded against police racism and for the next few days there were pitched battles between black people of all ages and the overwhelmingly white police. That summer there were further clashes between black people and police in Rochester, Patterson, Jersey City, Elizabeth, Chicago and Philadelphia. Then in August 1965 Watts in Los Angeles exploded and over several days became the biggest urban disturbance in the US since 1943. Eventually the National Guard were called in and the death toll started to rise. In all, 34 people were killed and almost 4,000 people were arrested. Some $35 million in damage had been done. But the biggest conflicts were yet to come. In 1967 Newark and Detroit went up and the scale of the rebellion changed dramatically. Of Detroit, Chris Harman notes:

> With the "spontaneity" there was a high degree of improvised organisation. At one point a group of a hundred snipers—mainly blacks with military experience in Vietnam—had laid siege to a police station. The looting was not "random", but directed against stores whose owners were hated. And, for the first time, there was some involvement of whites alongside blacks; some of the looting was by integrated groups, and the police complained about the presence of "white terrorists" among the snipers.[24]

Harman concludes that Black Power was the slogan not just of student activists, "but of millions of black workers in the Northern cities".[25] Although seen by most as radical, the slogan carried contradictions at its heart. For the black youth fighting the police in

Watts, Black Power meant a collective challenge to the state—getting your own back on the police who oppressed you by pelting them with rocks and firebombs, and forming black organisations. But for the black businessman it could mean something very different, something more individualistic. Black Power for them meant more black ownership, more black representation, more black managers—in short, capitalism, but with a black face.

There was also a rise of cultural black nationalism which emphasised black people's African heritage. With slogans such as "Black is beautiful" the movement had a major impact on music, fashion and self-image. For example, it was responsible for the growing unpopularity of skin lightening creams and hair relaxing. But by de-emphasising politics, cultural nationalism also ran the risk of demobilising people by suggesting that embracing a black culture was in itself a way to fight racism.

This was the context in which Huey P Newton and Bobby Seale, two college students from Oakland, California, formed a new organisation in 1966 called the Black Panther Party for Self-Defense. They were firmly on the revolutionary wing of the Black Power movement and drew their inspiration from a range of sources. They were impressed by the civil rights movement's ability to mobilise large numbers but they found King's stress on non-violence and his demand for integration into "white society" too meek. The Panthers were more attuned to Malcolm X, specifically his ideas of revolution, and to his commitment to black self-defence against racism. The Panthers were also influenced by Maoism—the ideas developed by China's Communist leader Mao Zedong. Mao's strategy was an elitist one, which stressed the role of a self-proclaimed and committed revolutionary vanguard, but these ideas influenced many 1960s radicals who wanted an alternative to the Stalinism of the Soviet Union.

Together Seale and Newton drew up a ten-point programme for the Panthers. It included demands for an end to police brutality, the release of all black prisoners and exemption of black men from military service. It ended with a demand for "land, bread, housing, education, clothing, justice and peace—all power to the people".

Newton had studied law and knew that all US citizens had the right to bear arms. He and Seale decided that one of the first objectives of the Panthers would be to end police harassment in their community. They recruited and armed young men and women to "patrol the pigs"—following police patrols through the ghettos of Oakland.

The Panthers wore a uniform of black leather jackets, black trousers and blue shirts. After watching a film about the French resistance to the Nazis, Seale added a black beret. Not surprisingly, the state did not accept the right of the Panthers to patrol the police, let alone to do so with their own arms and uniform. In the spring of 1967 Assemblyman Don Mulford brought forward a bill to outlaw the carrying of loaded weapons. The Panthers responded by organising an armed march on the state capital. Seale recalled the day in his memoirs:

> On 2 May 1967 we went across the bridge to Sacramento with a caravan of cars. There were 30 brothers and sisters—20 of the brothers were armed... A lot of people were looking. A lot of white people were shocked, just looking at us. I know what they were saying: "Who in the hell are those niggers with guns".[26]

California's governor, Ronald Reagan, who was on the lawn of the state legislature, took one look and ran. In front of hundreds of reporters Seale read a proclamation that put the Panthers on the national map.

Within months of the protest the party grew from about 50 members to over 5,000, as new activists joined and started operations in towns and cities across the US. Eldridge Cleaver was among them. He had a concept of building a party from among the "brothers on the block", or what he sometimes called the "lumpen proletariat". He argued that those with the least to lose, those without jobs and commitments, were the section of society most open to revolutionary ideas, a concept borrowed from the revolutionary Frantz Fanon, whose book *The Wretched of the Earth* argued that oppressed people had a right to use violence against their oppressors.

The growth of the Panthers coincided with a wider radicalisation across US society. In 1967 over 100,000 joined a New York rally against the Vietnam War. The anti-war mood fed other demands—for black rights, for equality for women and for gay liberation. The connections were there to be made. Black people made up 13.5 percent of all enlisted army personnel and 22.4 percent of the war's casualties, but only 3.4 percent of the officers.[27] The Panthers differentiated themselves from other black nationalist organisations by making alliances with predominantly white, left wing groups such as Students for a Democratic Society and the Peace And Freedom Party. Any organisation that stated its opposition to capitalism and imperialism was a potential ally.

However, there was a weakness within the growing rebellion. There were very few sustained confrontations between US workers and their bosses in the 1960s. This reinforced the Panthers' emphasis on the most marginal sections of the black community, along with the minority of white students and committed white revolutionaries.

The problem with this approach was exposed when the US ruling class launched a violent crackdown on the Panthers. The group found that they had no mechanism to counter the violence of the state. The "brothers on the block" strategy had enabled the Panthers to find thousands of young people who were prepared to engage with revolutionary politics, but when it came to gun battles, it soon became clear that the state was much better armed. The Panthers' leadership largely overlooked the millions of black and white workers in factories, offices and mines, who had the power to hit US capitalism where it was most vulnerable. They regarded these organised workers as being both "enslaved" and at the same time bought off by the system. Newton argued, "We're exploited not only by the small group of the ruling class; we're oppressed, and repressed by even the working class Whites in the country".[28]

The Panthers' orientation on the "brothers on the block" was responsible for their success and their ultimate demise. Largely unemployed ghetto youth were often dependent on a mixture of casual work, welfare payments and sometimes petty crime, and this tends not to encourage collective organisation. The ghetto could be at the centre of political rage at racism and the system, but it could also be a place where people were at their most atomised, and where those around you are seen as potential competitors and enemies in the battle to survive.

Despite this weakness, the Panthers did enjoy considerable support. This was reinforced after 1968, when the party started a series of community programmes. To the armed resistance of "patrolling the pigs" they now added the notion of "serving the people", setting up feeding centres that provided breakfasts for up to 250,000 children a week. They also launched medical clinics and community controlled schools—all of which exposed the wilful neglect of the state.

In practice the twin strategies of "patrolling the pigs" and "serving the people" pulled in different directions. Armed conflict with the state pushed in a revolutionary direction, albeit an adventurist one, while feeding centres pushed in the direction of reformist community politics that sooner or later led to compromise with the state. For the time being the Panthers could appear to follow both strategies and continue to wield mass appeal. A nationwide poll conducted for *Time* magazine in 1970 revealed that 9 percent of the black population (about 2 million people) considered themselves to be "revolutionaries".[29] The *Wall Street Journal* asked black people in New York what they thought about the Panthers and were shocked at what they heard: "I dig the Panthers...they are not just advocating militancy; they're talking about economic and political power. Right now they are backing up what they preach, and that's why the man is coming down on them," said one interviewee.[30] The US establishment was terrified by the presence of armed groups of self-declared revolutionaries winning mass support at the height of the Cold War. FBI chief J Edgar Hoover labelled the Panthers "the greatest threat to internal security of the country".

When an unarmed Newton was shot in the stomach by police during a confrontation, many people were shocked but not surprised. During the clash a police officer was killed and Newton was sentenced to three years in prison. The battle to free Newton became one of the focal points for both the black liberation movement and the left across the US. Leading radical figures pledged their support. Actor Jane Fonda argued:

Revolution is an act of love. We are the children of revolution, born to be rebels. It runs in our blood... [The Panthers are] our revolutionary vanguard; we must support them with love, money, propaganda and risk.[31]

But despite widespread support for Newton and the Panthers, the state persecution continued. By late 1968 Eldridge Cleaver was on the run from the police and was ultimately forced into exile in Algeria. Seale was put on trial with a number of white radicals for allegedly starting a riot in Chicago—a case which saw him bound and gagged in the courtroom. The following year Chicago Panther leader Fred Hampton was shot dead by police while in his bed during a raid on the party offices there. In that year the police targeted every office of the party and 27 Panthers were killed—a further 749 were jailed or arrested. In 1969 another Panther leader, David Hilliard, made a speech in which he called President Richard Nixon a "motherfucker" and went on to say, "We will kill Richard Nixon. We will kill any motherfucker who stands in the way of our freedom." As a result Hilliard joined the long list of Panthers who found themselves on trial.[32] For a small revolutionary organisation, the loss of so many leaders and activists made life virtually impossible.

What remained of the Panthers, now led by Elaine Brown, sought to moderate their activities in order to avoid further losses. They directed ever more resources towards the community programmes and election campaigns. In practice the reformist strategy had won out over the revolutionary one. The Panthers had elicited enormous support but when the state moved to smash them, the organisation did not have the means to hit back, primarily because it had written off the potential of the organised working class. But not all revolutionaries who had grown up alongside the civil rights movement were to make the same mistake.

## DRUM

This spirit of Black Power and urban rebellion could not but help find an expression in America's factories—and the heart of industrial America, Detroit. The city which had seen one of the biggest urban uprisings in 1967 was now to be the centre of a new battle that took place on the car production lines. Groups of revolutionary black workers concluded that the state crackdown on the riots proved that such community revolts did not take full advantage of the specific power that the working class has at the point of production.

Until the 1960s many unions had helped keep black labour out of the industries it organised and out of their ranks. But by the end of the decade millions of black workers were members and they were demanding the right to proper representation in all types of jobs, access to promotion—and seats at the union leadership's table. The United Auto Workers union was regarded as one of the most progressive on issues of race but it had only one black member on its 26-person executive, and black candidates often found themselves blocked.

A crucial workplace struggle involved a group of black socialists on the Dodge car production line. They formed the Dodge Revolutionary Union Movement (DRUM) in mid-1968 with the aim of combining Black Power with workers' power. One worker even dedicated a poem to it:

> Deep in the gloom of the fire-filed pit
> Where the Dodge rolls down the line
> We challenge the doom while dying in shit
> While strangled by a swine...
> For hours and years with sweated tears
> Trying to break our chain...
> But we broke our backs and died in packs
> To find our manhood slain...
> But now we stand for DRUM's at hand
> To lead our freedom fight,
> And now till then we'll unite like men
> For now we know our might...
> And damn the plantations and the whole Dodge nation...
> For DRUM has dried our tears...
> And now as we die we have a different cry
> For now we hold our spears!
> UAW is scum...
> OUR THING IS DRUM!!![33]

Detroit was the home of car production in the US, with tens of thousands working on the production lines, day and night. One in four workers were black but 99 percent of foremen and 90 percent of skilled tradesmen were white. DRUM was formed to fight discrimination in and outside of the plant and was prepared to organise unofficial strikes to achieve its goals. The situation inside Dodge was ripe for an explosion and DRUM activists knew the same conditions existed in every other factory in the city. Before long there were major unofficial strikes and the movement spread from one car manufacturer to another until DRUM was able to form an umbrella group, the League of Revolutionary Black Workers.

The strength of the revolutionary unions when compared to those who organised solely in the community was that organised workers had more power to hit profits. Car production was hit every time workers downed tools and the companies were often forced to give in to demands. Not a single member of DRUM was shot, put on trial or jailed during the period the organisation existed. The revolutionary unions did not confine themselves to the car plants, but they had a clear idea of where their power lay. As league executive member John Watson said:

> In one factory we have 10,000 people who are faced with the same brutal conditions... When you go out into the community, the interests of the people...are going to be much more dispersed... Just in terms of expediency there are greater possibilities in the organisation of the plant... The kinds of action which can be taken [in the community] are not as effectively damaging to the ruling class as the kinds of actions which can be taken in the plant.[34]

But there were tensions between socialists and nationalists within the revolutionary union movement and the question of how and whether to relate to white workers was to show up weaknesses among both. Few among them believed that they should seek to organise white workers, even during the wildcat strikes. Many refused to even hand their leaflets to sympathetic white workers who had refused to cross their picket lines. This allowed the bosses to play divide and rule. It also allowed the main union, the UAW, to present itself as the one force that would represent everyone. As struggle spread across the car plants in the wake of a dip in production after 1969, many white workers were to display a militancy that took black radicals by surprise. At one General Motors plant 4,000 workers erected barricades during a major strike in 1970. And white workers were to strike alongside black workers against the victimisation of black activists in the very plants where the revolutionary union movement was strongest. Yet few in the ranks of the revolutionary union movement questioned the logic of organising black workers separately, even when they numbered less than half of the workforce.

A single example illustrates what might have been possible if the leadership of the movement had a different vision of the working class. The editor of *The Stinger*, issued by black auto workers at the Mack Avenue Chrysler plant in Detroit, explained:

> It is true we are fighting discrimination against black workers in the shop as one of the most important questions of our lives. But that isn't the only question. The reason many of the white workers in our shop also read—and even support—*The Stinger*, is that we are raising the question of inhuman conditions of all workers in production. Automation speed-up and the inhumanity of the company and the union bureaucrats is against workers as a whole. That is why *The Stinger* is fighting, and why white workers have told us they are glad we are distributing it.[35]

The radical movement in the plants began to decline from 1969 as the general level of militancy in the car industry fell. But the existence of DRUM and other organisations had forced the employers and the main unions to change some of their most racist policies out of fear that a similar rising would occur again and they marked a high point in the influence of revolutionaries upon the organised working class in the US.

The downturn in struggle inside the factories was matched outside them. The movement that had once put hundreds of thousands on the streets now appeared increasingly introverted and fragmented. The assassination of Martin Luther King in 1968 as he sought to organise striking garbage workers in Memphis and a new poor people's march on Washington was a sign for some that the radical phase of the movement had come to an end. A minority began to believe the only way to now secure reforms for black people was to fight from within the system, not against it.

**Black reform**

By the early 1970s the revolutionaries of the civil rights and Black Power eras found themselves stranded as the high tide of revolt receded. President Nixon's attempts to create a buffer between the state and the black urban poor led to money being channelled into the cities to bolster black businesses and the black middle class more generally, and also to new community programmes that sought to undermine those started by groups such as the Black Panthers. People who had entered politics out of a desire to bring about radical change were lured by the possibility of directing the growing federal government funds towards the poorest black communities.

The massive increase in the numbers of black people registered to vote during the 1960s led to an expansion of the number of black elected officials—one that continued to climb at an unprecedented rate. In March 1969 there were 994 black men and 131 black women who held office around the country. By May 1975 this figure had more than tripled, to 2,969 black men and 530 black women.[36] Yet the Southern states contained more than half of these new politicians. The battle was on to win the Northern cities which had been the site of the last decade of struggle.

Most of those seeking office and those actually elected were from the black middle class—doctors, lawyers, entrepreneurs and college professors—rather than the black working class. Together they began to plan a strategy to take over the running of the main cities. Organisations, such as the National Black Political Assembly, were formed as alliances of radicalised black business types and black nationalists. They hoped that by establishing new city administrations they would create an alternative centre of power in the US. Upon entering office, however, their dreams were to be cut down as financial crisis gripped national and local government. Soon cities that had recently celebrated the election of their first black mayors and the appointment of the first black chiefs of police found that, along with the rest of the country, funds had dried up and swingeing cuts were the order of the day. The promises made to the urban poor, black and white, quickly turned to dust and soon black unemployment in ghettos returned to the 50 percent mark. Meanwhile, the black elite found themselves a place in the boardrooms and exclusive clubs where the US ruling class plotted the country's future.

Confidence among black workers was hit by both the decline of the movement and the rapid erosion of union militancy as the recession took hold. Black political life, which for almost a decade seemed to be radicalising ever further to the left, seemed now to return to the centre and the Democratic Party, although this was much blacker than before. Those figures who had made their names in the movement now traded on them to win elections, knowing that the economic crisis meant they could make not a bit of difference to those who elected them. In such circumstances, the black separatists of the Nation of Islam, which had been marginal at best during the struggles of the late 1960s, began to make a return under the leadership of Louis Farrakhan—the man who had once declared that Malcolm X was "worthy of death". Yet somewhere beneath the surface the simmering rage that gave rise to the struggles of the 1930s, the 1950s and the 1960s remains. From time to time, usually following a police outrage, we can catch a glimpse of it as hundreds, sometimes thousands, spontaneously erupt against oppression.

The story of black resistance in the US is one that teaches us the centrality of class. It explains how the ruling class of the South used racism and segregation laws to divide opposition and maintain its rule. It also tells of how those divisions could be broken down in the huge class confrontations of the 1930s. The way in which reformers became revolutionaries in the fights against racism in the decades that followed confirms our analysis that racism is an intrinsic part of capitalism and cannot be legislated out of existence any more than it can be changed when confronted with moral good. But it also shows us that class divides exist even among people who share a similar oppression. The battles over strategy in the civil rights movement—and over the meaning of Black Power—were ultimately class questions. Lastly, the struggle shows that changing the skin complexion of those at the top of society is no guarantee of real changes to life at the bottom.

The election of Barack Obama as the first African-American US president in 2008 reignited the hopes of millions who were inspired by this history. They projected onto him their dreams of a society that could move beyond race. Yet a poll carried out for CNN indicated that the wealth gap between blacks and whites doubled during his first term so that white Americans had 22 times more wealth than African Americans.[37] In short, racism and its effects remain deeply entrenched. If there is a lesson to be learned, it is that only by workers' own struggles can the racial divide be breached.

## CHAPTER 8

# How do we fight racism today?

Esme Choonara

EVERY STRATEGY for fighting racism is underpinned by an analysis of its causes and how it is sustained. We argued in the first chapter that racism is not natural and that race has no basis in scientific fact. It is an invention of capitalism, born of the need to justify slavery and later used to maintain the rule of the capitalist class. It follows, therefore, that the fight against racism should be linked to the struggle against the system that created and perpetuates it.

This Marxist analysis contrasts with the pessimism of those who see racism as expressing "natural fears" or being part of "human nature" and for whom the best that we can aim for is to contain the worst impulses of racism or to escape it by separating off its victims.

Many black nationalists, for example, see all white people as part of the problem, or at best as unreliable allies in the struggle for liberation. It flows from this that black people should organise themselves separately. Others, such as liberals and reformists, are more likely to see racism as an irrational hangover from a previous era—and so the key is to gradually educate the negative ideas away or to use the state to legislate them away. Their strategy is often to seek positions of influence in the system, rather than to rely on a struggle to change society.

In this chapter we will explain the Marxist case in three sections. First we will ask whose interests racism serves and how it functions. Second, we will look at some recent debates around racism and finally we will look at where we go from here in the fight to eradicate racism.

## 1   How does racism work?

### Who benefits from racism?

One of the key questions for those trying to combat racism is to work out who has an interest in challenging it. As we have seen in earlier chapters, black nationalists look primarily to other black people to oppose racism. Marxists by contrast look to the potential unity of black and white workers. To scrutinise which of these is likely to be more effective, it is useful to consider who benefits from racism.

Clearly black people—and other groups oppressed by racism—lose out in a racist society. But our day to day experience also leads many people to assume that all white people benefit from racism—after all, racism is not just a set of ideas but involves black people being systematically discriminated against in education, health, jobs, politics, housing, the criminal justice system and many other areas of life. If you are black you experience direct racist comments, abuse and violence not from "the capitalist system" at large, but from individual white people.

However, contrary to this surface appearance, not all white people do benefit from racism. In particular, white workers do not benefit materially from racism. This has been tested by a number of academic studies especially in the US. For example sociologist Al Syzmanski compared the position of black and white workers in 50 states of the US to look at the effects of racism on white wages. He found that "the higher the black earnings relative to white, the higher white earnings relative to whites elsewhere in the US". He concluded that "white workers appear to actually lose economically from racial discrimination".[1]

Similarly, US economist Michael Reich looked at income distribution in 48 metropolitan areas. Like Syzmanski, he found that the greater the divide between black and white incomes—in other words, the greater the racist discrimination at work—the greater the inequality between white incomes themselves. He explained that racist divisions in the workforce drive down every worker's wage:

> Racial inequality exacerbates racial antagonisms and divisions between black and white workers. White workers develop racist

attitudes and feelings that make it more difficult for them to ally with blacks and to see their common class interests against capital. The greater the racial income gap, the deeper are the divisions between black and white workers and the weaker are unions and class solidarity. The consequence of these racial divisions is that the collective strength of labour is weakened in its bargaining with capital over the wage rate and income shares. Capitalists gain and white workers lose, and the income differences between capitalists and white workers are increased.[2]

He also looked at service provision, in particular education and welfare, and again found empirical evidence that racist divisions lead to an inability to fight effectively for better services, leading to poorer services for both black and white working class people.

So although life is much clearly much harder for black people, white workers are themselves adversely affected by racism. This is true both in the narrowest sense of their immediate income and in the more general sense of undermining the ability to build solidarity to resist attacks on their living standards.

## Ruling class racism

Racism, then, doesn't benefit white workers. As we have seen from its origins in slavery, it serves the interests of the ruling capitalist class, and it is this class that benefits from racism. It may seem counter-intuitive to say that racist ideas today come from the top of society. After all, when politicians attack immigration or multiculturalism, they often say that they are simply "listening to real concerns" among their electorate. This is the mantra that has justified Labour's treacherous slide to the right on immigration over past decades. However, politicians do not just reflect already existing racism—they help to foster and inflame such ideas. They are aided in this by all the institutions of capitalism.

Racist ideas permeate the media. Racism is strongly embedded in the state—most obviously in the police treatment of young black and Asian men, but also through other areas such as education, where there is a constant battle over the treatment of black and Asian children, over racist exclusion policies, a fight over the curriculum and so on. Racism endures in part because it does not just exist at the level of ideas—it is so central to capitalism that it is structured into the functioning of society.

This is not to say that racism operates purely as a clever conspiracy by our rulers. As Marx pointed out when looking at divisions between Irish and English workers, some of the ruling class are indeed conscious of the advantages of using racism to divide and discipline the working class. But for others, it is a less thought through strategy, often reflecting deep prejudices absorbed from generations of a ruling class schooled in empire.

For politicians and the capitalist class more generally, racism provides useful scapegoats onto which they encourage workers to project their grievances. This scapegoating often takes the form of politicians and the media whipping up lurid scare stories about immigration or "terror" threats that actually bear very little, if any, resemblance to reality.

At the time of writing, for example, the Tory-led coalition government is attempting to create panic directed at migrant workers from Eastern Europe. Prime Minister David Cameron has managed to combine two Tory prejudices, claiming, "Ending the 'something for nothing' culture is something that needs to apply in the immigration system as well as in the welfare system".[3]

Cameron's claims that new immigrants from the EU are placing an unbearable demand on housing, services and welfare have no basis in fact. In reality, Eastern European migrants are proportionally much less likely to claim benefits, use the NHS or live in social housing than other people in Britain. To take just one example, a report in the *Guardian* in March 2012 pointed out that of the 2 million migrants to Britain from the eight countries that joined the EU in 2004, fewer than 1 percent—only around 13,000—had claimed jobseeker's allowance.[4]

But scare stories around immigration are not about fact; they are about racist scapegoating. They attempt to cast the world into one divided between the "home nation" and the migrants who threaten that nation's way of life or economic foundations. This creates both a useful diversion for the problems that are actually caused by the politicians and the capitalist class themselves, and an attempt to bolster a common national identity that disguises the opposing interests within it and encourages workers to identify with their "own" ruling class.

What politicians and other ruling class figures say has an impact on racism throughout society. When politicians blame immigrants or target Muslims, it gives confidence to racists to spout their lies, stir up race hate or carry out racist attacks.

### Why do some white workers accept racist ideas?

It is clearly in the interests of the capitalist class to spread racist ideas, but why do some white working class people accept them, especially if they do not actually gain by doing so?

One reason workers may accept some racist ideas is economic competition. Capitalism is a dynamic global system but a brutally unequal one that forces millions to travel to new parts of the world looking for work. This creates the contradictory phenomenon of bringing workers into a collective situation with the potential power to challenge their bosses and the system more generally, while simultaneously atomising each individual in the labour market.

Workers everywhere are forced to compete with others for jobs, housing and so on, and new groups of migrant workers are often portrayed as economic competitors. As we have seen, employers frequently use the threat of bringing in migrant workers to try to discipline the existing workforce, or try to foster divides among the workforce for example by paying different rates to different groups of workers. Scapegoating can appeal to workers—it can make more sense, or seem more "realistic", to resent other workers of a different background than to realise the importance of solidarity in a common struggle.

The best response for the established workforce is to unionise new workers and to try to fight for equal wages. But the way in which economic competition structures workers' lives means some can be open to fears about other groups of workers and to racist ideas.

Second, one of the reasons that racist ideas can take hold is because although white workers actually lose out materially from the effects of racism, they may still feel that they are superior. W E B Du Bois described this as a "psychological wage" which he identified as one of the tools used to divide black and white workers in the Southern US states after the defeat of the Radical Reconstruction that followed the abolition of slavery.

Du Bois's term has been misused by some on the left to try to prove that white workers do indeed benefit from racism—that the "psychological wage" actually represents a material gain or that racist ideas are not intimately linked to capitalism. But Du Bois is actually driving the point home that racism is used to benefit the ruling class. It is worth quoting his explanation at length as it shows how this "psychological wage" is used to perpetuate both racism and economic exploitation. Du Bois argued that a deliberate racist campaign in the South:

> drove such a wedge between the white and black workers that there probably are not today in the world two groups of workers with practically identical interests who hate and fear each other so deeply and persistently and who are kept so far apart that neither sees anything of common.
>
> It must be remembered that the white group of labourers, while they received a low wage, were compensated for by a sort of public and psychological wage. They were given public deference and titles of courtesy because they were white. They were admitted freely with all classes of white people to public functions, public parks and public schools... The newspapers specialised in news that flattered the poor whites and almost utterly ignored the Negro except in crime and ridicule.
>
> On the other hand, in the same way, the Negro was subject to public insult; was afraid of mobs; was liable to the jibes of children and the unreasoning fears of white women; and compelled almost continuously to submit to various badges of inferiority. The result of this was that the wages of both classes could be kept low, the whites fearing to be supplanted by Negro labour, the Negroes always being threatened by the substitution of white labour.[5]

In other words, white workers may be being battered by their bosses and the system in general, but they may feel that at least they are somehow better than black people, Muslims or whoever the latest scapegoats are, and they may at times be incited to protect that perceived superiority. Marx was making a very similar point when he described English workers feeling themselves "part of the ruling nation" in regard to Irish workers.

Finally, there is also a broader question of why people under capitalism may accept ideas that are not in their own material interests. Racism is only one example of this. Many people accept, even if only partially, many of the myths of capitalism: that there is an enduring fixed human nature, that capitalism is the only way to organise things, that the state is neutral, that those who work hard can get ahead. This is in part because of the alienation of working class people under capitalism—the lack of control over our lives and the functioning of society. Fortunately ideas are not fixed in people's heads, and these myths are often challenged by the reality of people's experiences, especially by the experience of struggle.

## 2 Debates around racism

### Is there a white privilege?

The idea of "white privilege" is a new form of the argument that all white people benefit from racism. The theory is most popular in the US but has also found its way into the movement in Britain and has been taken up by a number of bloggers, activists, academics and those working in "diversity" training.

White privilege is based on the idea that because all black people are oppressed by racism, all white people gain an "unearned advantage" simply by virtue of being white. There are many versions of this theory, but they share in common the idea that whiteness brings with it both material advantage and complicity in the functioning of racism. This is reflected in a move among some activists away from talking about racism at all, to using the term "white supremacy".

Many proponents of privilege theory also suggest that all white people are conduits of racism, even if unwilling ones. For example, author Frances Kendall argues, "Any of us who has race privilege... is racist by definition".[6] This theory pessimistically casts all white people as prisoners of their whiteness—the best they can do is to own up to and confront their role in oppressing others, but they can't completely break from it.

For many activists who embrace elements of privilege theory, it is for them simply an assertion that oppression exists and that it is wrong. This is a good starting point. But privilege theory doesn't give us the tools we need either to understand racism or to effectively challenge it and the system that breeds it.

Theories of white privilege build on earlier forms of identity politics and share many of their weaknesses. An increasingly inward-looking form of identity-based politics took hold in the 1980s and 1990s both in Britain and the US. It represented a shift away from tackling questions of structural inequality to more subjective ones about competing "identities". It expressed the idea that only those who experience oppression can really understand or challenge it. This led to fragmentation of the movements against oppression and for many activists in Britain a pull into the Labour Party—notably in the case of racism, into the Black Sections.

In Britain, as we have seen, this was in part the product of a decline in wider class struggles and movements against the fascist National Front that had previously formed the basis for broad and militant mobilisations against racism and fascism. The struggles of the 1970s and the social explosions such as the riots in many major cities in 1981 and again in Tottenham and Brixton in 1985 forced the state to change its approach from direct repression to one that also involved attempts to co-opt a layer of black activists. This meant a state-sponsored programme of funding targeted at "ethnic groups" that further encouraged the breaking down of solidarity into narrower forms of identity politics based on ethnic origin and competition for resources.

Identity politics was also given a boost by the rise in academia of post-Marxist and postmodernist theories that held that the era of "big narratives" was over and that an analysis based on class was simply reductionist. This involved a recasting of notions of power away from the central functioning of how a capitalist class maintains its rule towards a more diffuse "multi-dimensional" understanding of power.[7]

Power resides, according to this argument, not just in the structures of society and the domination of a capitalist ruling elite, but is spread throughout society in interactions between individuals. Identity politics was often, therefore, a recipe not just for fragmentation of the struggles against oppression, but a move away from attempting to directly challenge the system and the state towards a focus on the individual.

Privilege theory is in many ways the flip side of identity politics—it accepts the same framework, but turns it on its head to concentrate not on the oppressed, but on the alleged oppressor. The role of the oppressed is to understand and challenge their own oppression; the primary role of the privileged is to acknowledge and confront their own privilege—to "check your privilege", as the popular phrase puts it. This approach is not as new as it might seem—much of the literature around white privilege has come from those involved in "diversity training" who have a model very similar to that of the Racial Awareness Training embraced by many local authorities in the 1980s and discussed earlier in this book.

Some proponents of privilege theory do recognise that racism has material roots or that it is structured into societal inequalities. Tim Wise, for example, one of the most influential white privilege theorists in the US, accepts that the origins of racism are bound up with capitalism and economic dominance. However, he suggests that after slavery racism becomes so deeply entrenched that "white racism can now take on an auto-pilot effect" in which it is sustained not by the ruling elites and the needs of capitalism, but by white people themselves. So racism as a power structure becomes detached from capitalism.[8]

And even where structural inequalities are identified, the emphasis throughout privilege theory is still on educating and challenging individual attitudes, primarily through self-scrutiny. As Kendall puts it, "Those of us who are white and, by definition, have white privilege must engage in sustained self-examination about how our race affects our lives. If we don't fully understand our individual and collective roles in maintaining a system of white superiority, our relationships with people of colour remain superficial".[9]

Of course there is nothing wrong with white people being self-critical about how their behaviour or attitudes may reflect or reinforce racism. It is important to challenge all manifestations of racism—including individual acts of racist language and assumptions. However, a strategy for defeating racism—a huge systemic inequality—cannot rest on the individual self-reflection of progressive individuals. A much larger struggle is needed both to make material change to the conditions of racism and to shake up and drive back wider racist ideas.

To seek to iron out individual attitudes before meaningful struggle is possible is to approach the question the wrong way round. Most people who enter into struggle, whether against racism, sexism, for workers' rights or some other campaign, bring with them contradictory ideas. They may accept some reactionary ideas, while rejecting others. It is precisely in the process of struggle for change that people gain new insights into how capitalism functions and can rapidly break down old assumptions and prejudices.

On the face of it, it is not surprising that privilege theory can appear to make some sense: it is clear that in a racist world a white person is more likely than a black person from a similar class background to get a job, get into university, not be in prison, not be stopped and searched by the police, not face racist abuse or attack. But to see this as an unearned privilege is to look at oppression in only the most superficial terms and to miss the bigger picture of how racism works for the benefit of the ruling class. And we should ask whether it is really an advantage not to be attacked, abused, discriminated against, or a right that everyone should have.

One problem with understanding racism as functioning primarily through white people's "unearned advantage" is the implicit suggestion that the privileged should own up and give up their advantage. *Guardian* columnist Ally Fogg, in a comment piece that is actually fairly critical of privilege theory, suggests that maybe we should stop saying that women are underpaid by 20 percent in the workforce and consider instead that men are 20 percent overpaid.[10] It is worth reflecting on where this approach leads us—maybe to a conclusion that men should have their wages cut in line with women in the name of equality?

Peggy McIntosh, one of the earliest and best known proponents of privilege theory, describes privilege as an "invisible knapsack". She argues, "White privilege is like an invisible weightless knapsack of special provisions, assurances, tools, maps, guides, codebooks, passports, visas, clothes, compass, emergency gear and blank checks".[11] Yet it is obvious that not all white people will really share all these invisible advantages. White working class people or oppressed white groups such as some Eastern Europeans will be denied these "special provisions" and "blank cheques".

Some privilege theorists acknowledge this by talking of "intersectionality". So someone can be "privileged" in one area and disadvantaged in another, as for example with a white woman, or an able-bodied black person. Furthermore different oppressions—based on "race", sexuality, gender, class, etc—intersect and impact on each other. This approach has the benefit of recognising that there are relationships between different oppressions in society and they can't be examined entirely separately, but it still tends to reduce people to a sum of their oppressions (or lack thereof). As with identity politics in general, power then becomes something that happens not through the structures and domination of capitalism as an economic system, but through the relationships between individuals. Class becomes just one of many unequal relationships, instead of being the fundamental relationship at the heart of the system—and the one which provides the key to transforming it.

A Marxist political strategy flows from this understanding of the relationship between exploitation and oppression. We will return to this point.

Without this approach, the number of possible sources of privilege just keeps growing. The Transformative Justice Law Project of Illinois, for example, lists many forms of privilege that activists should check including education privilege, body size privilege, "life on the outside" privilege (it is a privilege not to be in prison!) and "passing privilege", which they describe as "the privilege to be able to 'pass' as a more privileged group, such as a light skinned person of colour passing as white".[12]

This shows many of the flaws of this line of argument. It is a recipe for fragmentation and moralistic squabbling rather than solidarity—light skinned people are more privileged than dark skinned, white women are less privileged than white men and so on. It reflects an approach based on the primacy of the individual and focused on challenging and educating people in regard to language and attitude. The effect of this is to reduce the question of structural inequalities to myriad gradations of individual privileges. It is a very disarming theory—seeing us all as prisoners of our privileges and unable to build a genuine movement of solidarity without first going through a process of self-denunciation for any "privileges" we may have over others. The logic of this is to replace political strategy and debate with moral appeal—in other words, it matters less what is said than who is saying it.

### Why is there no unity between oppressed people?

Sadly, unity of the oppressed is not inevitable or automatic. The ruling class attempts to foster and institutionalise competition and animosity between groups of people of different ethnic backgrounds or nationalities. Sometimes black or Asian workers can accept racist ideas and prejudices about other groups such as newer immigrants. It can be extremely frustrating to see how quickly black, Asian and Irish people can seem to forget the abuse and obstacles they or their parents or grandparents faced when they first came to Britain. But some sections of the left and the wider movements do make these links—pointing for example to the similarities in the way that first Jewish, then Irish and now Muslim people have been treated as the "enemy within" in British society.

Just as black and white unity is not automatic, a political fight must be waged to draw out the common experiences and interests of different sections of the oppressed. In the wake of the 2011 riots for example, activists in Hackney, east London, helped to organise a 2,000 strong march demanding better facilities and futures for young people, bringing together groups and individuals of different backgrounds. Those involved in organising the march included some people from Turkish and Kurdish backgrounds. This was important to try to overcome attempts to divide local people and to portray the riots as anti-Turkish after some local Turkish shopkeepers had faced damage and theft from their shops.

To say that black people can accept some racist ideas and prejudices is not, however, the same as saying that they are racist. In particular we should be clear that there is no such thing as "reverse racism" by black people against white people. The argument that reverse racism exists is sometimes an expression of the idea that anti-racism has gone too far and that white people are now disadvantaged or oppressed. This is clearly not the case. More often, however, the argument is based on confusion between prejudice and racism. Black people may accept all sorts of ideas that circulate in society—about others, about white people or even about themselves—but racism is about more than ideas; it is about structural inequality. So if a white person is racist towards a black person, they are reflecting the dominant ruling class ideas and the structural inequalities of society. If a black person is abusive or negative about white people, this is a reaction to racism.

Often one of the most destructive ways that oppression works is by the oppressed themselves internalising negative ideas about themselves. The US writer and activist James Baldwin captured this in an open letter to jailed black activist Angela Davis:

> When I was little I despised myself; I did not know any better. And this meant, albeit unconsciously, or against my will, or in great pain, that I also despised my father. And my mother. And my brothers. And my sisters. Black people were killing each other every Saturday night...when I was growing up; and no one explained to them, or to me, that it was intended that they should; that they were penned where they were, like animals. Everything supported this sense of reality, nothing denied it: and so one was ready, when it came time to go to work, to be treated as a slave.[13]

Baldwin goes on to explain that this is why it was so important to have a new generation of black activists in the US who challenged racism head on. With that resistance, as we saw in the previous chapter, came a sense of pride and dignity and self-assurance that we see repeatedly in struggles throughout history.

## Are white workers losing out?

One reason it is important to remember that racist ideas come from the ruling class is that there have been repeated attempts to portray white workers as the most racist group in society.

In part this reflects a ruling class prejudice that sees all working class people as ignorant and uneducated. But the image of the embittered racist white worker has also been taken up more widely by the media and politicians in recent years, accompanied by arguments that white workers are losing out. There have been intermittent flurries of media and academic speculation that white working class boys are now the main disadvantaged group in education[14] and many commentators arguing that "the white working class has been left behind".[15] Labour MP and poverty tsar to the coalition government Frank Field has argued that the white working class are now so alienated that they should attend citizenship ceremonies.[16]

White workers are generally portrayed in these arguments as caught between the decline of traditional manufacturing and the rise of multiculturalism that has eroded their "way of life". They are seen as disorientated, bitter, confused and easy fodder for the far-right.

It is true that more than 30 years of neoliberalism and attacks from both Tory and Labour governments have destroyed some working class communities, devastating industries such as mining and textiles, and leaving many areas scarred by poverty and deprivation. But this is not unique to white people. The bitterness felt by many white workers is the same anger felt across the working class. In fact black and Asian workers still suffer much higher rates of poverty and unemployment.

Often the arguments about "white workers" are based on a very narrow version of what the "working class" might mean. The working class constantly changes, and has always done so. So many traditional industries may have been destroyed (although we should not exaggerate this), but other areas of work have moved centre stage such as the public sector or newer industries such as supermarkets, IT and call centres.

Defining white workers by their "whiteness" instead of their class is about seeing them in competition with other ethnic groups. The argument is based on the supposed failure of multiculturalism—it has threatened the British "way of life" and in fact has gone too far in giving special attention to minority ethnic groups.

As Wendy Bottero explains in a study by the Runnymede Trust:

> In this media flurry, it is the whiteness of the white working class which is the real focus of attention. This is a debate which pitches the interests of the white working class against those of other ethnic groups and migrant workers, and it is no coincidence that this sudden concern about the ethnic identity of the working class has emerged at a time of over-heated public focus on questions of ethnic and religious citizenship. Ironically, the latest attack on multiculturalism comes through the championing of a new excluded "cultural" minority—the white working class.
>
> After a long period of quiet on the "class" front, it would be good to see questions of inequality, and of the working class, back on the public agenda. But so far, this is a sound-bite debate, in danger of writing "class" out of the question of inequality altogether.[17]

White workers are not a separate group, just as black workers are not. They are today part of a multiracial workforce that has drawn in people from across the world. Many studies show that working class lives have become more integrated, not less, over past decades. The myths of segregation have been dealt with in an earlier chapter, but just to take one example of the growing integration among working class people, we can note the rapid increase in those born of racially mixed relationships. In fact recent census data shows that "mixed race" was the fasted growing ethnicity in the decade from 2001 to 2011.

### Why are workers in the Global South oppressed?

The appalling level of absolute poverty and deprivation in much of the Global South has led many to conclude that all Westerners must benefit from this immiseration. Just like the argument that white workers benefit from racism, this reflects a superficial reading of how inequality works. Crucially it hides the real bonds of exploitation and potential solidarity that workers across the world share.

The idea that workers in the West benefit from the oppression of the Global South is not a new one. At the turn of the last century a similar argument held currency that attempted to explain the hold of reformism on workers in advanced capitalist countries as reflecting the material position of a layer of workers who supposedly benefited from the fruits of empire. Both the black writer W E B Du Bois and V I Lenin, the leader of the 1917 Russian Revolution, separately concluded that this layer of workers formed a "labour aristocracy". Many black nationalists and others went further still, arguing that all workers in the industrial heartlands of the capitalist countries had been materially bought off by the fruits of empire and colonialism and so had a stake in capitalist exploitation of the colonies.

These theories are wrong. As Alex Callinicos points out, the theory of the labour aristocracy is:

> an extremely poor guide to the behaviour of the Western working class during the heyday of classical imperialism in the late 19th and early 20th centuries. Aside from the flaws in its economic arguments, the theory does not explain why the most plausible candidate for the title of "labour aristocrats", the skilled metal workers, formed in all the main European industrial centres—Petrograd, Berlin, Turin, Sheffield, Glasgow—the vanguard of the great surge of working class revolt at the end of the First World War.[18]

More importantly, these theories ignore the commonalities of exploitation faced by workers across the globe. It is true that in the poorest countries of the Global South wages are a tiny proportion of those in the richest Western countries, and that absolute poverty is evidently much higher.

But exploitation is not just about levels of poverty and suffering. It is about the economic relationship by which capitalism extracts profits from workers. That is the driving force of the economy worldwide. And exploitation as understood in this way can actually be greater in more advanced capitalist countries. In fact one of the reasons that many parts of the Global South are so poor is that they are bypassed for investment as higher profits can often be extracted from a more highly trained workforce with a more developed infrastructure in the West or in parts of a handful of newly industrialised countries.

Marx recognised in the *Communist Manifesto* that capitalism drags all corners of the globe into its brutal system, creating a global working class. No nation on earth is now without its own elite and a ruling capitalist class.

To say that workers across the world have a common interest is not to say that they share identical conditions or to deny that some are treated far worse than others. But all workers, wherever they are in the world, are exploited for capitalist profit. This is why internationalism is not just a matter of the principle of standing in solidarity with others—it is a reflection that capitalism is a global system and that the struggles for liberation of workers or oppressed people in different parts of the world are linked.

Russian revolutionary Leon Trotsky explained this in 1930: "If we take Britain and India as polarised varieties of the capitalist type, then we are obliged to say that the internationalism of the British and Indian proletariats does not at all rest on an identity of conditions, tasks and methods, but on their indivisible interdependence".[19]

It is not just an interesting question of theory to recognise the common interests of workers across the world. There is a long radical tradition of Western workers making common cause with those oppressed by slavery, colonialism or racist oppression. For example when working class radicals in Sheffield organised a mass meeting in April 1794, they passed a unanimous resolution calling for the ending of the slave trade and the emancipation of black slaves. "Wishing to be rid of the weight of oppression under which we groan," they declared, "we are induced to compassion with those who groan also".[20]

## 3    Fighting back

### Black nationalism: class or community?

Black nationalists see the unity of black people as the key to fighting racism. As we have seen, there have been many forms of organised black nationalism over the past decades, including those who see all white people as the problem and more radical groups such as the Black Panthers in the US or the Asian Youth Movements in Britain in the 1970s who saw themselves as part of much wider struggles in society. Some have looked to attempts to create a self-reliant black capitalism and some have attempted instead to confront and challenge capitalism. What unites them is a strategy based on black self-organisation.

Britain has not seen black nationalist organisations on the same scale as the US. There are a few reasons for this. Black populations in Britain are smaller and tend to be less segregated than in the US. There are not ghettos in Britain in the same way as in some US cities. It is also the case that the relatively recent history of the brutality of US slavery at home as well as abroad hangs over the history of anti-racist struggles in the US in a way that it doesn't in Britain.

In Britain there have been smaller more piecemeal attempts to build black-only groups and self-defence campaigns, as well as attempts at demanding that anti-racist organisations should be "black-led". But even without large-scale black nationalist organisations, the ideas of black self-reliance can still take on a common currency.

Black nationalist ideas in general agree—either overtly or by implication—with the idea that all white people benefit from or are complicit in racism and therefore cannot be won to a sustained struggle against racism. Instead some black nationalists look to an alliance of all black people—across classes—to what they may call the "black community". But notions of community are very vague and ignore some of the stark difference that exist with such "communities". For example there are 10,000 Muslim millionaires in Britain.[21] Meanwhile two thirds of children in families of Pakistani or Bangladeshi origin, who make up around half of Britain's 1.6 million Muslims, are born into poverty.[22]

A Muslim millionaire may well suffer racism, and we must oppose that. However, that person has a stake in the system as it is—it makes them very rich. So although they may be in favour of measures that help to advance individuals facing racism, they have no material interest in a consistent collective struggle to end racism.

Some black nationalists are themselves aware of the way class divides "community". For example British activist John La Rose, who was a member of the Race Today Collective, once explained,

"The organisation to which I belong makes its position absolutely clear. We are part of the perspective of struggle to change British society—it is part of the working class, the black working class and unemployed perspective in Britain, and we are in opposition to the black middle classes".[23]

La Rose is right to draw out the class differences among black people. However, there is no discrete group called the "black working class" any more than there is a "white working class". The working class is on the whole very mixed and becoming increasingly so. And black people are a minority in Britain—for class struggle to have a chance of success they must unite with others, crucially with white workers who make up the majority of the workforce.

Organised black nationalism in Britain was incorporated to a large degree in the 1980s by an overlapping strategy that we could call black reformism. As we have seen, previously militant struggles that confronted the state and challenged the capitalist class were largely replaced by the turn of a number of individuals towards the Labour Party and securing positions in local or national government or state advisory bodies.

We shouldn't dismiss the aspiration to have more black representation at all levels of society—it is part of demolishing the lie that black people are inferior to white people. Winning better representation can give black and Asian people confidence. However, getting more black and Asian MPs elected is not in itself enough to deal with the very real problems faced by the majority of black and Asian people in Britain who remain blighted by the daily reality of racism.

Criticising black nationalism as a strategy is not to deny that oppressed people should play a central role in resistance. It is unthinkable that there would be any struggles in Britain today against racism or other injustice that don't involve many black people in the forefront of those battles. Look for example at the mobilisations against the racist English Defence League in recent years, which have seen large numbers of young Asian men take to the street alongside multiracial trade unions and left organisations. But the Marxist view is that the most powerful weapon we have in the fight against racism is united working class resistance.

## Class struggle and the fight against racism

Class struggle can create the conditions for overcoming racism. Rising militancy gives confidence that change is possible, and makes it easier to direct anger away from scapegoats and towards the real enemy—the bosses and the government. It can lay the basis for overcoming divisions between different groups of workers. However it is not inevitable that rising struggle automatically eliminates racism. We have seen that in the 1960s and 1970s some groups of workers had to fight the racism in their unions as well as from employers. Struggle creates the possibilities for unity, but this potential is shaped by political and union organisation and the wider ideological climate.

For example, a wave of unofficial strikes in the construction industry in early 2009 saw a battle over the slogan "British jobs for British workers"—a slogan first raised by then Labour Prime Minister Gordon Brown. Socialists and others argued that this was the wrong slogan for the campaign to adopt and the wrong direction to take the dispute. The arguments started to have an impact, and within a few months the "British jobs" slogan had lost prominence. Many Polish workers also joined the picket lines at Drax power station in North Yorkshire, helping to win a significant victory for all construction workers.

One of the reasons that the question of racism should be of primary importance to the whole working class movement is not just that racism is morally repugnant and unjust. Racist divisions, as we have seen, hamper the possibility of effective class struggle.

Emphasising the centrality of class doesn't mean that the only important battles take place in the workplace. As we have seen, social explosions such as the riots of the 1980s or in 2011 can express the rage and frustration that many feel over a range of issues including racism. These explosions can have an impact on the state, even if they can also be quickly contained. Justice campaigns and wider movements against racism and fascism also help to drive racism back. Mass mobilisations against fascism have repeatedly not only driven the Nazis back, but also helped to create a broader anti-racist culture.

Understanding the role of class, however, can also help to inform the strategy for these wider political campaigns. Marxists insist that white workers are not inherently racist and can be part of the solution, not the problem, and that workers organised through the unions can bring social weight to any campaign. So, as we saw in chapter 3, the huge campaign following the racist murder of Stephen Lawrence involved hundreds of people, black and white, petitioning and campaigning over the issue, as well as the Lawrence family winning support and funding from the trade unions to sustain the long-running campaign.

There is a long, often hidden, history of workers in Britain making common cause with migrant workers or with those facing slavery or the brutality of empire abroad.

The first widespread use of petitioning by working class people in Britain was the huge petitions raised as part of the campaign to abolish the slave trade. More working class people signed these petitions in solidarity with others than signed the Charter which was about securing their own rights.[24] When Gandhi visited mill workers in Lancashire in 1931, thousands came out into the streets to greet him, even though many of them were out of work as a result of the cotton boycott Gandhi was leading in the campaign for home rule in India. As one local historian wrote, "Gandhi was received with sympathy and affection by the Lancashire cotton workers, even though they were the ones hit hardest by the boycott".[25]

There are also many more recent examples of the power and potential of organising black and white workers together. A series of bus strikes in London in 2006 proved how a truly multiracial workforce can collectively organise to make a difference. One union activist described organising in a bus garage with "550 drivers mainly drawn from Europe, Africa and Asia potentially speaking up to 44 different languages".[26] Strikes brought these workers together, in the process creating a strong and united group of workers. Outsourced cleaners in London also won better wages after a lively campaign bringing together many different nationalities. Many of the cleaners involved brought their own powerful traditions of organisation and resistance to the campaign.

Bosses who attempt to use migrant workers to undercut wages or undermine union organisation do not always get away with it. For example, when Polish agency workers were bussed in to attempt to break a Post Office dispute over privatisation and pay in 2007, pickets at Watford climbed onto the bus, explained the dispute, and the Polish workers voted not to go into work.[27] Several unions, including Unite and the GMB, have taken up specific campaigns to recruit and organise new migrant workers.

Many bus companies have employed a specific tactic of recruiting workers directly from Poland after it joined the EU in 2004. But rather than allow this to divide the workforce, many Polish workers have been part of disputes in recent years. In 2005 *Socialist Worker* reported on a bus strike at First Bus in Staffordshire that gives a glimpse of workers' unity in action. One Polish driver told the paper:

> I started working for First Bus a few months ago. I'd only been here about a month when I first heard that there was a possibility of strike action.
>
> This action is really important. They pay us less here than they do in the rest of the country—it makes no sense and so we have to fight. The drivers here have been absolutely great to me and the rest of the Polish drivers. Even the management treat us all the same. British or Polish we all get treated badly.[28]

This pattern has been repeated in numerous bus strikes including in Aberdeen in 2008 and 2009 and in Liverpool in 2010.

Every major strike in recent years—in the post, civil service, London Underground, education and across the public sector—has shown the multiracial nature of today's working class. There have also been a few examples of the potential not just for building unity at work, but for taking up specific arguments around racism. For example, around 300 postal workers in Wolverhampton—black, white and Asian—walked out unofficially in 2003 in an inspiring protest against racism. The same office saw 100 workers walk out over racism again in 2006, with one worker telling *Socialist Worker*, "We weren't prepared to let racism exist in this office. There's a tradition of taking action over racism".[29] Thousands of postal workers also effectively risk their jobs every election by refusing to deliver election addresses for fascist parties.

Black and Asian people in Britain are a vital part of the working class today. Despite facing higher unemployment rates than their white counterparts, the majority of economically active black and Asian adults are in work and are far from marginal to the functioning of the British economy. The National Health Service, for example, simply couldn't function without large numbers of black and Asian workers. Almost 20 percent of qualified nurses, midwives and health visitors in England are from minority ethnic groups—including over 50,000 black and Asian people working in these professions.[30] Around 17 percent of healthcare scientists and over 12 percent of qualified therapeutic, scientific and technical staff are from minority ethnic groups.

There are large numbers of black, Asian and other minority ethnic groups in many other industries. For example at the time of writing there were around 184,000 minority ethnic workers in manufacturing in the UK, 356,200 in transport and communication, 920,000 in public administration and 269,000 working in caring and leisure.[31] Almost a tenth of civil service workers are from non-white minority ethnic groups, and the figure is even higher among some of the lower grades.[32]

Black and Asian people are, then, a key part of today's multiracial working class. They are also a key part of the trade union movement. Black people are actually more likely to be in unions than white people, and Asian workers are not far behind (union density for black workers was 27.7 percent in 2011 as compared to white workers at 26.4 percent and Asian workers at 21.6).[33] So a strategy based on working class unity is both necessary and realistic.

### Reform or revolution?

Many critics of Marxism argue that an analysis based on class is reductionist—that it ignores or downplays questions of oppression or expects oppressed people to "wait for the revolution" to secure their liberation. For example, white privilege theorist Tim Wise argues that "left activists often marginalise people of colour by operating from a framework of extreme class reductionism, which holds that the 'real' issue is class, not race".[34]

It should already be clear that for socialists our strategy involves an urgent and immediate fight against racism in all its forms. Apart from anything else, it is highly unlikely that we could see successful class struggles without challenging and overcoming racist divisions in the working class. As Marx wrote in *Capital*, "Labour cannot emancipate itself in the white skin when in the black it is branded".[35]

However, class is not just one of a series of inequalities that we face. It is defined by exploitation—the basis of a live and antagonistic relationship between the two great classes under capitalism, the capitalist class and the working class. As we have seen, the rise of racism is intrinsically linked to and sustained by capitalism. This does not mean that distinct forms of oppression can be reduced to class—racism and sexism for example have their own dynamics and affect all classes—but the unlocking and defeating of this oppression is intimately linked to the struggle against capitalism.

This is not automatic: a political battle must be waged to overcome ruling class ideas, including racism. Lenin made this point in 1902 when he wrote that socialists should not restrict themselves to narrow economic and workplace struggle. He wrote that for socialists the model should not "be the trade union secretary, but the tribune of the people, who is able to react to every manifestation of tyranny and oppression, no matter where it appears, no matter what stratum or class of the people it affects".[36] So socialists should take up every issue of inequality and oppression. Lenin doesn't leave it at that. He goes on to say that socialists should also be "able to generalise all these manifestations and produce a single picture of police violence and capitalist exploitation". So socialists should oppose every manifestation of injustice, but attempt to draw out from it a more general political picture of how society works.

Marxists stand in a tradition of socialism from below—the self-activity of the working class to effect change and ultimately to liberate all humankind. This is in contrast to ideas of change from above, such as those represented by the Labour Party or a range of activists who see the key to change as securing positions of influence within the state. At the time of writing we have a greater number of black and Asian MPs than at any time in British history and a black president in the most powerful country in the world, yet the reality for most black and Asian people is that life is getting harder. This is because it is not enough just to get people into positions of power—it is necessary to challenge the logic and power of the capitalist state altogether. This requires mass activity, crucially mass resistance by workers.

Despite its declining base, many working class people in Britain still look to the Labour Party to deliver change and to promote equality. Many Labour Party members are committed anti-racists and actively involved in campaigning against racism. Yet, as we have seen in earlier chapters, the Labour Party in office—and often in opposition too—consistently fails those affected by racism. This is less to do with which individuals are in the leadership—though some such as Tony Blair have carried out unforgivable atrocities such as the Iraq War and the ratcheting up of Islamophobia—than a reflection of the logic of a reformist electoral party.

The main aim of the Labour Party when in opposition is to win elections. That is why it panders to racist myths, hoping to pick up votes but helping to further entrench such scapegoating in the process. In office the project of running a capitalist state means accepting the rules of international capitalism—military and economic competition to stay ahead of your rivals. This means accepting and promoting the idea of a "national interest" that must be defended. This focus on nation obscures the divisions of class, and encourages workers in Britain to identify with their "own" rulers, rather than see that they have far more in common with other workers across the world. This logic is why, as we have seen, Labour has been responsible for some of most appalling treatment of immigrants such as the scapegoating of a small group of Asians from Malawi in 1974 or forcing Asian women entering Britain to undergo "virginity tests" in 1976. More recently Labour leader Ed Miliband chose the *Sun* newspaper to reassure people that a future Labour government would be much harder on immigration, writing, "The Labour Party I lead will listen to people's worries and we will talk about immigration... We know low-skill immigration has been too high and it should come down".[37]

The alternative to such opportunistic pandering to racism would be to make a clear argument that migrants are not to blame for the problems people face and to start to take steps to address those problems. But this would mean challenging the logic of neoliberalism and austerity and the rights of employers to ruthlessly exploit workers of all backgrounds. In other words, it would mean challenging capitalism and the sanctity of the nation state. Such a fundamental challenge cannot be instituted from enlightened individuals on high, but requires mass struggle from below.

Revolutions are the highest point of class struggle and bring with them the most far reaching flux in ideas and the potential for liberation. The Russian Revolution of 1917—the only successful workers' revolution to date—brought with it a huge change in established attitudes, for example a sea change in ideas about the role of women and the status of Jewish people.

Many leading figures in the revolution were Jewish—in a country where anti-Semitism was probably the most severe of any country prior to the rise of fascism in Germany. The new revolutionary society made huge strides in establishing legal equality for the oppressed— legalising homosexuality, giving women equal rights with men in voting and employment. But the leaders of the revolution also recognised that there should be a fight to dig out the roots of oppression from the new society and to spread this work internationally. Nations that had been oppressed by the Russian Empire were given the right to self-determination. Many black, Asian, Caribbean and African activists were inspired by the example of the Bolsheviks and the Russian Revolution and joined the newly formed Communist Parties across the world.

The Bosheviks—the party that had led the revolution—set up the Third Communist International (known as the Comintern) which among other issues debated questions of national liberation and strategies for organisation. The Bolsheviks, in the middle of civil war and the spreading threat of famine, also established a Congress of the Peoples of the East in Baku, Azerbaijan, in 1920 where over 2,000 delegates, mostly from Asia, debated questions of liberation, colonialism and how to spread the revolutionary struggle.

Other high points of struggle also show the potential for change.

The early days of the revolution that swept Egypt at the beginning of 2011 showed an inspiring degree of solidarity between Muslims and Christians—who have traditionally been oppressed in Egypt. Many Muslims rushed to defend Christians from the violence of the Egyptian state. The revolution also brought many women out into the streets and squares, playing a key role in the protests. None of these gains are permanent and, just like the Arab revolutions themselves, they are contested and can be rolled back. Yet the lesson is still that the highest points of struggle create new possibilities for overcoming oppression.

Marx argued that revolution is necessary both because the ruling class will not voluntarily relinquish power and because it is necessary for the working class to go through the process of liberating themselves in order to shed the old prejudices of capitalist society: "Revolution is necessary, therefore, not only because the ruling class cannot be overthrown in any other way, but also because the class overthrowing it can only in a revolution succeed in ridding itself of all the muck of ages and become fitted to found society anew".[38]

### How should we organise today?

Socialists should always be at the forefront of struggles against racism. In Britain, as we have seen, socialists—black and white— have been central to successful mass struggles against fascism for the last four decades. We have also been at the forefront of combatting Islamophobia and supporting justice campaigns against police racism and deaths in custody. Socialists in Britain also have a proud history of defending asylum seekers and challenging anti-immigrant myths both through argument and in practice. We have fought for the unity of black and white workers and against attempts to divide workers along racial or national lines.

Short of a revolutionary mass struggle, revolutionary socialists are only a minority in the working class. This is one reason why a central part of our strategy is the united front—campaigns that reach out to wider forces, bringing revolutionaries together with Labour Party members, other trade unionists, community groups and individuals in a common struggle on specific issues.

Such united campaigns are crucial to building broad enough mobilisations to have an impact against racism or fascism. Being serious about fighting racism means being open to working with many others including those who have very different strategies or understandings of racism.

But as we have seen there are many competing ideas about how best to fight racism. United front campaigns are testing grounds for these different strategies, and socialists have much experience, ideas and energy to offer to these debates. Our understanding of the link between racism and capitalism means that we can be optimistic about being able to win white workers away from racism, emphasising the role of black and white unity and linking the fight to wider class struggle.

Today we face a highly contradictory situation: the level of general racist attitudes among working class people has declined massively since the 1950s or 1960s, yet we still face vicious state racism, repeated attempts at fascist mobilisations and nasty scapegoating of migrant workers and Muslims.

As we have seen throughout this book, many racist attitudes have been driven back over the past 60 years through increased intermixing, united class struggle and sustained anti-racist activity. Yet racism endures and indeed evolves, creating new scapegoats and changed rhetoric at the same time as resurrecting old prejudices. And just as racism can be driven back, it can rise or surge forward again.

The economic crisis that has swept the globe since 2008 has brought with it brutal austerity and increased scapegoating. Yet it has also created crisis in the ideas at the top of society, volatility and mass protests in much of the world and a resurgence of interest in questions of class. This can make it easier for anti-racist activists to point to the wider problems with capitalism, and the need for unity. It can also offer opportunities to build multiracial resistance on many fronts.

Every generation that has faced racism has fought back bravely. But future generations should not have to keep repeating these struggles. Our fight must be for more than just equality under the brutal and destructive capitalist system—we want real liberation.

As James Baldwin put it:

> We know that a man is not a thing and is not to be placed at the mercy of things. We know that air and water belong to all mankind and not merely to industrialists. We know that a baby does not come into the world merely to be the instrument of someone else's profit. We know that democracy does not mean the coercion of all into a deadly—and, finally, wicked—mediocrity but the liberty for all to aspire to the best that is in him, or that has ever been.[39]

Marxists offer a unique insight into racism—its origins in the brutal establishment of capitalism and its role in maintaining that barbaric system. More importantly, Marxism locates the force—the working class, both black and white—that offers the potential to most effectively challenge racism and also the chance to abolish it once and for all.

# Further reading

## The roots of racism: slavery and colonialism

Alex Callinicos, *Race and Class* (Bookmarks, 1995)

Eric Williams, *Capitalism and Slavery* (University of North Carolina Press, 1994)

W E B Du Bois, *Black Reconstruction in America 1860-1880* (Free Press, 1999)

C L R James, *The Black Jacobins* (Penguin, 2001)

Adam Hochschild, *Bury the Chains: The British Struggle to Abolish Slavery* (Pan, 2012)

Robin Blackburn, *The Making of New World Slavery* (Verso, 2010)

John Newsinger, *The Blood Never Dried: A People's History of the British Empire*, 2nd edition (Bookmarks, 2013)

## The black British experience

Peter Fryer, *Staying Power: The History of Black People in Britain* (Pluto, 2010)

Rozina Visram, *Asians in Britain: 400 Years of History* (Pluto, 2002)

Mike Phillips and Trevor Phillips, *Windrush: The Irresistable Rise of Multi-Racial Britain* (Harper Collins, 2009)

A Sivanandan, *Communities of Resistance: Writings on Black Struggles for Socialism* (Verso, 1990)

A Sivanandan, "From Resistance to Rebellion: Asian and Afro-Caribbean struggles in Britain", *Race & Class* (October 1981)

Asian Youth Movements archive, www.tandana.org

Chris Harman, "The Summer of 1981: A Post-Riot Analysis", *International Socialism* 14 (autumn 1981), www.marxists.org/archive/harman/1981/xx/riots.html

David Widgery, *Beating Time: Riot 'n' Race 'n' Rock 'n' Roll* (Chatto & Windus, 1986)

Audrey Farrell, *Crime, Class and Corruption: The Politics of the Police* (Bookmarks, 1992)

Paul Gilroy, *There Ain't no Black in the Union Jack* (Routledge, 2002)

Doreen Lawrence, *And Still I Rise* (Faber and Faber, 2007)

David Gillborn, *Racism and Education: Coincidence or Conspiracy?* (Routledge, 2008)

Hassan Mahamdallie, *Defending Multiculturalism: A Guide for the Movement* (Bookmarks, 2011)

*Reading the Riots* (Guardian/LSE report, 2011), www.guardian. co.uk/uk/interactive/2011/dec/14/reading-the-riots-investigating-england-s-summer-of-disorder-full-report

Gary Younge, *Who Are We—and Should it Matter in the 21st Century?* (Viking, 2010)

### Islamophobia

Chris Harman, "The Prophet and the Proletariat", *International Socialism* 64 (autumn 1994), www.marxists.org/archive/harman/1994/xx/islam.htm

Deepa Kumar, *Islamophobia and the Politics of Empire* (Haymarket, 2012)

Arun Kundnani, *The End of Tolerance: Racism in 21st Century Britain* (Pluto, 2007)

Liz Fekete, *A Suitable Enemy: Racism, Migration and Islamophobia in Europe* (Pluto, 2009)

Liz Fekete, *Integration, Islamophobia and Civil Rights in Europe* (Institute of Race Relations, 2008), www.irr.org.uk/pdf/Integrationreport.pdf

Nissa Finney and Ludi Simpson, *"Sleepwalking to Segregation"? Challenging Myths of Race and Migration* (Policy, 2009)

Peter Oborne and James Jones, *Muslims Under Siege: Alienating Vulnerable Communities* (University of Essex, 2008), www.channel4.com/news/media/pdfs/Muslims_under_siege_LR.pdf

Islamophobia Watch is a useful resource for up to date statistics: islamophobia-watch.com

*Say it Loud*

The Institute of Race Relations produces many reports, books and
pamphlets as well as the journal *Race & Class*: www.irr.org.uk

**Fighting fascism**

Leon Trotsky, *The Struggle Against Fascism in Germany*
(Pathfinder, 1971)

Phil Piratin, *Our Flag Stays Red* (Lawrence & Wishart, 2006)

Donny Gluckstein, *The Nazis, Capitalism and the Working Class*
(Haymarket, 2012)

Robert Paxton, *The Anatomy of Fascism* (Penguin, 2005)

**Lessons from America**

Glenda Elizabet Gilmore, *Defying Dixie: The Radical Roots of Civil
Rights, 1919-1950* (W W Norton & Co, 2009)

R Kelley, *Hammer and Hoe: Alabama Communists during the Great
Depression* (University of North Carolina Press, 2006)

Mark Naison, *Communists in Harlem During the Depression*
(University of Illinois Press, 2005)

Manning Marable, *Race, Reform and Rebellion: The Second
Reconstruction and Beyond in Black America, 1945-2006* (Palgrave
Macmillan, 2007)

J M Bloom, *Class Race and Civil Rights Movement: The Changing
Political Economy of Southern Racism* (John Wiley & Sons, 1987)

Clayborne Carson (ed), *The Eyes on the Prize: Civil Rights Reader:
Documents, Speeches and Firsthand Accounts from the Black
Freedom Fighters, 1954-1990* (Prentice-Hall, 1992)

Manning Marable, *Malcolm X: A Life of Reinvention*
(Penguin, 2012)

Malcolm X, *The Autobiography of Malcolm X* (Penguin, 2007)

Malcolm X Oxford Union debate (1964), www.youtube.com/
watch?v=Dmzaaf-9aHQ

Chris Harman, *The Fire Last Time: 1968 and After* (Bookmarks, 1998)

Clayborne Carson, *The Black Panthers Speak* (Da Capo Press Inc, 1995)

Bobby Seale, *Seize the Time: Story of the Black Panther Party and
Huey P Newton* (Black Classic Press, 1991)

*The Black Power Mixtape 1967-1975* (documentary on the movement,
available on DVD)

Dan Georgakas, *Detroit: I Do Mind Dying: A Study in Urban Revolution* (South End Press, 1999)

*Finally Got The News* (documentary on the League of Revolutionary Black Workers), www.youtube.com/watch?v=RgJd_MvJVzg

## Key writings in the classical Marxist tradition

The Marxists Internet Archive provides a brilliant resource for finding writings by Marx, Lenin and others in the Marxist tradition.

For Marx's key passage on how racism was used to divide and rule English and Irish workers, go to www.marxists.org/archive/marx/works/1870/letters/70_04_09.htm

Marx also wrote widely on India and colonialism. These writings have been collected in Iqbal Husain (ed), *Karl Marx On India* (Tulika Books, 2006).

V I Lenin's *What Is To Be Done?*, which includes the argument that socialists should be the "tribune of the people" is available in full at www.marxists.org/archive/lenin/works/1901/witbd/

Lenin and other figures on the international left debated national and colonial questions at the second congress of the Communist International in 1920. These are collected in John Riddell (ed), *Workers of the World and Oppressed Peoples, Unite! Volume One of The Communist International in Lenin's Time* (Pathfinder, 1991).

John Riddell (ed), *To See The Dawn: Baku, 1920* (Pathfinder, 1993) records the proceedings of the First Congress of the Peoples of the East. The manifesto of this congress gives you a taste of the inspirational gathering: www.marxists.org/history/international/comintern/baku/manifesto.htm

# About the authors

**Talat Ahmed** is Lecturer in South Asian History at the University of Edinburgh and a member of the editorial board of *International Socialism*. She is the author of *Literature and Politics in the Age of Nationalism: The Progressive Episode in South Asia, 1932-56* and is working on a forthcoming book on Gandhi.

**Weyman Bennett** is a long time socialist activist and campaigner against racism and fascism and is the joint national secretary of Unite Against Fascism.

**Esme Choonara** is a member of the International Socialism editorial board and the author of *A Rebel's Guide to Trotsky*.

**Hassan Mahamdallie** contributed to *Tell It Like It Is: How Our Schools Fail Black Children*. His publications include *Crossing the River of Fire: The Socialism of William Morris*, *Black British Rebels: Figures from Working Class History* and *Defending Multiculturalism: A Guide for the Movement* (editor). He covered the Stephen Lawrence Inquiry for *Socialist Worker*.

**Gary McFarlane** is a journalist and the equality officer for NUJ London Magazine Branch. He is a long time socialist activist based in Tottenham.

**Ken Olende** writes for *Socialist Worker* and is a part time lecturer for the Workers' Educational Association.

**Yuri Prasad** is a socialist based in London and has written for *Socialist Worker*.

# Notes

### Introduction: Say it loud

1  "Man killed in shooting incident involving police officer", *Daily Telegraph*, 4 August 2011, www.telegraph.co.uk/news/uknews/crime/8682655/Mark-Duggan-killed-in-shooting-incident-involving-police-officer.html

2  "Man killed in shooting incident involving police officer", as above.

3  Prime Minister David Cameron, speech to parliament, 11 August 2011, www.publications.parliament.uk/pa/cm201011/cmhansrd/cm110811/debtext/110811-0001.htm column 1051.

4  See for example Kiran Stacey, "UK riots: Is this the moment Boris loses his shine?", *Financial Times*, 9 August 2011, blogs.ft.com/westminster/2011/08/uk-riots-is-this-the-moment-boris-loses-his-shine/#axzz1sIY8MIAv

5  The exchange can be viewed on YouTube: Newsnight—Harriet Harman & Michael Gove—Heated Debate 1 London Riots 09/08/2011. A transcript of part of the exchange is available at www.guardian.co.uk/politics/wintour-and-watt/2011/aug/10/michaelgove-harrietharman

6  Hazel Blears MP, speech to parliament, 11 August, as above, column 1062.

7  David Lammy MP, speech to parliament, 11 August, as above, column 1060.

8  R v Blackshaw & Others [2011] EWCA Crim 2312 at paragraph 17. This judgment can be found at www.bailii.org by typing the word "Blackshaw" into the case law search.

9  R v Blackshaw & Others, as above, at paragraph 1.

10  R v Blackshaw & Others, as above, at paragraph 4.

11  And in fact, the "riots" that Jordan Blackshaw and Perry Sutcliffe were convicted of inciting via social media never actually occured.

12  Ministry of Justice statistics cited in "Riots broken down: who was in court and what's happened to them?", *Guardian* datablog, 15 September 2011, www.guardian.co.uk/news/datablog/2011/sep/15/riot-defendants-court-sentencing#data

13  "England riots: 'The whites have become black'", *Newsnight*, 12 August 2011, www.bbc.co.uk/news/uk-14513517

14  A full copy of the report can be found at www.guardian.co.uk/uk/interactive/2011/dec/14/reading-the-riots-investigating-england-s-summer-of-disorder-full-report

15  This panel chaired by Darra Singh, the Chief Executive of Job Centre Plus and a former chief executive of the London Borough of Ealing and Luton Borough Council, was hand-picked by the prime minister, deputy prime minister and leader of the opposition, in short the leaders of all three main parties.

16  David Lammy, *Out of the Ashes* (Guardian Books, 2011).

17  "Metropolitan police commissioner's message on racism—video", Guardian, 3 April 2012, www.guardian.co.uk/uk/video/2012/apr/03/metropolitan-police-bernard-hogan-howe-racism-video

18  www.channel4.com/news/met-police-racism-figures-reveal-120-cases-one-dismissal

19  Sir William Macpherson of Cluny, *The Stephen Lawrence Inquiry Report* (The Stationery Office, 1999), paragraph 6.34.

20  Patrick Wintour, "Blair vows to root out extremism—Lawyers and Muslim groups alarmed", *Guardian*, 6 August 2005, www.guardian.co.uk/politics/2005/aug/06/terrorism.july7

21  Gary Younge, *Who Are We: And Should*

*it Matter in the 21st Century?* (Viking, 2010).

22  Simon Hallsworth and David Brotherton, *Urban Disorder and Gangs* (Runnymede, 2011), p9.

**Chapter 1:**
**The roots of racism**

1   Robin Derricourt, *Inventing Africa* (Pluto, 2011), p57.

2   Derricourt, as above, p60.

3   W E B Du Bois, *The Negro* (Humanity Books, 2002), p27.

4   www.aaanet.org/stmts/racepp.htm

5   C L R James, *Modern Politics* (Bewick Editions, 1973), p124.

6   Peter Alexander, *Racism, Resistance and Revolution* (Bookmarks, 1987), p2.

7   Chris Harman, *A People's History of the World* (Bookmarks, 1999), p245.

8   Jeffrey B Perry (ed), *A Hubert Harrison Reader* (Wesleyan, 2001), p53.

9   Eric Williams, *Capitalism and Slavery* (Andre Deutsch, 1964), pp19-20.

10  Peter Fryer, *Staying Power* (Pluto, 1984), p148.

11  Quoted in Fryer, as above, p159.

12  Quoted in Fryer, as above, p152.

13  Fryer, as above, p94.

14  Brian Kelly, "The Material Origins of American Racism" (Unpublished article supplied by author), p9.

15  Kelly, as above, p10.

16  Kelly, as above, p16.

17  Kelly, as above, p17.

18  Kelly, as above, p24.

19  Kelly, as above, p26.

20  Kelly, as above, p29.

21  Adam Smith, *The Wealth of Nations*, chapter 7, www.marxists.org/reference/archive/smith-adam/works/wealth-of-nations/book04/ch07c-2.htm

22  Karl Marx, *Capital Volume One* (1867), chapter 26, www.marxists.org/archive/marx/works/1867-c1/ch26.htm

23  Robin Blackburn, *The Making of New World Slavery* (Verso, 1997), p572.

24  Karl Marx, *Capital Volume One* (1867), chapter 31, www.marxists.org/archive/marx/works/1867-c1/ch31.htm

25  Fryer, as above, p34.

26  Karl Marx, *The Poverty of Philosophy* (1847), chapter 2, www.marxists.org/archive/marx/works/1847/poverty-philosophy/ch02.htm

27  Norah Carlin, "Was There Racism in Ancient Society?", *International Socialism* 36 (autumn 1987), p92.

28  "Pope St Miltiades", *Catholic Encyclopedia* (1913), en.wikisource.org/wiki/Catholic_Encyclopedia_(1913)/Pope_St._Miltiades

29  Fryer, as above, p136.

30  Jacques Gernet, *A History of Chinese Civilization* (Cambridge University Press, 1996), p292.

31  Abram Leon, *The Jewish Question* (Pathfinder, 1970), p128.

32  Christopher Allen, *Islamophobia* (Ashgate, 2010), p27.

33  Allen, as above, p27.

34  Blackburn, *The Making of New World Slavery*, as above, p39.

35  Blackburn, *The Making of New World Slavery*, as above, p103.

36  Olaudah Equiano, *The Interesting Narrative of the Life of Olaudah Equiano* (Digireads, 2009), p28.

37  Adam Hochschild, *Bury the Chains: The British Struggle to Abolish Slavery* (Macmillan, 2005), p64.

38  Fryer, as above, pp128-129.

39  Quoted in Angela Davis, *Women, Race and Class* (Women's Press, 1981), p9.

40  C L R James, "Revolution and the Negro" (1939), www.marxists.org/archive/james-clr/works/1939/12/negro-revolution.htm

41  Hochschild, as above, p259.

42  Toussaint L'Ouverture, *The Haitian Revolution* (Verso, 2008), p6.

43  C L R James, *The Black Jacobins* (Penguin, 2001), p72.

44  See Chris Harman, "Haiti: Pawn In Their Game", in *Socialist Worker Review*, no 85, March 1986, www.marxists.org/archive/harman/1986/03/haiti.html

45  Fryer, as above, p70.

46  Fryer, as above, p60.

47  Fryer, as above, p71.

48  Adam Hochschild, "Radicals and rebels behind the abolition of slavery", *Socialist Worker*, 24 March 2007.

49  Fryer, as above, p50.

50  Hochschild, "Radicals and rebels behind the abolition of slavery", as above.

51  Hochschild, "Radicals and rebels behind the abolition of slavery", as above.

52  Karl Marx, "Letters: Marx to Sigfrid Meyer and August Vogt, 9 April 1870", www.marxists.org/archive/marx/works/1870/letters/70_04_09.htm

53  Alex Callinicos, *Race and Class* (Bookmarks, 1992), p35.

54  Philip S Foner, *Organized Labor & the Black Worker 1619-1981* (International, 1981), p4.

*Say it Loud*

55     Charles Darwin, *The Descent of Man* (1871), darwin-online.org.uk/content/frameset?viewtype=text&itemID=F937.1&pageseq=181

56     Quoted in Robert O Collins, James M Burns, *A History of Sub-Saharan Africa* (Cambridge, 2007), p105.

57     Quoted in Howard Zinn, *A People's History of the United States, 1492 to the Present* (Harper Collins, 2001), p26.

58     www.kipling.org.uk/poems_burden.htm

59     Bruce Berman and John Lonsdale, *Unhappy Valley: Conflict in Kenya and Africa* (James Currey, 1993), p19.

60     Most notably in Niall Ferguson, *Empire: How Britain Made the Modern World* (Penguin, 2004).

61     Quoted in Kevin B Anderson, *Marx at the Margins* (University of Chicago Press, 2010), p34.

62     Ron Ramdin, *The Making of the Black Working Class in Britain* (Wildwood House, 1987), p36.

63     Lydia Potts, *The World Labour Market* (Zed, 1990), p63.

64     Vijaya Teelock of the Mauritian Truth and Justice Forum, in a talk at the University of London, 21 March 2012.

65     Potts, as above, p64.

66     Manning Marable, *Race, Reform and Rebellion* (Macmillan, 1991), p32.

67     Chris Harman, "The Return of the National Question", in Alex Callinicos (ed), *Marxism and the New Imperialism* (Bookmarks, 1994), p196.

68     Harman, "The Return of the National Question", as above, p243.

69     Leon, as above, p238.

70     Marable, as above, p4.

71     W E B Du Bois, *Black Reconstruction in America, 1860-1880* (Free Press, 1998), p8.

72     Eric Foner, *Reconstruction: America's Unfinished Revolution 1863-1877* (Harper & Row, 1988), p27.

73     Foner, as above, p142.

74     Foner, as above, p288.

75     Frederick Douglass, *The Life and Times of Frederick Douglass* (Wordsworth, 1996), p305.

76     This section based on my article "Racism and class solidarity in history of the US South", *Socialist Worker*, 22 September 2007, www.socialistworker.co.uk/art.php?id=13018

77     Ahmed Shawki, *Black Liberation and Socialism* (Haymarket, 2007), p44.

78     Jack M Bloom, *Class, Race and the Civil Rights Movement* (Indiana University Press, 1987), p30.

79     In part based on my review of Perry's *Hubert Harrison* that appeared in *International Socialism* 123 (summer 2009), www.isj.org.uk/index.php4?id=571&issue=123

80     Jeffrey B Perry, *Hubert Harrison: the Voice of Harlem Radicalism, 1883-1918* (Columbia University Press, 2009), p162.

81     Perry, as above, p183.

82     Perry, as above, p279.

83     This section is in part based on my article, "Marcus Garvey: a liberating legacy of challenging racism", *Socialist Worker*, 12 July 2008, www.socialistworker.co.uk/art.php?id=15420

84     Peter Linebaugh and Marcus Rediker, *The Many-Headed Hydra* (Verso, 2000), p319.

85     Ramdin, as above, p28.

86     John Saville, *1848: The British State and the Chartist Movement* (Cambridge University Press, 1987), p104.

87     Fryer, as above, p242.

88     George Orwell, *Collected Essays, Letters and Journalism* volume 1 (Penguin, 1970), p471.

89     Harman, *A People's History of the World*, as above, p552.

90     C L R James, *A History of Negro Revolt* (Research Associates, 1994), p72.

91     Nigel Harris, *Thinking the Unthinkable* (IB Tauris, 2001), p46.

92     Paul Foot, *Immigration and Race in British Politics* (Penguin, 1965), p126.

93     Fryer, as above, p366.

94     Fryer, as above, p376.

95     Madge Dresser, *Black and White on the Buses: The 1963 Colour Bar Dispute in Bristol* (Bristol Broadsides, 1986), p39.

96     Partha Sarathi Gupta, *Power, Politics and the People* (Anthem, 2002), p204.

97     Robert Winder, *Bloody Foreigners* (Abacus, 2004), p341.

98     Foot, *Immigration and Race in British Politics*, as above, p161.

99     Foot, *Immigration and Race in British Politics*, as above, p172.

100    Foot, *Immigration and Race in British Politics*, as above, p44.

101    Paul Foot, *The Rise of Enoch Powell* (Penguin, 1969), p113.

102    Alexander, as above, p153.

103    Tony Cliff, "The Labour Party in Perspective", *In the Thick of Workers' Struggle, Selected Writings Volume 2* (Bookmarks, 2002), p1.

104    Ramdin, as above, p156.

105    Fryer, as above, p334.

106 James P Cannon, "The Russian Revolution and the Black Struggle in the United States" (1959), www.marxists.org/archive/cannon/works/1959/black.htm

**Chapter 2:**
**From confrontation to compromise: Black British politics in the 1970s and 1980s**

1 A slogan adopted by many of the Asian Youth Movements. The website www.tandana.org carries a digitised archive of Asian Youth Movement leaflets, posters and other political ephemera.

2 www.guardian.co.uk/uk/2011/may/08/home-office-virginity-tests-1970s.

3 A Sivanandan, *Communities of Resistance* (Verso, 1990), p83.

4 C L R James, *Beyond a Boundary* (Hutchinson, 1963), p66.

5 archive.tribunemagazine.co.uk/article/4th-may-1973/10/mansfield-workers-new-step-against-racialism

6 CIS Special Report, "Racism: Who Profits?", *Counter Information Services Anti-Report*, no 16 (Autumn 1976), p22.

7 Jack Dromey and Graham Taylor, *Grunwick: The Workers' Story* (Lawrence and Wishart, 1978), p102.

8 Hassan Mahamdallie, "Muslim Working Class Struggles", *International Socialism* 113 (winter 2007), p111.

9 Peter Alexander, *Race, Resistance and Revolution* (Bookmarks, 1987), p154.

10 See www.tomrobinson.com/trb/rar.htm

11 Paul Foot quoted at www.tomrobinson.com/trb/rar.htm

12 en.wikipedia.org/wiki/Daily_Telegraph

13 Chris Harman, "The Summer of 1981: A Post-riot Analysis" in Chris Harman, *Selected Writings* (Bookmarks, 2010).

14 John Rex and Sally Tomlinson, *Colonial Immigrants in a British City* (Routledge, 1979), p217.

15 *Race Today*, March 1978.

16 Harman, as above, p281.

17 In "Redemption Song", one of his finest final songs which, unusually, he performs solo on the album *Uprising*.

18 A Sivanandan, "From Resistance to Rebellion: Asian and Afro-Caribbean Struggles in Britain", *Race and Class*, vol 23, 2-3 (October 1981), p140.

19 Scarman Report (HMSO, 1981), pp204-206.

20 Cited in Sivanandan, *Communities of Resistance*, as above, p93.

21 Kalbir Shukra, *The Changing Pattern of Black Politics in Britain* (Pluto, 1998), p94.

22 Esme Choonara and Yuri Prasad, "The crisis of black leadership", *International Socialism* 136 (Autumn 2012).

23 www.margaretthatcher.org/document/103485

24 Sivanandan, *Communities of Resistance*, as above, p94.

25 www.guardian.co.uk/commentisfree/2008/oct/06/race.labour

26 Andy McSmith, *Faces of Labour: The Inside Story* (Verso, 1997), p129.

27 Lewisham Racism Awareness Training Unit, *Black Awareness Programme*, 9-10 August 1984.

28 Ian Macdonald, *Murder in the Playground* (Longsight Press, 1989) .

29 *New Statesman*, 27 May 1988.

30 Robert Miles and Annie Phizacklea, *White Man's Country* (Pluto Press, 1984), p108.

31 *Economist*, 18 September 1993.

**Chapter 3:**
**A defining struggle:**
**The Stephen Lawrence campaign**

1 Statement of Doreen Lawrence, 8 March 1998, Appendix 6, *The Stephen Lawrence Inquiry*, Appendices (The Stationery Office Limited, February 1999).

2 Quoted in Alban Pryce, "Immigration: Dealing With The Race Card", *Socialist Review*, March 2005.

3 Institute of Race Relations, "Black Deaths In Custody", 11 November 2002, www.irr.org.uk/news/black-deaths-in-custody/

4 Institute of Race Relations, "Deaths With A (Known or Suspected) Racial Element 1991-1999", 8 November 2002, www.irr.org.uk/news/deaths-with-a-known-or-suspected-racial-element-1991-1999/

5 The best account of the Stephen Lawrence murder, investigation and inquiry is Brian Cathcart, *The Case of Stephen Lawrence* (Penguin Books, 2000).

6 Continuation of Statement of Doreen Lawrence, 11 June 1998, Appendix 6, *The Stephen Lawrence Inquiry*, Appendices, as above.

7 *Mail* on Sunday, 17 October 1993.

8 The Report by Detective Chief Superintendent Barker of his Review, November 1993, Appendix 13, *The Stephen Lawrence Inquiry*, Appendices, as above, p1.

9 On Barker's evidence at Macpherson see Cathcart, as above, pp341-343.

10   Report by the Police Complaints Authority on the Investigation of a Complaint against the Metropolitan Police Service by Mr N and Mrs D Lawrence, Appendix 2, *The Stephen Lawrence Inquiry*, Appendices, as above, p13.

11   Continuation of Statement of Doreen Lawrence, 11 June 1998, Appendix 6, *The Stephen Lawrence Inquiry*, Appendices, as above.

12   www.dailymail.co.uk/news/article-2080159/Stephen-Lawrence-case-How-killers-finally-brought-justice.html

13   Quoted in "Stephen Lawrence murder: How unions played a role in fighting for justice", *Socialist Worker*, 14 January 2012, www.socialistworker.co.uk/art.php?id=27157

14   *The Stephen Lawrence Inquiry, Report of an Inquiry by Sir William Macpherson* (The Stationery Office Limited, February 1999), Chapter 3, p6.

15   See Cathcart, as above, pp312-314.

16   *The Stephen Lawrence Inquiry, Report of an Inquiry by Sir William Macpherson*, as above, Chapter 3, p3.

17   Audrey Farrell, *Crime, Class and Corruption* (Bookmarks, 1992), p9.

18   See Cathcart, as above, p47.

19   Final Submissions With Regard to Part 1 of The Stephen Lawrence Inquiry On Behalf of Mr and Mrs Lawrence, p21.

20   *The Stephen Lawrence Inquiry, Report of an Inquiry by Sir William Macpherson*, as above, Chapter 8, p43.

21   *The Stephen Lawrence Inquiry, Report of an Inquiry by Sir William Macpherson*, as above, Chapter 8, p45.

22   Sir Paul Condon, testimony to the Stephen Lawrence Inquiry, 1 October 1998, author's notes.

23   Stokely Carmichael and Charles V Hamilton, *Black Power: The Politics of Liberation in America* (Pelican Books, 1969), p20.

24   Ben Bowling and Coretta Phillips, "Policing ethnic minority communities" (LSE, 2003). Available at LSE Research Online: eprints.lse.ac.uk/9576/. See also Ben Bowling and Coretta Phillips, *Racism, Crime and Justice* (Longman, 2002), p158.

25   Farrell, as above, p125.

26   Public meeting, "Stephen Lawrence Inquiry", Ealing, 8 October 1998, author's notes.

27   See *The Stephen Lawrence Inquiry, Report of an Inquiry by Sir William Macpherson*, as above, Chapter 6, pp20-42.

28   Gallup/*Daily Telegraph* Poll, 8 February 1999. Summary can be found at "Confidence in Police Declining", BBC news report, news.bbc.co.uk/1/uk/275156.stm

29   ICM/*Guardian Poll*, Guardian, 9 February 1999.

30   Public Meeting, "Stephen Lawrence Inquiry", Manchester, 13 October 1998, author's notes.

31   Public Meeting, "Stephen Lawrence Inquiry", Birmingham, 13 November 1998, author's notes.

32   Kwesi Menson, speech to public meeting, Brixton, September 1998, author's notes.

33   Testimony to the Michael Menson inquest, Hornsey Coroner's Court, north London, 7-16 September 1998.

34   See "Michael Menson Killer Jailed for Life", *Guardian*, 22 December 1999, www.guardian.co.uk/uk/1999/dec/22/race.world5

35   Police Federation Annual Conference, May 1999, Blackpool Winter Gardens, all quotes from author's notes.

36   For press coverage of the Macpherson report see "The Press, the Police and Macpherson", CARF 49, April/May 1999, www.irr.org.uk/carf/feat26.html

37   All quotes cited in *Socialist Worker*, 13 March 1999.

38   Paul Boateng, *London Evening Standard*, 13 May 1999.

39   Paul Gordon and David Rosenberg, *Daily Racism: The Press and Black People in Britain* (Runnymede Trust, 1989), p15. *The Daily Mail* ran the headline "IT'S NO TO SCARMAN—Police must not have their hands tied" (7 December 1981). Compare with "Why we must not let the PC lobby destroy the police" (*Daily Mail*, 12 August 1999) and "Why we must not let race lunacy handcuff the police" (*London Evening Standard*, 23 March 1999).

40   *Hansard*, 29 March 1999.

41   See report in *The Voice* newspaper, 26 July 1999.

42   NOP/IPPR/OLR survey, 5 February 1997.

43   Vikram Dodd, "All hype and no action. So what is new: Six months after Macpherson's report, racism is actually worse", *Guardian*, 24 August 1999, www.guardian.co.uk/uk/1999/aug/24/race.world?INTCMP=SRCH

44  Nick Hopkins and Sarah Hall, "David
    Copeland: A quiet introvert obsessed
    with Hitler and bombs", *Guardian*,
    30 June 2000, www.guardian.co.uk/
    uk/2000/jun/30/uksecurity.sarahhall

45  *The Report of the Commission on the
    Future of Multi-Ethnic Britain* (Profile
    Books, 2000). It can be accessed at www.
    runnymedetrust.org/projects/meb/
    report.html

46  All quotes from Hassan Mahamdallie,
    "Outcry greets new report, Right wing
    wants to cover up racism", *Socialist
    Worker*, 21 October 2000.

47  See Hassan Mahamdallie, "Blunkett
    trashes anti-racist fight", *Socialist Worker*,
    25 January 2003, www.socialistworker.
    co.uk/art.php?id=2690

48  *Hansard*, 21 October 2005, www.
    publications.parliament.uk/pa/
    cm200506/cmhansrd/vo051021/
    wmstext/51021m01.htm#51021m01.
    html_sbhd3

49  Doreen Lawrence quoted in Nicholas
    Watt, "Jack Straw: Charles Clarke
    was wrong to shut down Stephen
    Lawrence group", *Guardian*, 16 January
    2012, www.guardian.co.uk/politics/
    wintour-and-watt/2012/jan/16/
    jackstraw-davidblunkett

50  Doreen Lawrence quoted in "Doreen
    Lawrence: Britain still blighted by
    racism", *Guardian*, 3 January 2012,
    www.guardian.co.uk/uk/2012/jan/03/
    doreen-lawrence-britain-blighted-racism

51  "Stephen Lawrence: Home office orders
    police probe review", BBC News, 1
    June 2012, www.bbc.co.uk/news/
    uk-england-london-18297462

#### Chapter 4:
#### A promise betrayed: Racism after Macpherson

1   These had been the words that Jack Straw
    used when he presented Macpherson's
    report to parliament on 24 February
    1999, hansard.millbanksystems.
    com/commons/1999/feb/24/
    stephen-lawrence-inquiry

2   "Getting it, Getting it Right",
    Department for Education and Skills
    Priority Review paper, September 2006,
    p16, www.emas4success.org/acrobat/
    WholeSchoolPlanning/DCSFGuidance/
    Gettingitgettingitright.pdf

3   Recommendation No 12, *Stephen
    Lawrence Inquiry Report* (The Stationery
    Office, February 1999).

4   19 year old Zahid Mubarek was murdered
    in Feltham Young Offenders Institute in
    March 2000 by Robert Stewart, a racist
    psychopath. The inquiry into his death
    was published in 2006 and identified a
    casual disregard for racism, officers in
    denial and victimisation of black staff.
    The report can be downloaded at image.
    guardian.co.uk/sys-files/Guardian/
    documents/2006/06/29/volume_one.pdf
    and similar but volume two pdf. Eighteen
    year old Anthony Walker was murdered
    by four white youths in Huyton,
    Merseyside in July 2005. Merseyside
    Police immediately acknowledged that it
    had been racially motivated and his killers
    were convicted within four months.

5   "UK Politics Phillips accuses Livingstone
    of racism", *BBC News*, 16 June 1999, news.
    bbc.co.uk/1/hi/uk_politics/369935.stm

6   This phrase was incorporated into the
    title of the article—*Daily Mail*, 19
    January 2009.

7   *Daily Mail*, 19 January 2009.

8   Paul Lewis, "Black fireman says he was
    tasered and abused by Met", *Guardian*,
    20 April 2012. This was one of a stream of
    stories run by the *Guardian* in March and
    April 2012.

9   This became law as the Equality Act 2010
    c15.

10  www.redcross.org.uk/What-
    we-do/Refugee-services/
    Refugee-facts-and-figures

11  *Stephen Lawrence Inquiry Report*, as
    above, 45.15.

12  Reprinted in Brian Richardson (ed), *Tell
    It Like It Is: How Our Schools Fail Black
    Children* (Bookmarks, 2005).

13  David Lammy caused controversy when
    he raised the question of parents feeling
    frustrated that they were not allowed
    to impose discipline on their children
    by smacking them when those children
    misbehaved.

14  See for example David Simon, "Education
    of the Blacks: the Supplementary School
    Movement", in Richardson (ed), as above,
    pp66-73.

15  Cited in David Gillborn, *Racism and
    Education: Coincidence or Conspiracy*
    (Routledge, 2008), p100.

16  Gillborn, as above.

17  Gillborn, as above, p104.

18  Richardson (ed), as above, pp92-94.

19  "They Never Give Up On You", *Report
    of the Children's Commissioner School
    Exclusions Inquiry Executive Summary*,

p12. The highest rate of exclusions was among those from Gypsy, Traveller and Roma backgrounds.

20  See for example David Gillborn and Heidi Safia Mirza, *Educational Inequality: Mapping Race, Class and Gender: A Synthesis of Research Evidence* (OFSTED, November 2000).

21  Gillborn and Mirza, as above, p18.

22  Gillborn and Mirza, as above.

23  Department for Education, Statistical First Release 03/2012, 9 February 2012.

24  See for example Mike Shiner and Tariq Modood, "Help or Hindrance? Higher Education and the Route to Ethnic Equality", *British Journal of Sociology of Education,* cited in Lola Young, "Accentuating the Positive", in Richardson (ed), as above, p147. See also *Race into Higher Education*, a 2010 report by Race for Opportunity. www.bitc.org.uk.

25  Established in 1992, these "new" universities had formerly been known as "polytechnics". The Russell Group meanwhile is a body of 20 self-styled "leading UK universities".

26  *Stephen Lawrence Inquiry Report*, as above, 45.8.

27  Ministry of Justice Statistics on Race and the Criminal Justice System 2010 (October 2011), p35.

28  Peter Ackroyd, *London: The Biography* (Chatto & Windus, 2000), p269.

29  In 2000/1 for example a total of 5.2 million crimes were recorded by the police, a 2.5 percent fall. Crime measured by the British Crime Survey fell by 13 percent between 1999 and 2000—Home Office Criminal Statistics England and Wales, December 2001, p24.

30  First introduced by the Crime and Disorder Act 1998—1998 c. 37.

31  *Stop and Think*, Equality and Human Rights Commission Report on Stop and Search (March 2010), p9, www.equalityhumanrights.com/key-projects/race-in...stop-and-think/

32  Ministry of Justice, *Statistics on Race and the Criminal Justice System 2010.*

33  *Stop and Think*, as above, p10.

34  See for example the research paper "Police-initiated Stop Practices in the United Kingdom—Where are we Now?" written by Lee Bridges, Emeritus Professor, School of Law, University of Warwick, August 2011.

35  This was the desperate claim made by Met Commissioner Bernard Hogan-Howe in an address to staff on 3 April 2012. It followed front page stories in the *Guardian* on 31 March and 3 April 2012.

36  www.parliament.uk/Templates/BriefingPapers/Pages/BPPdfDownload.aspx?bp-id=SN00634

37  Jason Bennetto, "Police and racism: What has been achieved 10 years after the Stephen Lawrence Inquiry Report?" (EHRC 2009), p14, www.equalityhumanrights.com/uploaded_files/raceinbritain/policeandracism.pdf

38  *Statistics on Race and the Criminal Justice System*, as above, pp51-52. The report advises a note of caution in considering these figures, but the disparity remains stark.

39  *Spectator*, 18 August 2011.

40  David Cameron, "Fightback" speech in local Witney constituency, 15 August 2011, www.number10.gov.uk/news/pms-speech-on-the-fightback-after-the-riots/

41  "Theresa May says most rioters were not in gangs", *BBC News*, 8 September 2011, www.bbc.co.uk/news/uk-politics-14834827

42  David Lammy, *Out of the Ashes* (Guardian Books, 2011), p33.

43  Lammy, as above, p109.

44  Ackroyd, as above, p270.

45  Ackroyd, as above, p151.

46  Ackroyd, as above, p271.

47  Ackroyd, as above, p271.

48  www.londonstreetgangs.com

49  See for example "Met launches major crack down on gang crime", www.london.gov.uk/media/press_releases_mayoral/met-launches-major-crack-down-gang-crime

50  *Archbold Criminal Pleading, Evidence & Practice 2012* (Sweet & Maxwell, 2012), Paragraph 18-15, p1846.

51  This was established by the case of Allen v Ireland [1984] 1 WLR 903.

52  I am grateful to Michael Magarian QC, Stella Harris and Tatyana Eatwell who hosted a seminar entitled "Joint Enterprise; a Fair Doctrine" at Tooks Chambers. I have shamelessly plagiarised their work. The video can be seen on YouTube by typing "Who killed Deon?" into the search engine.

53  NHS Statistics on Drug Misuse: England 2010, www.ic.nhs.uk/webfiles/publications/003_Health_Lifestyles/Statistics_on_Drug_Misuse%20_England_2010.pdf p6

54  Independent Advisory Panel on Deaths in Custody: End of Term Report February 2012. The IAP is a Ministerial Board which brings together the Ministry of Justice, Home Office and Department of Health.

55  See for example Inquest's website, www.inquest.org.uk and that of the United Families and Friends Campaign, uffc-campaigncentral.net

56  IPCC Press Release, "IPCC concludes investigation into death of David Emmanuel aka Smiley Culture", www.ipcc.gov.uk/news/Pages/pr_ipccconcludes investigationintodeathofdavid emmanuelakasmileyculture.aspx

57  Naomi Klein, *No Logo* (Flamingo, 2000). See the section "Hip hop Blows Up the Brands", p93. This brilliant book is now available online at ivanlefou.fr/repo/others/Naomi%20Klein%20-%No%20Logo.pdf

58  When Viv Anderson was picked to play against Czechoslovakia on 29 November 1978.

59  www.guardian.co.uk/media/2004/apr/22/football.raceinuk

60  Terry was acquitted of the charge at Westminster Magistrates Court as the judge ruled that it had not been proved beyond reasonable doubt that he had used the words as an insult. Terry was, however, banned and suspended following a separate Football Association hearing.

61  Lammy, as above, p194.

62  Office for National Statistics figures, www.nomisweb.co.uk cited in Lammy, as above, p80.

63  www.guardian.co.uk/society/2012/mar/09/half-uk-black-men-unemployed

64  First broadcast in October/November 2011.

65  Lammy, as above, p18.

66  The author of this chapter was invited to participate in a radio debate on precisely this topic in the summer of 2005. It is also the theme of Stanford professor Ralph Richard Banks's book entitled *Is Marriage for White People: How the African American Marriage Decline Affects Everyone* (Dutton Adult, 2011).

67  Alita Nandi and Lucinda Platt, *Ethnic Minority Women's Poverty and Economic Well-being* (Institute for Social and Economic Research, Home Office, September 2010), p4, www.homeoffice.gov.uk/publications/equalities/research/ethnic-minority-women-poverty/ethnic-minority-women's-poverty?view=Binary

68  Mary-Ann Stephenson, *TUC Women and the Cuts Toolkit* (Trades Union Congress, 2011), www.tuc.org.uk/equality/tuc-20286-f0.ctm p3

69  Zohra Moosra and Jessica Woodroffe, "Poverty Pathways: Ethnic Minority Women's Livelihoods", p15, cited in the *TUC Women and the Cuts Toolkit*, as above, p21.

70  Gill Kirton and Geraldine Healy, "Women and Trade Union Leadership Overview of UK Context", p8, hosted. busman.qmul.ac.uk/wtul/Files/17172.pdf

## Chapter 5:
### The rise of Islamophobia

1   Tony Blair's speech to Trades Union Congress, 11 September 2001.

2   *Economist*, 15-21 September, p15.

3   Quoted in P Sands, *Lawless World: America and the making and breaking of Global Rules* (Allen Lane, 2005), p174.

4   *Sun*, 12 September 2001.

5   news.bbc.co.uk/1/hi/uk_politics/4659933.stm

6   Tony Blair, *Guardian*, 6 August 2005.

7   Broadcast on 15 October 2010.

8   Quoted in *Daily Telegraph*, 19 January 2011.

9   Interview in *New York Magazine*, 26 April 2007.

10  Martin Amis, *Observer*, 10 September 2006.

11  Susan George, Attac weekly newsletter, 21 November 2001.

12  Chris Harman, "The Prophet and the Proletariat", *International Socialism* 64 (autumn 1994), p9. Available at www.marxists.org/archive/harman/1994/xx/islam.htm

13  See for example Anindya Bhattacharyya, "Racist ideas fuel the BNP", *Socialist Worker*, 20 June 2009, www.socialistworker.co.uk/art.php?id=18177

14  For an excellent analysis of this see Deepa Kumar, *Islamophobia and the Politics of Empire* (Haymarket Books, 2012).

15  *Sun*, 2 February 1979.

16  *Daily Mail*, 3 December 1979.

17  *Daily Mail*, 3 December 1979.

18  *Daily Mail*, 20 January 1981.

19  Interview with Fred Halliday in "The Iranian Revolution and its Implications", *New Left Review*, I/166

(November-December 1987), p36.

20   *Guardian*, 11 April 1980.

21   *Guardian*, 11 April 1980.

22   Saudi Arabia bought goods worth over £900 million per annum and was the UK's biggest market outside Western Europe and the US.

23   *Financial Times*, 25 April 1980.

24   *Guardian*, 11 April 1980.

25   *Guardian*, 11 April 1980.

26   *Guardian*, 11 April 1980.

27   *Socialist Worker*, 4 February 1978.

28   *Socialist Worker*, 11 February 1978.

29   www.number10.gov.uk/news/pms-speech-at-munich-security-conference/

30   Ray Honeyford, "Education and Race: An Alternative View", *Salisbury Review* (1984). The poem is part of "Inglan is a Bitch" by Linton Kwesi Johnson.

31   Honeyford, as above.

32   *Sunday Telegraph*, 27 August 2006.

33   Quoted in *The Roger Scruton Reader* (Continuum, 2009), p15.

34   *Daily Telegraph*, 8 September 1987.

35   *Telegraph and Argus*, 4 September 1987.

36   *Daily Telegraph*, 12 September 1987.

37   The Freedom Association organised Operation Pony Express in 1977, the clandestine sabotage of the Grunwick strike whereby post was retrieved and distributed during the night. They orchestrated black propaganda against members of CND claiming Joan Ruddock and Bruce Kent were communists. Throughout the 1980s they attempted to smear anti-apartheid opponents and vilify Nelson Mandela as a terrorist.

38   *Telegraph and Argus*, 9 September 1987.

39   *Telegraph and Argus*, 9 September 1987.

40   *Social Trends Survey*, 1989.

41   See interview in *Socialist Review*, April 1989.

42   Letters page, *Daily Telegraph*, 10 September 1987.

43   *Telegraph and Argus*, 4 September 1987.

44   Quoted in the *Times*, 17 February 1989.

45   *Daily Telegraph*, 16 January 1989.

46   *Daily Mirror*, 15 February 1989.

47   *Daily Telegraph*, 15 February 1989.

48   *Independent*, 16 March 1989.

49   Peregrine Worsthorne, "The Blooding of the Literati", *Sunday Telegraph*, 19 February 1989.

50   *Daily Telegraph*, 16 January 1989.

51   *Daily Telegraph*, 16 January 1989.

52   Fay Weldon, *Sacred Cows* (Chatto, 1989), p6.

53   Letter from John Pattern to Iqbal Sacranie dated 4 July 1989.

54   Gerald Marzorati, "Salman Rushdie: Fiction's Embattled Infidel", *New York Times Magazine*, 29 January 1989.

55   *Socialist Worker*, 18 February 1989.

56   *Socialist Worker*, 1 July 1989.

57   Samuel P Huntington, "The Clash of Civilizations?", *Foreign Affairs*, 72 (3), Summer 1993.

58   Huntington, as above.

59   Quoted in *Guardian*, 3 February 1995.

60   *Observer*, 12 September 1990.

61   Fred Halliday, "The Left and the War", *New Statesman and Society*, 8 March 1991, pp14-16.

62   Halliday, "The Left and the War", as above.

63   Quoted in *Tribune*, 22 November 1996, p7.

64   www.humanities.manchester.ac.uk/socialchange/research/social-change/summer-workshops/documents/sleepwalking.pdf

65   Nissa Finney and Ludi Simpson, *"Sleepwalking to Segregation"? Challenging myths of race and migration* (The Policy Press, 2009), pp128-129.

66   Finney and Simpson, as above, p124.

67   Danny Dorling, "Why Trevor Phillips is Wrong about race ghettos", *Observer*, 25 September 2005.

68   *Observer*, 11 November 2001.

69   *Guardian*, 26 November 2008.

70   monde diplo friends.org.uk/t_aproaart3.htm

71   *Socialist Worker*, 15 September 2001.

72   Tony Blair's speech to Labour Party conference 16 July 2005.

73   www.irr.org.uk/news/round-up-of-racial-violence/

74   Quoted in Vikram Dodd, "Guilty but Blair refuses to go", Guardian, 2 November 2007.

75   *Lancashire Telegraph*, 5 October 2006.

76   *Sunday Mirror*, 15 October 2006.

77   *Sunday Mirror*, 8 October 2006.

78   *Sunday Mirror*, 22 October 2006.

79   *Sunday Telegraph*, 8 October 2006.

80   *Sunday Telegraph*, 15 October 2006.

81   "Time for a More Liberal and 'Racist' Immigration Policy", *Spectator*, 19 October 1991.

82   *Sunday Telegraph*, 8 October 2006.

83   For an excellent analysis see Hassan Mahamdallie, "A History of Muslim Workers in Britain", *International Socialism* 113 (winter 2007).

## Chapter 6:
## Beating back the fascist threat

1    Paul Mason, BBC *Newsnight*, 17 October 2012.

2    mondediplo.com/2011/09/07farright

3    "Is the far right in decline in Britain?", *Daily Express*, 4 May 2012.

4    epp.eurostat.ec.europa.eu/ statistics_explained/index.php/ Unemployment_statistics

5    Martin Smith, "Eastenders: Have they knocked out the Nazis?", *Socialist Review* (April 1995), pubs.socialistreviewindex. org.uk/sr185/msmith.htm

6    Smith, as above.

7    In 1998 the ANL was given a membership list of BNP members in Tower Hamlets. When we compared them to lists of activists from the NF and BUF periods, we discovered that several local BNP activists had parents and grandparents who were in fascist groups stretching back to the 1930s.

8    en.wikipedia.org/wiki/ National_Front_(France)

9    *Patriot*, spring 1999.

10   *Searchlight*, August 2002.

11   *Patriot*, spring 1999.

12   "Lee Rigby death no excuse for reprisal attacks say family", *BBC News*, 31 May 2012.

13   Leon Trotsky, *The Struggle Against Fascism in Germany* (Pathfinder, 1971), p144.

14   www.marxists.org/archive/trotsky/1924/ ffyci-2/08.htm

15   en.wikipedia.org/wiki/ German_federal_election,_1928

16   *Trotsky*, as above, pp92-93.

17   Ernest Schmoger, *Memoirs of a Communist Activist* (publisher unknown), p19.

18   *Trotsky*, as above, pp138-139.

## Chapter 7:
## Lessons from America

1    Glenda Elizabeth Gilmore, *Defying Dixie: the Radical Roots of Civil Rights 1919-1950* (Norton, 2008), p44.

2    Joy Gleason Carew, *Blacks, Reds and Russians* (Rutgers University Press, 2011), p82.

3    Angelo Herdon, *Let Me Live* (University of Michigan Press, 2006), p88.

4    Robin D G Kelly, *Hammer and Hoe* (University of North Carolina Press, 1990), p113.

5    Gilmore, as above, p91.

6    Mark Naison, *Communists in Harlem During the Depression* (University of Illinois Press, 1983), p62.

7    As above.

8    As above, p158.

9    Manning Marable, *How Capitalism Underdeveloped Black America* (South End Press, 2000), p33.

10   *Current Population Reports* (US Department of Commerce, Bureau of the Census, 1971), p1.

11   Jack M Bloom, *Class, Race and the Civil Rights Movement* (Indiana University Press, 1987), p132.

12   Bloom, as above, p136.

13   Ahmed Shawki, *Black Liberation and Socialism* (Haymarket Books, 2006), p159.

14   Chris Harman, *The Fire Last Time: 1968 and After* (Bookmarks, 1988), p27.

15   Bloom, as above, p153.

16   Manning Marable, *Race, Reform and Rebellion: the Second Reconstruction and Beyond in Black America, 1945-2006* (Palgrave, 2007), p67.

17   Marable, *Race, Reform and Rebellion*, as above, p68.

18   Marable, *Race, Reform and Rebellion*, as above, p68.

19   Bloom, as above, p156.

20   Bloom, as above, p156.

21   Malcolm X, *Malcolm X Speaks* (Pathfinder, 1989), p12.

22   George Breitman, *The Last Year of Malcolm X* (Merit Publishers, 1979), p18.

23   Howard Zinn and Anthony Arnove, *Voices of a People's History of the United States* (Seven Stories, 2004), p401.

24   Harman, as above, p65.

25   Harman, as above, p66.

26   Bobby Seale, *Seize the Time: The Story of the Black Panther Party and Huey P Newton* (Black Classic Press, 1991), p153.

27   Marable, *Race, Rebellion and Reform*, as above, p98.

28   Philip S Foner (ed), *The Black Panthers Speak* (Da Capo, 1995), p71.

29   *The Afro American*, 23 May 1970.

30   *Wall Street Journal*, 13 January 1970.

31   Hugh Pearson, *The Shadow of the Panther: the Price of Black Power in America* (Addison Wesley, 1994), p209.

32   Foner (ed), *The Black Panthers Speak*, as above, p130.

33   Philip S Foner, *Organised Labor and the Black Worker* (Praeger Publishers, 1974), p410.

34   www.marxists.org/history/erol/1960-1970/watson.pdf

35 Foner, *Organized Labour and the Black Worker*, as above, p423.

36 Marable, *Race, Reform and Rebellion*, as above, p117.

37 "Worsening wealth inequality by race", money.cnn.com/2012/06/21/newseconomy/wealth-gap-race/index.htm?iid=EL

## Chapter 8:
## How do we fight racism today?

1 Al Syzmanski, "Racial Discrimination and White Gain", *American Sociological Review* 41, 1976, pp409-412.

2 Michael Reich, "Who Benefits from Racism? The Distribution among Whites of Gains and Losses from Racial Inequality", *Journal of Human Resources* vol 13, no 4 (Autumn 1978), p524.

3 David Cameron's immigration speech, 25 March 2013, www.number10.gov.uk/news/david-camerons-immigration-speech/

4 www.guardian.co.uk/uk/2013/mar/25/downing-street-defend-immigration-speech

5 W E B Du Bois, *Black Reconstruction in America 1860-1880* (New York, 1969), pp700-701.

6 Frances E Kendall, *Understanding White Privilege: Creating Pathways to Authentic Relationships Across Race* (second edition) (Routledge, 2013), p151.

7 Sharon Smith, "Mistaken Identity—or Can Identity Politics Liberate the Oppressed?", *International Socialism* 62 (spring 1994), pubs.socialistreviewindex.org.uk/isj62/smith.htm

8 www.timwise.org/f-a-q-s/

9 Kendall, as above, p1.

10 Ally Fogg, "'Check your privilege' isn't a trump card—it's a call for time out", Comment is Free, *Guardian*, 23 January 2013, www.guardian.co.uk/commentisfree/2013/jan/23/check-your-privilege-not-trump-card

11 Peggy McIntosh, "White Privilege and Male Privilege: A Personal Account of Coming to see Correspondences through Work in Women's Studies" (1988), reprinted in Michael S Kimmel and Abby L Ferber, *Privilege: A reader* (Westview Press, 2010), p14.

12 Transformative Justice Law Project of Illinois, 2012, *Checking Your Privilege*, www.tjlp.org

13 James Baldwin, "Open Letter to Angela Davis", in Angela Davis et al, *If They Come in the Morning: Voices of Resistance* (Philips Park Press, 1971), p20.

14 See for example the BBC's report, "White Working Class left behind", 27 March 2008, news.bbc.co.uk/1/hi/education/7316891.stm

15 www.telegraph.co.uk/news/politics/6989832/Have-white-working-class-Britons-been-left-behind-by-New-Labour.html

16 www.independent.co.uk/news/uk/politics/poverty-tsar-frank-field-white-working-class-need-own-citizenship-ceremonies-8559004.html

17 Wendy Bottero, "Class in the 21st century", in *Who Cares about the White Working Class?* (Runnymede Trust, 2009), pp7-15.

18 Alex Callinicos, *Race and Class* (Bookmarks, 1993), p41.

19 Leon Trotsky, *The Permanent Revolution*, Introduction to the German edition (1930), www.marxists.org/archive/trotsky/1931/tpr/prge.htm

20 Peter Fryer, *Staying Power: The History of Black People in Britain* (Pluto, 1984), p209.

21 www.power100.co.uk/index.php?id=22

22 www.guardian.co.uk/commentisfree/2007/apr/30/politics.homeaffairs

23 Quoted in Gus John, "30 years after the New Cross fire: challenging racism today", *Socialist Worker*, 10 September 2011, www.socialistworker.co.uk/art.php?id=26904

24 Fryer, as above, p213.

25 www.cottontown.org

26 www.socialistworker.co.uk/art.php?id=10422

27 Jane Hardy, "Migration, Migrant Workers and Capitalism", *International Socialism* 122 (spring 2009), www.isj.org.uk/?id=818

28 *Socialist Worker*, 29 October 2005, www.socialistworker.co.uk/art/7463/Bus+drivers%3A++%E2%80%98Bosses+treat+us+all+the+same+%E2%80%94+badly%E2%80%99

29 *Socialist Worker*, 23 May 2006, www.socialistworker.co.uk/art/8726/Wolverhampton+postal+workers+stand+up+against+racism

30 Health and Social Care Information Centre, *NHS Hospital and Community Health Service Workforce Statistics in England* (21 March 2013), www.hscic.gov.uk/searchcatalogue?productid=11216&to

pics=0%2fWorkforce&sort=Relevance&
size=10&page=1#top

31   www.nomisweb.co.uk/

32   www.ons.gov.uk/ons/rel/pse/civil-
service-statistics/2011/stb---civil-service-
statistics-2011.html#tab-Ethnicity

33   Trade Union Membership 2011
(Department for Business, Innovation
and Skills, 2012), www.gov.uk/
government/uploads/system/uploads/
attachment_data/file/16381/12-p77-trade-
union-membership-2011.pdf

34   Tim Wise, www.timwise.org/2010/08/
with-friends-like-these-who-needs-glenn-
beck-racism-and-white-privilege-on-the-
liberal-left/

35   Marx, *Capital*, vol 1 (Penguin, 1976),
p329.

36   V I Lenin, *What is to be Done?* (1902),
www.marxists.org/archive/lenin/
works/1901/witbd/iii.htm

37   www.thesun.co.uk/sol/homepage/news/
politics/4833976/Ed-Miliband-on-
immigration.html

38   Karl Marx, *The German Ideology* (1845),
www.marxists.org/archive/marx/
works/1845/german-ideology/ch01d.htm

39   Baldwin, as above, p22.

# Index